The Happiness Habit

The Happiness Habit

BRIAN COLBERT

Newleaf

Published by
Newleaf
an imprint of
Gill & Macmillan
Hume Avenue, Park West, Dublin 12
www.gillmacmillan.ie

© Brian Colbert 2010
978 0 7171 4776 2

Print origination by Carole Lynch
Printed by SPRINT-Print, Ireland

This book is typeset in Minion 11/15pt.

The paper used in this book comes from the wood pulp of managed forests. For every tree felled, at least one tree is planted, thereby renewing natural resources.

A CIP catalogue record for this book is available from the British Library.

10 9 8 7 6

Note: All NLP tools and techniques are used with the expressed consent of Richard Bandler and John La Valle.

Exercise on pg 201 © Genie Laborde, reproduced from *Influencing with Integrity* with permission of Crown House Publishing.

Dedication

To my three favourite people

Theresa, Dylan and Cian

Contents

Acknowledgments

This book would not have been possible without the inspiration and influence of some of the greatest creators of human excellence programs: Richard Bandler, John Grinder, John La Valle, Jim Rohn, Anthony Robbins, Robert Diltz, Maxwell Maltz, Stephen Covey, Nightingale Conant, Wayne Dyer, Napoleon Hill, Timothy Leary, Robert Anton Wilson, Michel Neil, Paul McKenna and many others. It has been a pleasure to learn from them.

I would like to acknowledge my business partner and friend, Owen Fitzpatrick, for all the fun times that we have at our seminars and for his support over the years.

The fuel for my motivation and direction in life comes mostly from my soul mate, best friend, life partner and business manager, Theresa, and our two creatively fun-loving, mischievous sons, Dylan and Cian.

Thanks to Sarah Liddy, Aoife O'Kelly, Jennifer Armstrong, Nicki Howard and all at Gill & Macmillan. Thanks also to Aoife Collins, Michael Connolly and Tony Parish. Thanks to my clients and our seminar delegates, without whom none of this would be possible.

Enjoy!

Brian Colbert

Foreword

For centuries people have sought excellence for themselves, striving to do the best they could, searching for ways to be the best they could be. Many messages have been delivered through the philosophers, teachers and so-called 'prophets' of their times. And while many of these made sense, they haven't really been able to affect people's behaviours and emotions in ways that would be long lasting. In the 1800s and 1900s interest in the psyche of people grew and more theories developed. In the 1970s a myriad of groups emerged offering theories, ideas and seminars that promised the elusive journey to excellence. Almost forty years later the one that continues to withstand the test of time successfully is NLP or Neuro-Linguistic Programming.

NLP focuses more on asking 'how' rather than 'why' and on applications rather than theories. Based on models, language and behaviour, NLP has proven to be unparalleled in its application when used as it was intended to be used so many years ago. It has also spawned many 'techniques' by people all over the world and, as any other well-founded technology, has been compromised by some that have wandered off the proven path of simplicity.

NLP is often challenged by academics and others who view its lack of scientific testing as some kind of failure. But the proof of NLP and its efficacy is in the success of those who have been able to change their lives, learn to achieve their goals and communicate more effectively with their loved ones, not in the labs of intellectuals. It is important to remember when reading this book that NLP was never an intellectual exercise, it is an interactive one. It requires 'doing', not just knowing. This book has exercises for you to 'do'.

The essence of this work is to be happy, making it a habit. More and more evidence is being published about the effects of people being happy and affecting their lives in a positive way mentally, physically and spiritually. Brian is offering you many ways to achieve this. What you have here is a very easy to read, easy to follow and easy to use book that Brian has used his experience and expertise to put together. Enjoy it and feel good!

John La Valle
Co-author of *Persuasion Engineering*® with Dr Richard Bandler,
and President of The Society of NLP ™

Introduction

Y ou hold in your hands right now an exciting opportunity that will dramatically transform you in ways you may have never dreamed.

Since my childhood I have had a burning passion for understanding human behaviour and have always focused on what makes people tick. I have spent almost all my life exploring, dismantling and investigating practical tools for personal development, change and transformation. I have read books, attended courses, studied gurus and modelled excellence. I have worked in business for years and even experienced the darker side of human behaviour.

As a therapist, mind coach and NLP master trainer, I have had the privilege of training thousands of people over the last fifteen years. I have witnessed first hand the powerful effect of these techniques on myself and on my clients and the many delighted seminar delegates that I have trained throughout Ireland, Britain, Europe, Brazil and America. What you are about to learn is powerful beyond measure. I have distilled what I have learned from the disciplines of NLP, Healing, Shamanism, Mysticism, Hypnosis and Magick and combined them in this book.

Whether you have had a tough past or are currently going through some challenges in your life, whether you are looking for a second chance or are simply curious and want to get ahead in life, this book will have something of benefit to you. Something that will hopefully offer you a further insight into the wonderful complexity that is the human condition.

This book is teaming with tools and techniques, which once used will serve to release the powerful creative force that is in you and this in turn will make you so much happier that you did. Time and time again I have had the good fortune to meet people who tell me of the great transformations that have taken place in their lives as a result of using these simple but powerful and effective tools of

1

change. Much and all as I would like to take credit for them I have learned the majority of them from some of the world's greats such as Richard Bandler, John Grinder, Robert Anton Wilson, Win Wenger, Aleister Crowley, Timothy Leary and many more.

If I am to take credit for anything it will be for my capacity to bring a variety of disciplines together and make them work as one unit. My focus is your happiness. This book will provide you with the tools to achieve happiness.

One set of tools that I have used, which dominates the pages, is NLP. NLP is a transformational, feel-good, mind and mood management technology that helps you to build confidence, stay positive, face adversity, overcome challenge and persuade more easily. NLP stands for Neuro-Linguistic Programming. Neuro refers to your brain and how to run it better. Linguistic refers to language and this includes body language. Programming refers to your ability to learn how to program your brain and other people's brains for positive results.

NLP originated in the early 1970s when Richard Bandler, a student at the University of California, Santa Cruz, was transcribing taped therapy sessions of the Gestalt therapist Fritz Perls. Richard recognised particular language patterns and behaviour structures that determined Perls' success. He showed his findings to one of his lecturers, John Grinder, a linguist, and together they decided to model other successful therapists, such as Milton Erickson and Virginia Satir. As a result NLP 'the science of success' was born. NLP has become a global phenomenon. From its early roots as a therapeutic tool it has spread its wings across the world of business, politics, sports and comedy. Notable users of NLP include Bill Clinton, Andre Agassi, Tony Blair and Jimmy Carr. Nowadays NLP is an essential tool for anyone in the helping professions, from life coaches to GPs and even your dentist.

Much of my focus is centred around the latest research findings on happiness. Dr Michael Fordyce published the results in 1977 of the world's first comprehensive experiment designed to increase personal happiness. He later refined this in 1983. In 1980 New

Zealand scientists S. Lichter, K. Haye and R. Kammann also conducted happiness-increase experiments. Their combined research has become known as 'the science of happiness-increase'. Their findings demonstrated that individuals could be taught to increase their happiness dramatically (by an average of 25 per cent) through training. I know the tools in this book will do far more than that.

Here are the findings of some of this research:

- Happy people consider that life has a purpose.
- Happy people spend up to 50 per cent less time than their unhappy counterparts thinking about unpleasant experiences.
- Happy people actively 'sort' for the positive when bad things happen.
- Happy people keep records, journals and/or diaries and write down their goals.
- Happy people choose long-term, inter-related goals involving career, education, family and geography, which amount to about 80 per cent of life satisfaction.
- Happy people compete to better their best and avoid negative comparisons with others.
- Happy people choose co-operation over competition where possible.
- Happy people focus regularly on what they are grateful for in life.
- Happy people actively seek the company of other happy people.
- Happy people are more likely to be healthier.
- Happy people are more likely to live longer.
- Happy people are more likely to marry.
- Happy people tend to have more fulfilling lives.
- Happy people are more likely to have friends.
- Happy people are more generous.
- Happy people are more creative.
- Happy people enjoy their jobs more.
- Happy people tend to earn more.
- Happy people are more likely to be more active.

- Happy people are more likely to have more energy.
- Happy people like to keep others happy.
- Happy people make happiness a priority.

By applying your mind, building the skills and remaining consistent, and by making your happiness a priority, you will experience outstanding results in your life.

I have kept this book as brief and to the point as I can. To fast-track your progress I have devised a series of core questions and processes that need to be addressed for you to bring about profound positive change in your life.

Your journey of change works on eight different levels. This book will teach you how to optimise and transcend each level for maximum progress and effect.

The Eight Levels of Change

This chart highlights the eight core areas that I will be concentrating on in this book in order for you to achieve permanent and positive change in your life.

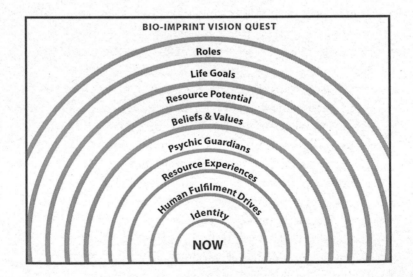

The Eight Underlying Questions

Each of the eight core areas is driven by a single question. The question for each level is reflected in that level. If you compare this chart with the previous one you will see the core area and its relevant question in the corresponding level.

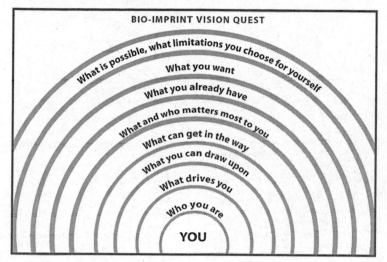

BIO-IMPRINT VISION QUEST

What is possible, what limitations you choose for yourself

What you want

What you already have

What and who matters most to you

What can get in the way

What you can draw upon

What drives you

Who you are

YOU

The Eight Levels: Expansion One

Each core area is influenced by a number of factors. For example the core area 'Roles' (i.e. the ones you perform in life) is affected by 'The time you have' and 'the spaces (e.g. jobs and activities) you occupy'. This expanded chart is shown on page 6. It may not mean very much to you right now, however, you will find it a useful reference tool once you have read the book.

The Eight Levels: Complete Chart

This chart, on page 281, is a summation of the entire book. In it you will see that I have merged the previous three charts. So be sure to revisit all of these charts as you read the book and after you read the book.

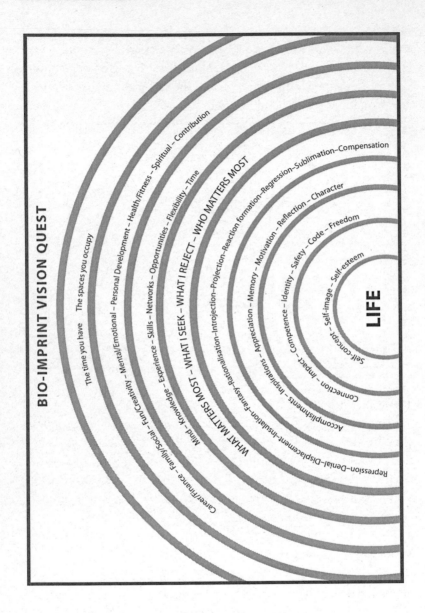

These charts will serve to jog your memory and realign your focus in seconds so that you can continue to concentrate on what matters most and live a life that's more fulfilling, fun-filled and successful.

My advice is that you read this book from start to finish and do each exercise as it is presented to you. All change requires an expenditure of effort and the more you give to each of the exercises the more life will give back to you. Most exercises are clearly explained before you are invited to engage with them; however, some things are best left unexplained as they will make greater sense when you do them. There are a number of exercises throughout the book that I am certain you will enjoy and use often.

Chapter 1 gets straight into the action. You will be made aware of the power of your breathing on your imagination and how it impacts on the quality of your thinking. This is followed by an invitation to breathe in a way that will start things changing. Next you will be invited to establish a starting point for your journey. To set some overview, 'Big Picture' goals and then to establish what gets in the way of achieving them. There are a number of overview exercises to give you that starting point, along with some funda- mental questions that represent the core focus of the book. At the end there is a little experiment for you to try.

Chapter 2 introduces you to the concept of running your brain and addresses the absolute need for behavioural flexibility in order to be continuously happy.

Chapter 3 addresses the source and causes of negative thinking and provides a powerful, simple, effective solution.

Chapter 4 gets a little more technical and teaches practical applications of thinking. It shows you how to collapse negative feelings and how to build positive ones in a very simple way.

Chapter 5 takes you on a journey of self-discovery and prompts you to explore your skills, attributes and qualities, many of which are often hidden, overlooked or forgotten. It encourages you to use them to get you into a more positive and resourceful state to make more changes in your thinking and consequently in your life.

Chapter 6 teaches and demonstrates effective goal-setting in a way that suits the brain and leads to sustainable feelings of motivation.

Chapter 7 deals with how to overcome worries by explaining how and why they operate in the manner that they do and what you need to do to deal with them.

Chapter 8 investigates how to handle challenges, problems and obstacles and helps you clear a path to happiness.

Chapter 9 teaches you the power of words and how to use them to talk yourself into success.

Chapter 10 looks at how to deal with conscious and unconscious conflict and how to create a more harmonious life experience by being cognisant of each other's life values.

Chapter 11 addresses the challenges of interpersonal interactions and explores the rules of engagement for effective relations with others.

Chapter 12 uses personality-profiling techniques to deepen your understanding of how people are and why they do what they do.

Chapter 13 reveals the fundamental drives of all human beings. These drives give rise to your values.

Chapter 14 creates and assigns your chosen values.

Chapter 15 brings things to a conclusion. It provides the template for your Bio-Imprint Statement and gives a quick review and overview of how to ensure continued happiness.

Let me take this opportunity to wish you well. I trust you will enjoy this book and my hope for you is that you experience the same or greater levels of balance, harmony and happiness that I have had in my life since studying and taking on board these learnings.

Journey well!

CHAPTER 1

Setting the Agenda for a Happier You

Imagination is the beginning of creation. You imagine what you desire, you will what you imagine and at last you create what you will.

George Bernard Shaw

The Breath of Life

The first thing you take when you come into this world is a deep breath and the last thing you will take on passing into spirit is another deep breath. You know how important it is to breathe but do you realise how fundamental it is for optimum brain functioning and succeeding in life? Your happiness literally depends on it!

Recent research from the field of emotional intelligence has revealed the wisdom behind what your mother used to tell you when you were stressed, 'Just take a few deep breaths and you will be okay.' We now know that the process of taking a few deep breaths activates the thinking portion of the brain and reduces the impact of the feeling part of the brain. In short, it helps you to think more rationally.

Breathing affects the quality of your thinking and the quality of your thinking is what determines the results you get from life. Despite its necessity, many of us fail to breathe properly.

Yoga teachers have known for centuries that where breath flows consciousness follows. Being mindful, being in the moment, being fully present is determined by how you allow yourself to breathe.

Taking a few good quality, deep breaths makes you fully aware of your body. By taking you away from the everyday hustle and bustle, it gives you back control of your mind and leaves you centred. It grounds you and reminds you to be in the here and now.

If you take a look around you, you will find that people breathe differently; some high up in their chest, some from their mid-section and others from their tummy. The ones that breathe from their tummy are the ones that are fully present in their world. The ones whose breathing is often fast and shallow and is located in their mid-section are often the ones with the biggest problems. They may even be hunched up as if they are getting ready to fold over. The ones that breathe higher are in such a hurry that life passes them by.

Breathing opens the gateways to alternative states of consciousness. The shaman's breath takes him deep into earth on his vision quest to the spirit world and takes him back again to lead his tribe. The medicine man reduces his breath and slows down his heart almost to a standstill to get insight so that he can help his patient. The modern healer uses her breath to guide her trance and dance between both worlds so that she can make the unknown known and bend reality to her will.

If you are breathing from your chest – that is, if when you take a breath you do it like the smoker does – you only go so deep (you will know this if your chest feels restricted most of the time) and that's not good. You need to go all the way. If you stop halfway through and hold on too tightly then that's what happens in your life as well. You will 'go with the flow', so it makes sense to breathe better, it's as simple as that.

Breathing affects the movie-making capacity of your imagination. Everything that is or ever will be is first born in your imagination. To get the best from this book I want you to be making the best-quality mental movies possible so that the limits in your life are governed only by the limits of your imagination, which itself is limitless.

So the first thing I am going to ask you to do is to breathe!

Exercise: The Breath of Life

As time goes on this simple technique will condition you to breathe more deeply in general and that can only be good. Obviously you can't breathe like this all of the time, if you did you would be likely to hyperventilate.

1. Take a deep breath, counting slowly 1-2-3-4, then pause.
2. Hold on to this breath, counting silently 1-2-3-4, then pause.
3. Exhale slowly and very gently, releasing this time to the count of 1-2-3-4-5-6-7-8. By the time you reach 5 you will need to push the remaining air out of your lungs.
4. Repeat this process ten times at least.

If you do this exercise sitting down be aware that you may feel light-headed for a few moments so take care when exerting yourself.

I know that by the count of eight you would probably have dropped the baby and grabbed on to dear life, but believe me exhale until it feels like you have nothing left and then squeeze out some more so that your lungs will empty. This will benefit you in many ways.

Do this about ten times at first and then whenever you become aware of the need to improve your breathing. The first ten times it can feel particularly spacey. It's called oxygen, your body needs it, your body loves it but it may not be used to it, so when you take off the stranglehold you had on it, it may just feel like a rush to the head.

Stop for a few moments and do it now. Nobody need notice if you do it quietly. Wherever you are now, whether you are in company or not, go ahead: softly, gently and slowly inhale to the count of four. Hold to the count of four and exhale ever so slowly to the count of eight until you feel a spacey sensation inside your head or a tingling sensation in your hands or both.

Enjoy the freedom it will give you. Once you have done it take a break, raise your head from the pages, have a look around you for a few moments and let your breathing come back to normal before returning to the text again.

That doesn't take very long does it? So from here on in try to be more aware of your breathing, especially when you want to feel better and re-centre yourself. Once you are aware of it, you'll regularly grab a few good deep breaths – oxygenate and off you go again.

The Circle of Life

Now I want to establish a quick overview of where you are at this point in your life. In order to develop the habit of happiness you first need to establish where you are now, and then you can decide where you want to go in the future.

People are constantly changing. You are changing. You are moving in one of two directions, either backwards or forwards. You don't get to stand still. People often say they feel stuck in life. They are not stuck, they are probably going backwards.

You need to learn how to go forward more of the time. Once you start to learn that, you can start to give shape, depth and dimension to your levels of happiness.

Exercise: The Circle of Life

This exercise only takes a few minutes. Take a look at the diagram on page 15. You are going to see what I call 'the Circle of Life'. It's a wheel that is used to give you an indication of where you are at this moment in time. It's like taking a snapshot of your life right now.

I want you to look at the Circle of Life and in each grid plot where, in your opinion, you are now. So, for example, if you choose Personal Development as a starting point, take note of where you reckon you are now. You will see that there are grades from one to ten and what I want you to do is to mark out where you are on each of those grids.

What's really important in this exercise is that you mark out where you are, not where you want to be. Let's look at it this way: I am doing the exercise and for Health and Fitness I put down a mark of five. I'm reasonably fit, I'm not Olympic fit but I'm reasonably fit, I'm fit enough, you know. (Fit for nothing as my Dad used to say jokingly.) I don't want to be a ten, I'm not interested in being a ten,

I might push it and go up to a seven or say a seven and a half. That's all I will ever want. What I am suggesting to you is that you don't have to be a ten in everything, it's just wherever you want to be, you get to choose. Perfection is not required, neither is it desirable. Striving for perfection is classic self-sabotage stuff, you can never get there because perfection requires you to measure your destination against something better all the time. That's why perfectionists are so stressed, as soon as one mountain is reached they just see a better one on the other side – what a bore!

So plot out where you are in each of the areas. There is a section for 'Contribution'. Contribution means giving back. By giving back I mean unconditional giving back. For example, you might work for the Samaritans, you might visit your elderly next-door neighbour or you might make a donation to a particular charity. One of the principles of abundance, one of the principles of wealth is based on the concept of Contribution. If you look at the most successful people in the world they often have particular charities or causes that they give to. This frees up energy – if you are giving you are better able to receive. It just seems to work that way.

Now I know some cynical people are thinking that rich people only give to charity because of the tax incentive, but that is precisely the point: when you give you get.

Buckminster Fuller, a famous architect, designer, author and inventor, recognised that there is enough for everyone. In his analysis of the condition of 'Spaceship Earth' he concluded that during the 1970s humanity had attained the relevant knowledge and resources such that competition for necessities was not necessary anymore. Co-operation had become the optimum survival strategy. 'Selfishness,' he declared, 'is unnecessary and hence-forth unrationalizable' and he even went so far as to say, 'War is obsolete.'

You too have all that you need to get all that you want. However, it is a question of becoming aware of that before claiming power over it. Everyone has the ability to choose a better life. That too is a skill and the fortunate thing is it can be learned. Just like happiness is a skill that can be made into a habit. Once you are happy the rest of it becomes easier.

This book is not interested in laying blame on your past for the person you are today. This book is about self-awareness, but awareness by itself isn't enough. Once you become aware of who you are, you have to learn how to work with it and sometimes through it. This may call for change.

Quantum physicist Dr Amit Goswami says that real change requires accessing 'a non-ordinary state of consciousness'. To help you do this, I have prepared a specially designed hypnotic CD, entitled *Mind Whispers: Developing the Happiness Habit*, to accompany this book. You will find it attached to the inside back cover. Listening to this CD daily for a couple of weeks will facilitate this state of non-ordinary consciousness. But for now I am going to ask that you complete the Circle of Life chart opposite.

The aim of the next part of the exercise is to help you focus your brain on the Big Picture and to keep it there throughout this book. So I am now going to ask you to be a little more specific. In the Circle of life you have identified the areas that you want to improve or focus on. These are your Big Picture goals. Now I am going to ask you to be a little more specific about your chosen areas and note in some more detail your Big Picture goal or goals. One line or even a couple of words is plenty for now.

For example, if I feel I need to have more fun in life then under the heading 'Fun' I might add the following first steps:

1. Do a bungee jump – Search the Internet to find out where.
2. Go snowboarding – Phone Dave to book a session.
3. Take a holiday – Drop by the travel agents today.

For now, keep it brief, simple and to the point. I have included some prompts to help you on your way. It is not necessary that you answer the prompt questions, only that you select at least one goal in each area of importance. However, the more the merrier! Be sure to run each goal through the '60 Second Goal Setting' criteria.

The Circle of Life

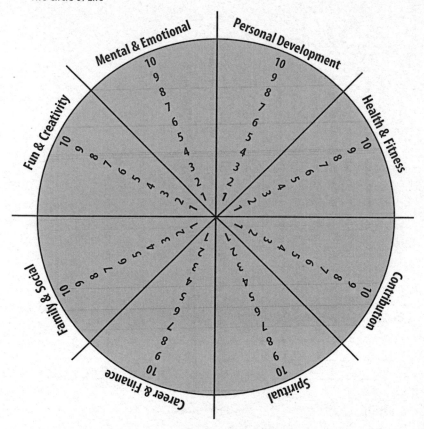

Please take up a pen and complete the chart by circling or marking where you feel that you currently stand in relation to the above stated areas of your life. The number of points you can assign ranges from one to ten. One is the minimum amount of points and means you are totally dissatisfied and ten is the maximum and means you are totally satisfied (i.e. there is no room for improvement). Once you have completed the chart, connect the points.

Next repeat the exercise, this time marking out where you would like to be in a year or six months from now. You can use a different colour of pen to do this.

Now you have an overview and a number of more specific targets to aim for and a means with which to track your progress.

Big Picture Goals: 60 Second Goal Setting

- What do you want?
- When do you want it?
- What will you see, hear and feel when you have it?
- What's your first step?

Health and Fitness   **First steps**

Prompt: What can you do to improve your health? How fit do you want to be?

1 _____   _____

2 _____   _____

3 _____   _____

Contribution   **First steps**

Prompt: What would make you feel really good about yourself if you do it?

1 _____   _____

2 _____   _____

3 _____   _____

Spiritual   **First steps**

Prompt: What about your soul?

1 _____   _____

2 _____   _____

3 _____   _____

Career and Finance   **First steps**

Prompt: What is your ideal job? How much money do you want to make in a year?

1 _____   _____

2 _____   _____

3 _____   _____

Family and Social   **First steps**

Prompt: Who is important to you? What about your friends?

1 _____   _____
2 _____   _____
3 _____   _____

Fun and Creativity   **First steps**

Prompt: What would you love to do? What do you dream about doing?

1 _____   _____
2 _____   _____
3 _____   _____

Mental and Emotional   **First steps**

Prompt: What do you want to learn? How do you want to feel most days?

1 _____   _____
2 _____   _____
3 _____   _____

Personal Development   **First steps**

Prompt: What else is there to include as a goal here?

1 _____   _____
2 _____   _____
3 _____   _____

What Stops You?

Now that you have decided what you want, it's time to assess what stops you from becoming or being who and how you want to be. Whether you want to see yourself radiating with confidence or filled with happiness. Whether you are drawn to the idea of being an outstanding communicator or being the one that lights up the room when you walk in. Whether you'd like to see yourself in a fulfilling relationship, with a partner, among friends or even family. What stops you?

What do you want for yourself? I cannot know exactly what that is, but I do know that you already know, if only on a deeper level. If you're not already aware I can help you identify it. What is it that has stopped you? What is it that has prevented you thus far from becoming your better self? The self that you know deep down inside you can be. That you want to be. That you deserve to be. Isn't it time right now to start to make that happen? This truly can be your time to shine.

Identify right here and now what it is that stops you. What prevents you from being who you want to be? If you can identify that, I hope to help you get past it so that the only question you're left with is: What *can* stop me? I don't need to answer that one, do I?

What I am asking you to do now is to find out what gets in your way. I am not asking you *why* you have not got to where you want to go. I am asking you *what* gets in the way. Please think about it for a few moments.

You're reading this book for a reason and when you think it through you know most of the obstacles can be narrowed down to one or two reasons. The same stuff that keeps cropping up time and time again. But what I want you to do is begin to notice what it is that gets in your way. I want you to start to note it down in the space set out on page 20.

Keep in mind that this is not a counselling session. I am not interested in eliciting pain or tears. I am not interested in your life story to date. You cannot undo what is already done so there is no use in complaining about it. All that produces is more of the same. My guess is that you have had enough of that already. I am not interested in the blame game either. I am not looking for a long and tedious rendition of a sob story. You know the kind that goes 'When I was a little helpless innocent child they took my soother away from me.' I just want you to list down what stops you now – that's all. The best thing about the past is that it is over. You are here, in the now. You can be strong and you can take control. Things will work out so much better this way.

If up until now you believed that you were not confident enough, well then that's what stops you. If you have being saying to yourself 'I'm not a good people person', well that's what stops you. If you've been saying 'I'm depressed', then that's what stops you. If you have been saying 'I'm too irritated most of time', then that's what stops you. I want you to put short labels on it, just one or two words. I will show you some examples of what I mean below.

Please forgive my apparent lack of sensitivity but I am not focusing on the negative because that is precisely where we are headed away from. My interest here is solely focused on your life getting better and your happiness becoming habit. I want you to create the starting points, the place where your journey of personal evolution and change begins. Once you identify that and decide it's time to break free of it, your life becomes absolutely magical. It becomes much more fulfilling, more enjoyable and more exciting. Once you target and label what has been in the way up until now, you know where the fences around your freedom are. The fences that you are going to jump past, break through or smash down to have the life you want. You may have up to five or six big reasons. Once you know them, the rest of it gets easier. So go for it!

In the box are some typical reasons offered up by the thousands of people I have trained to date. Read them and let them prompt your own.

Lack of motivation
Tension
Inner conflict
Fear of failure
Fear of change
Lack of direction
Poor communication skills
Procrastination
Feeling stupid
Putting others first
Lack of confidence
Overactive mind
Lack of time
Stress
Lack of skill
Lack of confidence
No self-belief
Low self-esteem
Feelings of inadequacy
Indecision
Fear of relationship difficulties
Lack of focus
Hesitation

Exercise: What Stops You?
Write down in point format, in the left-hand box only, all the things that have stopped you from succeeding so far. What has gotten in the way? What prevented you thus far from getting to where and who you want to be?

Step 1: Challenge	Step 2: Conversation
What stops you?	What does the solution look and feel like?

Once you have completed the list of what stops you in the left-hand box, I want you to take each point in turn and write down the solution in the right-hand box entitled 'Conversion', again in point format. Don't think about the mechanics of *how* to do this just yet, that will come later. For now all I want you to do is to produce what you believe is the solution to the challenge. For example, if you wrote down 'fear of failure', the solution is 'success'. If you wrote down 'too shy', the solution is 'confidence'. If you wrote down 'procrastination', the solution might be 'decisiveness' and so on.

When you have that done I want you to keep in mind that you are going to get through it and you are going to sort it out. When you know what the target is, you know what you want to get over, what you want to get past, we can set it up so that you can do that. Now I can't get you a new house, but if you want a new house and that's what you stated, then what I can do is to set up the mental skills, the capacity, the ability for you to be able to get the house. If you get through all that has stopped you up until now, then you get what you want and my job is well done. But I like to be thorough so I have even better plans for you, I want to give you more than you ask for. I think it is a good thing if you make people feel better just because you can, don't you?

Work Smarter Not Harder

Now that we have our starting point we can begin the process of making it all happen. No matter what, if only theoretically, it is possible to come up with solutions for all of the things you have listed. When you do, you get to be happier. You get to have the life you want.

Most of us have been led to believe that if we work hard and struggle to survive everything will work out. In Japan many truck and cab drivers and people who work long hours to survive take amphetamines, which they call 'shabu' (we call them 'meth' or 'ice'). Amphetamines fool you into thinking you can achieve anything, without tiredness or hunger. Chronic abuse can lead to problems including psychosis, paranoia and aggression. It can cause a variety of physical health problems including damage to the liver, kidneys or stomach. Paranoid delusions are common amongst heavy users. Hitler was addicted to amphetamines.

Successful people often don't work that hard, they just work smarter. They use time differently and often they use other people's time too. I take stage hypnotist Paul McKenna's advice on the matter. Paul says, 'Programme your own mind before someone else does.' If you don't have a plan for how you want things to turn out for you,

you can bet your bottom dollar someone else has one for you. If you experience daily tension and irritation it may be because you have been fulfilling someone else's dreams and your unconscious is knocking on your door to tell you to wake up, your freedom is on the line.

It's time that you take a deep breath in and start to feed your unconscious with the right suggestions, the nicest images and the best outcomes. Start to use your mind, your imagination and your creative intelligence so that you can begin to program in ideas, the fuel that will support you from moment to moment. Once this happens, then you are ready to make good decisions. You are ready to claim your personal freedom. Your future will already be looking brighter. You don't have to have everything down to a fine art. We don't all have to be the Michelangelos of this world. You just have to master the art of living a life worth living and that's what you are now beginning to do.

Many of us hesitate and say, 'Well I'll get to that later'. But with time, you can never tell for sure how much of it you have. That's why it is important to make every moment count. I often ask the question:

WHAT WOULD YOU DO IF YOU WEREN'T DOING THIS?

And if the answer is 'anything', then I know I am not making the moment count. Get into the habit of asking yourself:

IS WHAT I AM DOING REALLY WORTH DOING?
DOES IT MAKE ME HAPPY?

And if you act on this each time you ask, soon you will be making more and more moments count. You don't have to go changing everything at once. If you are changing some things all of the time you will get there quicker than you thought.

Imagine a loaded gun was put to your head right now, and the trigger was about to be pulled and you were asked:

HAVE YOU BEEN MAKING EACH MOMENT COUNT?

Could you say you've been doing the best that you can? Because if you can't, it is time that you change things so that you can and you do. Change things so that at the end of each day, you can look back and smile.

Exercise: The Final Month

Consider what you would do if you were informed that you were being granted one final month to complete your life on this earth after which, without pain or incident, you would no longer be a part of the life you now know. You are also told that you will be given sufficient extra time to say your goodbyes and to get your technical affairs in order in the appropriate way, so those matters can be excluded here.

Gerry French, a good friend of mine, was in the audience the first time I presented 'The Final Month' exercise to a group. After setting up the exercise and explaining what I wanted the group to do I noticed Gerry sitting motionless, his arms folded and a stubborn look on his face. I said to him, 'Gerry! What's the problem?' To which he responded indignantly, 'What do you mean, what's the problem?' Surprised by his lack of co-operation, I asked him, 'Are you not doing the exercise?' To which he replied, 'Sure there's no f**king point I'll be dead in a month!' Now although he was joking, this is not the point of this exercise. In another seminar in Scotland, I overheard one of the delegates arranging his funeral; that is not the point either. This is an exercise in positive thinking.

So, using the present tense, I want you to write down overleaf what you are going to do over the next thirty-one days, what you are going to do with your final month?

_____

_____

_____

_____

_____

_____

_____

_____

_____

_____

_____

_____

Epitaph: What would you most like to be remembered for and how would you have it written on your headstone?

_____

_____

_____

Now that you have completed this exercise, look and see if there is anything on your list that you could already be doing. You know it is important. Your happiness depends on it. You know what to do!

Some people think, 'I can't be doing that, what would people think?' Well why can't you? Is it because it just doesn't feel right? That's just part of the 'selfishness is bad and you'll burn in hell for it philosophy' put forward by people who know no better. Selfishness is not a bad thing, it's a good thing. Selfishness opens the door to selflessness. In order to be selfless you need to be selfish first, that way you can give freely and with compassion.

Success Requires Clear Positive Thinking

Decisions and beliefs are alike. Indecision is about not believing that you know the right answer – as if there could only be one. You have to believe in yourself. Think of those people who psych themselves up with the same gusto every year before setting out their New Year's Resolution. They usually end up in exactly the same place they started a little later because they lack self-belief. You need to give yourself permission to have a go and be prepared to be wrong.

You need to trust your intuition. Joe Vitale, contributor to Rhonda Byrne's world-famous book *The Secret*, states, 'As with most things in life, there's little to be afraid of, and wealth and glory await right around the corner. All you have to do is step forward and do the things you're being nudged to do from within.' Your greatest resource is your intuition, if you start to listen to your intuition you will always find a way. I have not met anyone who could say that their intuition did not serve them for most if not all things. Your intuition is your inner guidance missile. If you want, it can be your god talking through you. Some people mistake feelings for intuition, but they are not the same. Your intuition produces a feeling, but it also produces with it a sense of what to do that is right. It involves 'a push' or 'a pull' in a particular direction that holds with it a sense of knowing that this is the right thing to do. Often independent of logic, or of the presenting 'evidence', it whispers faintly in the background of your mind. It is always there, so set it free and let it guide you.

How to Charm Reality from Your Desires

Try this little experiment:

1. Bring to mind a goal that you have never really invested a whole lot of thought, time or effort into achieving. One that is what you might consider just a little bit outside your scope. One that would leave you grinning from ear to ear for weeks if it were to happen. You know the type that can fill you with pride and make you sing and laugh and dance for joy! Take a few moments to imagine just how cool that would be and enjoy the feeling that goes with it.
2. Now think how grateful and thankful you would feel if it actually happened.
3. Imagine what it could be like if it actually is happening now.
4. Notice how your body is responding.
5. Be playful, allow yourself to be entertained by the prospect.
6. Give the feeling space to build.
7. Decide now to dip just momentarily into that feeling a handful of times each day over the next week.
8. Go on about your daily business now as if nothing much has changed. You have played an imagination game that feels good. You have agreed to remind yourself over the next few days, more for the sake of the feeling it gives than the consequences it may produce. At some point in your day, something will happen that will catch your attention and make you think for just a moment. When that happens STOP and LISTEN. Is this your intuition nudging you in a particular direction? If it doesn't appear to fit with what you are doing, yet you notice a gentle pull towards it that feels right to you, I invite you to follow and see where it takes you. Life may never be the same again! You will be consciously experiencing The Law of Attraction at play!

CHAPTER 2

How to Build the Habit of Happiness

Take charge of your thoughts. You can do what you will with them.

Plato

Conscious Versus Subconscious

onsider when you were just an infant and you were learning to walk. You didn't get all the way up off the ground on your shaky little legs only to fall on your bum and say, 'Well this is not really working out for me, this walking thing.' And then when you tried it again you didn't say, 'Nope I don't think so.' You tried it one more time and never gave up. You got up every single time. You looked at where you were going and even with wobbly legs you began to focus on where you wanted to go, to focus on what it was you wanted to have. When you were crawling about you had the idea that walking would improve things for you, if you could just get there. Mummy's there and Daddy's there and they are beckoning, 'Come on, come on, come on you can do it ... come to Mummy.'

And you did. Eventually you toddled right over to your mother's arms. The reality is, if you focus on where it is you want to go, you will get there. The problem for most people is that they give up too easily.

Our brains love what they already know, what's habit. However, our brains can only learn by doing different things, new things. As you got older, rather than respond instinctively as you did as a child, you began to think about things and you began to choose immediate comfort over change. But the devil you know is not always better than the devil you don't. Each time you hesitate, a little more uneasiness builds and builds until it becomes unbearable. It lingers in the background of your mind as a nagging feeling that you are better than this, while your old brain says you can't keep going on changing things willy-nilly.

The Laws of Repetition and Association

Both parts of the brain have their useful functions. The older part, to build and keep habits, works through The Law of Association and The Law of Repetition. Once it finds something that works, it keeps on seeking it out and doing it over and over again so that it feels natural. This is the part of the brain that is responsible for your habits. It is good for learning and remembering stuff. It is good for learning how to ride a bike, drive a car, swim, speak etc. But it's not perfect in that it has not got a lot of discernment. It is based on the here and now and does not take into account the future consequences of not repeating something. For example, you might be familiar with the following scenario inside your head:

'I think I feel like having some chocolate tonight.'
Oh but that's not very healthy
'I want chocolate.'
But all those extra calo–
'I want chocolate, I want chocolate now!'
But . . .
'But nothing, never mind your butt, I want chocolate, lovely sumptuous chocolate, adorable melt-in-your-mouth chocolate. I'm dying here, where's the goddamn chocolate! It's party time! I love chocolate! Isn't life great! Ah for the good things in life.'
Oh I really shouldn't . . .
'Shut the hell up brain I'm eating here! Yeah baby, now that's what I'm talking about.'
Honey, do I look fat in this?

Ask yourself which part of your brain you have been using more of lately. Is it the habit part (the lazy part) or is it the creative part (the innovative part)?

Your brain is constantly building new neural nets for the 'old brain' to manage. Once the net is built by the conscious part of your mind, it is handed over to the non-conscious mind or the automatic mind (the 'old brain'). However, once handed over, it can only survive if it is exercised. The neural net is much like a muscle and like any muscle you have to use it or lose it.

Your brain is made up of billions of neurons. Neurons are the tiny brain cells that make up your nervous system. If you could imagine a huge crowd of people at a live music performance all chatting away to one another, each having their own interests and concerns, this would be similar to what's going on with the neurons inside your brain at any given time. Each time you experience something, a message travels from one neuron to another and imprints itself on your brain. This leaves a trail much like you do if you walk through long grass in a field. The brain acts on these imprints and creates interconnecting pathways or networks between the neurons, so that the next time you experience the same thing, such as riding a bike, driving a car or learning a new skill, your brain uses this same path. As a result, the skill becomes easier and you can do it with less effort.

It's like what happens when the band strikes the first note of your favourite song, as soon as you hear it you immediately recognise and recall every note of it, because the brain has your 'favourite song' pathway already imprinted. These interconnected pathways are called neural networks, you know them as memories and often experience them as habits. In the case of your favourite song, learning to recall all the different elements – the vocals, the drums, the bass, the lead, the keyboards – all feels easier because of the positive emotion it stirs in you. However, when learning new skills or creating behavioural change our emotional approach tends to be different. Change can feel temporarily uncomfortable or even fearful depending on how long you have been slacking off. But once the older brain gets the experience clocked up a few times, it will work on making it feel natural to you. That's just the way it is. The brain, once given the opportunity, will normalise anything. Have a look around you at what some people consider normal.

The Kayan women of Burma and Thailand consider it normal and beautiful to wear multiple neck rings (brass coils), which give them the appearance of having an elongated neck. The coils, which are applied from the age of five onwards, are added to once the weight of the previous brass coil pushes down the collar bone and compresses the rib cage, thereby making space for a new one. After ten years or so these women say that the coils feel like a natural or normal part of their body. The brain has normalised the sensations that go with this.

Some people consider it normal to go to the gym every second day. Some people consider it normal to eat curry for breakfast, dinner and tea. Some people consider it normal to read five or six books a week. These people are not different from you, they have just done different things more times than you and now they are carrying on as normal. (Well, at least their version of normality!) All of this comes from the older brain, the habit-forming brain, or what psychologists call the unconscious or subconscious part of the brain.

You have done this many times yourself. You now have skills, capacities and abilities that at one point were unfamiliar, unknown or even apparently impossible to you, but with perseverance you succeeded. You can now read but there was a time when you couldn't.

But for now your questions are:

WHAT DO YOU WANT TO FEEL NORMAL TO YOU?

WHAT HABITS DO YOU WANT TO BUILD?

We like to think that life is supposed to be easy all of the time – and life can get to be a lot easier – but it's supposed to be challenging too. Wouldn't it be boring if everything was so easy?

Have you ever thought about those pivotal times, those defining moments that let you know that you are growing as a person? Times when it feels like you're evolving, developing, transforming into something better, someone to be proud of. They were the times when it was most challenging. It could be changing jobs, taking on a course of study or ending a relationship. You got through that and you said to yourself 'Well it didn't kill me . . . and what doesn't kill you makes you . . .' so you end up being a much better person because of it.

Things are often not as difficult as you might think, but they are as difficult as you make them. And what you will learn throughout this book is how to begin to change your thinking so you can start to make things that were once challenging a lot easier. The next time – and there will be a next time – that you feel the emotional pull to hesitate, recognise that it is just your older brain doing its thing, attempting to keep the status quo, to play the same record again and again.

When people consult me in my clinic on an issue like weight management they often tell me that they have tried lots of things to keep fit, but they just lose their motivation after a while and say there is no point. The change required is too big, they don't have the time and they can't manage to fit it into their lives. This is because there is a threshold point where things change. When they try to do their exercise routine and fail to see the results they want at the pace they want, they get disillusioned. They claim they don't have the motivation, that it is too much hard work.

Now it is true that change very often requires effort, but these clients are used to effort. Many of them lead very busy lives and work hard to earn a living, so hard work is rarely the problem. Tiredness, exhaustion, exasperation and frustration are often the enemy. However, a lot of this is borne out of their mental approach to change as opposed to their physical approach. So when they try to add in an extra behaviour on top of an already hectic lifestyle, the brain decides that the change is not a good thing and pulls them back to 'normality'. Sometimes the brain doesn't know what's best for you. You have to learn how the brain works to get it to work for you.

This is your opportunity to take charge of your brain and let it know that it will get that familiar feeling once you have done it enough times. Because that brain is also a greedy brain and it just loves more of the same. However, to give it more of the same (i.e. that underlying feel-good feeling) you have to keep doing different things. It's all down to chemicals and thinking is chemical.

If, for example, you like chocolate, follow this sequence through. Buy a bar of your favourite chocolate. Bring the chocolate to your mouth and draw in the smell of it through your nose. Notice the delicious taste of it (you have taste receptacles in your nose). Now take the first piece and let it slowly melt in your mouth while you indulge in its rich decadent flavour. Slow everything right down as you and your taste buds relish the entire sensation. When you're ready, swallow it and track the feeling as you complete the process. Now take a second piece and restart the process. You will notice that after a while the freshness, the newness and the attraction reduces and what you are really doing is just satisfying a habit. What is happening is your habit mind is making you continue just for habit's sake (The Law of Association: I did it before and it tasted good, and The Law of Repetition: so if I keep doing this stuff I will continue to feel better). But that is not true.

The more you continue to do the same thing over and over again the less benefit you get from it. In fact if you think of it, the more you do something over and over again the more you need of it to feel the same as you felt at first. This is how out of control habits work. The drug addict calls this 'chasing the dragon'. It's the thing he knows will get him in the end. With overuse, as with over-indulgence, the sensation (nerve endings) gets saturated or dulled and so more is required to replace the original sensation, until eventually even that can't be reached.

Frank, a friend of mine, used to tell me with pride that he was a redhead which 'meant' he was fiery by nature. Over the years I witnessed his assumed identity wreak havoc on his relationships.

(I was tempted to suggest that he shave off his hair to see would his fire subside!) His belief led him to develop the habit of allowing himself to get angry with people and of justifying his behaviour afterwards as 'genetic' so to speak. He got sense in his later years and realised that all he was doing was feeding a habit borne out of the dubious belief that all redheads must be hotheads. Now he is so much happier and when he gets angry he realises it's not his hair that's making him do it. It is just a learned habit which he has the power to change. Frank is a much more amicable man now, he is in a successful relationship, life is improving and so is his temperament.

What's Seldom Is Beautiful

To survive and thrive you have got to do different things on a regular basis. Because that way you don't have to change everything all at once. If you do a little a lot then it gets dull, but if you do a lot a little then life gets to be more wonderful. You now know how the expression 'what's seldom is beautiful' came about.

You need challenge in your life. Challenge is not always a comfortable thing, but that does not mean that it is a bad thing. Challenge is about change, change is about survival and survival is about evolution, which is what keeps you on top of things. Each and every challenge is an opportunity to make you stronger, more successful, more resilient and more capable of dealing with whatever else comes your way. To succeed more readily you need to be on your own side, especially when you are creating and engaging with those challenges. Doesn't that make sense?

So by now some readers are working with me, while the others are thinking, 'He's probably not talking about me, he's probably talking to the rest of the readers so I'm not going to take this on board even though it's a good idea.' If you do what you have always done then you will get what you have always got and this book is about you changing your life around for the better, yes? Albert Einstein said that the definition of insanity is doing the same thing over and over again and expecting a different result! Sound familiar? If it does, then the solution is simple, it's time to change.

Far too many people hold back and say, 'You're not messing with my head.' I know, I have been there, I did the self-hate thing, I hated everything for a time until one day the penny dropped, 'Who cares? There you go whinging and moaning and no one gives a damn except yourself and you don't count because you don't even get on with yourself.'

Ashby's Law

In systems theory there is a principle called The Law of Requisite Variety, often referred to as Ashby's Law, which states that any member of a system needs a certain minimum amount of flexibility in order to successfully adapt and survive. When applied to your life this means that in order for you to consistently achieve your goals, you must vary the things you are doing over time to continue succeeding. Nothing stands still, things change, circumstances change, situations change, opportunities come and go, you change, your body changes, your resistance levels change and as such your success strategies need to change too.

Behavioural Flexibility Is the Key

In order for you to succeed you need to notice what is happening and if what you are doing is not working you need to do something else. For example, if walking worked to help you achieve your goal of losing weight before and you find that it is no longer working, this just means that you need to do something else. Most people notice this and they end up walking for longer and longer to get the same result. The only thing that has changed here is the distance and if that works well and good. However, what has happened is that the body got used to this level of exertion and is no longer challenged by it, so really it is time to do something more than a little different – that could mean swimming instead of walking, or running, or taking up yoga. At this point it is all about introducing that level of 'flexibility' to get the same result. You are simply keeping your eye on your target but getting there in a different way.

Exercise: The Law of Requisite Variety
Select three of your most important Big Picture goals from Chapter
1 and write down as many different routes to achieving each of these
goals as possible. The more avenues, the more possibilities for success.

Goal 1:

_____

_____

_____

_____

_____

_____

Goal 2:

_____

_____

_____

_____

_____

Goal 3:

_____

_____

_____

_____

_____

Bringing Your Brain on Board

Your brain is constantly processing what's happening to you. It is also taking note of what's happening around you. The details of every event are being stored as you encounter them. Because of the way your brain is organised when you recall (or imagine) an event it is a bit like re-living it. This is the reason we feel good or bad, happy or sad, energised or deflated. Our thoughts determine how we feel. Although our brains are similar, there are huge differences in how we access and use them. Learning how to run your brain is the fun part of building the habit of happiness.

Many of us think that in order to change how we feel we need to go to a therapist or a specialist. That is not always the case. You can change how you think about many things. In a moment I will show you how. The following exercises will help you. Each exercise will need to be read first and then tried with closed eyes afterwards.

Exercise: Eliminating the Negative, Option 1

This exercise can be done anywhere, even in company. The men in the white coats will not be called to take you away (at least not for doing this exercise anyway). This exercise is in two parts, steps one and two. Read step one of the exercise first and then close your eyes and do it. Afterwards do step two. Read it first, then close your eyes, do it and notice the difference!

Step One

- Take a moment to think about someone that annoys you, someone that irritates you or makes you angry.
- Bring that somebody to mind, using your imagination or your memory.
- If you can't think of a person, just think of a behaviour that irritates, annoys or makes you angry.
- Notice what you may be seeing, hearing and feeling as that person is doing the thing that provokes you.

- You can only get this right. So whatever elements or parts you recalled are perfectly okay.

You've just completed step one. Hold your judgment until you have completed step two. Remember, read through the instructions first, then close your eyes, do it and notice the difference!

Step Two
- Bring that person or behaviour to mind again.
- This time I want you to imagine that you are bringing the image, or the feeling or the sense of them right up close to you, so that they are practically breathing on top of you.
- Imagine the person is right 'in your face'. You know that sensation, that feeling that you get.
- Imagine they are breathing down your neck, complaining, moaning and whinging and giving out or doing their really annoying thing. You may take a few moments to make this vivid in your mind.
- You will know you are getting there when you notice differences in your experience.
- Next I want you to imagine as you look at that situation or person that the colour is being drained from the experience. The entire image is losing its definition. Imagine all the colour being drained from it so that the picture itself becomes like a faint black and white watermark.
- If it's not a picture you see, begin to notice the sounds in the experience and reduce the volume a little bit.
- If you are hearing the sound of a person's voice, turn down the volume a little bit too.
- Next imagine you can actually push that person or that image away, out further into the distance.
- Notice as it goes off further into the distance it begins to get smaller; it starts to shrink to the size of a tiny little pea.
- Imagine as it shrinks that the voice shrinks as well and the sound is more faint, even cute like the voice of a cartoon character.

- Hear that tiny person giving out to you now.
- Imagine a huge gigantic foot coming into the top right-hand corner of the image.
- Imagine this foot coming thundering down on top of them and making a squelching sound as it smashes the pea-like image you see there.
- Notice what that feels like now.

Typically once you have done this exercise you will have noticed something changed as soon as you changed the structure and content of the memory you had been storing. The most significant changes are in your feelings.

Memories are a bit like balloons. When you blow them up and then let the air out of them they do not go back to their original form. So the fact that a memory has been stored in a certain way through circumstance or experience doesn't mean that you have to keep it that way. It's your memory, you can do what you like with it. Remember it is a memory. It is not the actual event. It is not the actual person or situation it is just your brain's recording of it. No one gets hurt if you alter it. You have been altering memories throughout your life. The next time you blow something out of proportion, take a closer look at how that affects the pictures inside your head. Do a little mental housekeeping and adjust the memory until it fits.

If you didn't get the result you expected yet, that's okay. This is new to you. Perfection is not a requirement the first time. In fact perfection is never a requirement unless you make it one. So relax, you have only done this once. There are plenty of other exercises to come. Not everything works for everyone all of the time. There is plenty more to be getting on with. This does not mean that NLP is not for you. Hang in there, this is just the beginning.

Right now you are learning how to take control of your brain, of your thoughts and your thinking, rather than being subjected to them.

I have done this exercise many times at my seminars and have gotten all sorts of responses. From 'fun' to 'brilliant' to 'nothing happened for me' or 'now I feel really annoyed'. Others say things like 'I feel great now but what happens when I meet the person for real?' I tell them to wait and see (I know they will be pleasantly surprised). Still more say, 'I feel better but I need to do more' and that is also allowed. This stuff is all open, you have full permission to experiment and play with it. One way or the other your experience of it is your experience of it, no more and no less. Some things take more time than others. I do not expect you to do this only once. You can work on it some more later. In a few moments I am going to get you to do another variation of the same exercise.

I will continuously suggest ways of doing things, as I did in the previous exercise. They are not meant to be written in stone. Just do whatever works for you. Find your own freedom within it to mix and match, delete or include. Stick with the principle of the thing, which is to make you happier as a result of it.

Suzie, a very positive and successful 34-year-old businesswoman, came to see me because she was having a hard time dealing with her over-critical Mum. Her Mum grew up in different times and felt that Suzie ought to have long since settled down, found herself a good man, got married and had kids. Suzie was not ready for this. But her Mum was not letting go of it. Every time Suzie visited her Mum she left frustrated and deflated. She told me there were times she felt like strangling her Mum. That added to her problems because she felt guilty for even thinking the thought. I took her through the exercise but she hesitated and opened her eyes. She said, 'But I love Mum, I can't do that to her. I can't crush her. I know she can be annoying at times but she is an absolute treasure.' When I suggested that she leave out the part with the foot in it she relaxed and smiled and said, 'I can do that,' and she did.

As it was her Mum I thought that rather than getting rid of the negative associations why not amplify the positive loving feelings she had for her too. So I did the following exercise with her.

Exercise: Accentuating the Positive

1. This time think of someone that makes you feel good when you are around them. It can be someone you love, it can be a best friend, one of your joker pals whatever. (In Suzie's case it was her Mum.)

2. Now take this experience or this memory and as though you have a remote control for the movie screen of your own imagination, I want you to take the image and draw it closer.

3. Make it bigger, make it a little brighter.

4. Turn up the sounds and make it three-dimensional.

5. Imagine that person is right here with you now and breathe in the experience.

6. If they are saying something to you, make it clearer.

7. If it is appropriate, let the person draw nearer and let them give you a warm, affectionate hug. If it's your child let him run up to you, dive into your arms and nuzzle into your neck as his eyes sparkle with delight.

8. Once you have got the experience running take a deep breath in and savour the feelings.

9. Notice how much better that feels.

My guess is that for most of you this is an easier and a far better experience than the last exercise. Everyone has someone that can make them feel good and when you bring that person into your mind then you experience those same feelings all over again. It doesn't cost you anything except a thought. Now that is worth doing. If this experience made you smile, then you know how to be happy in an instant. Think about it! It only takes a few moments of your time to bring this experience into your mind and as soon as you do you begin to feel happier. If you can do this in such a short period of time the real question is: What else is possible?

Good feelings are available to you always. You just have to make use of them. Elderly people do this often, they reminisce about the good old days. They smile, laugh, giggle and flood their bodies with warm, glowing feelings and as they do so the good old days become the good day today. No matter what age you are, you have enough good memories inside you to last you a lifetime. But that is just for starters, I am not done with you yet. There is so much more we have yet to do so that happiness will feel second nature to you. Imagine the thought of getting up each day and knowing you have a choice in it. That you can be happy if you choose to be because you know how to make each moment count.

It doesn't matter what age you are, it doesn't matter what predicament you are in now. Somewhere, someone in your life makes you smile. Someone, somewhere in your memory, makes you giggle. It could be a friend from school. It could be a workmate. It could be someone that has passed on. Somewhere, someone can make you laugh still, can bring a big smile to your face, can brighten up your day. If you can't find someone you are not looking hard enough. If you can't find one leave down this book and go look for one. Even the most hardened heart will find it difficult not to smile back at a two-year-old child looking at the world with the freshness, enthusiasm, delight and curiosity that it deserves. If you still can't find it, you're just not trying, so get up off your arse, stop acting the Mick and find it. You deserve happiness, not sympathy.

In order for you to be annoyed with someone, peeved with them or depressed with life you have to be running pictures inside your head, you have to be saying things to yourself and you have to be generating feelings. Annoyance, depression, sadness and pessimism all work the same way.

At the age of twenty-one, Loren was beginning to find her feet in life. She had just finished college and was getting the finances together for a world trip before pursuing a career in the corporate world. Her first full-time job was on a production line in a sweet factory. The people were friendly and she made good friends there. However, her line manager didn't like 'college types' and was making life a living hell for her. He was arrogant, offensive, obnoxious and downright rude to her.

Loren told me she didn't want to make trouble for herself at this point. She didn't want to leave her job either. She said she wanted to hold out for a few more months to gather enough cash to go on her travels. Although this guy was unimportant to her, he was having a disastrous effect on her confidence and on her ability to enjoy her time there. With a torrent of emotion Loren said to me, 'I just can't seem to get him out of my head! He is always there hovering over me, waiting for me to screw up, which I inevitably do because he is scowling at me! Every day he has something to say for himself. Every day he does something on me. He's always on my back; he never leaves me alone to get on with it. I wish he would just clear off and leave me be!'

I knew to help Loren I would have to do something shocking. I looked at her and then distorted my face into a pouted grimace and scowled in disgust and replied, 'And yet you sleep with him?' Loren looked at me in horror and said, 'What do you mean?' To which I replied, 'But you do, don't you? You do, you really sleep with him!' Loren moved rapidly from shock to disbelief and asked me, 'What sort of planet are you on? You're missing the point completely!' Now that I had her full attention I said, 'Well isn't this what you do? When you have an argument with him you go off and you run the argument inside your head for hours and let it spoil your day? Then at night time when you get into bed and you're naked, you're still thinking about him, he's right there with you in the bed without your clothes on?'

Loren's jaw dropped and she squirmed with disgust, she was stuck for words. I knew my job was almost done. I had installed an image inside Loren's head that was so powerful that she decided enough was enough. It was time for her to put a stop to things. I continued, 'If your manager is annoying you, causing you grief, causing you pain or difficulty doesn't it make sense to try and stop the feelings as soon as he leaves your company? Isn't it bad enough that he annoys you once rather than you carrying it with you right through the day (or in some cases right through your life)?'

When your manager does that offensive act, walks away and you end up being annoyed – think about this, he is not there any longer, but yet you're still being annoyed at him. Perhaps that is understandable if the incident is very recent and he has just left. But as a therapist I get people who are still annoyed about some things that happened years ago. Not only has the person left their company but they may have also left the planet. Seems to me like an awful waste of energy that could be used on something more worthwhile.

You don't even like your manager and you are carrying on a conversation with him inside your head for the rest of the day, which only makes you feel bad. Then you complain about how you feel like crap because of him. How else would you expect to feel? Doesn't it make sense that when you recollect an annoying event, a depressing event or a pessimistic outlook that all you are doing is running a memory of it?

What's happening inside your head is that you've had an experience and you've stored it in a particular way, but not the best way. You could be having fun with it and he will never know except for the smile on your face the next time you see him. Just think about what you can get away with in your imagination. Think of all the fun you can have with it. You have a choice in how you store your memories, your experiences. Obviously your manager is right out of line and of course you deserve to be treated with dignity, courtesy and respect. You don't always get to choose what happens to you, however, but you do have a choice about how you respond to what happens to you. You can get bad memories and experiences and rip them apart, smash them up, burn them or do what you like to them. You can learn how to operate the software of your brain so that when someone's annoying you, you see what you can do to change it.

Loren was now ready to try the following technique.

Exercise: Eliminating the Negative, Option 2

1. Think of someone who annoys you. You can draw in a different person if you want or the same person that annoyed you before if you wish to do more work on that.
2. Imagine or visualise the person standing in front of you trying to give out to you, moan at you, complain to you or doing that

annoying thing that they do, but this time imagine them in the nude or perhaps wearing a pair of bloomers with love hearts on them.

3. Imagine, if you like, that on the middle of their face is a big, round, red clown's nose and on their feet are two huge, brown clown's shoes complete with red and white striped socks.
4. Look at them as they try to be taken seriously, finger pointing and gesturing with their clown's gloves trying to scold you.
5. Hear them go on and on as you admire their new clothes.
6. Imagine them doing that and try taking them seriously.

What does that do to the image? What happens to you? You just can't take the person as seriously can you? Remember there are no rules about how you do this. Just because the person gave you a bad experience didn't mean that you had to store it and run it as you experienced it. You might even blow it out of proportion! It makes sense for you to stop and say to yourself that this is your experience, your memory, your brain and so you will decide how to run it. You decide if you want to change it. You decide how to change it. This is about thinking. It is about beginning to look at the inside of your head and to clean it up so that you can get the habit of happiness.

Exercise: Your Secret Gift
Experiment with this over the next while.

1. Imagine that each person you meet today is deliberately conspiring to help you become happier.
2. Decide if you would like to become an inverse paranoid. And even if they treat you mean, just imagine that deep down they have your happiness at heart and that today may simply be their 'off' day. So, in your mind, forgive them for their actions and leave them be.
3. As you engage with each person whether it is for the first time or not, just imagine they want what's best for you.

4. Because of this I want you to give them your secret gift. Your gift can only be seen by you but it will be felt by both of you. Your gift needs to remain outside of your conversation, not to be spoken of but simply to be experienced. As soon as you see the person that you are about to engage with I want you to imagine them being cloaked in a shroud of light, bright, transparent light. Pick your own bright, light colour perhaps one from the colours of the rainbow.

5. Imagine this light is fuelled by a warm, loving feeling of care and curiosity. Visualise this feeling as coming from your heart and swirling out softly to surround and nestle this person in a glow of appreciation and interest.

6. Continue doing this occasionally throughout your interaction. Look for nothing in return, this is your gift.

7. Notice what happens and enjoy!

CHAPTER 3

The Cure to Toxic Thinking

The one thing you can't take away from me is the way I choose to respond to what you do to me.

Victor Frankl

Freedom of Choice

Psychiatrist Victor Frankl, who wrote the book *Man's Search for Meaning*, had the horrible misfortune of being held captive by the Germans during World War II. Frankl witnessed his family and friends being killed at the hands of the Germans in the concentration camps. When the war was over people asked him what it was all about, what the meaning was in all of it and what his view was on why the holocaust happened. Frankl said he had some good times in the concentration camps. He said there were the bad days: he saw people die, people being raped, punished and killed. But one of the things that he and his fellow captors realised while they were there was that they still had a certain level of control. The Germans had enormous power over them but there was one thing that they couldn't do and that was to take away the captives' ability and freedom to choose how they responded to any given situation.

> You can't always determine what happens to you, but you can always decide how you respond. If someone says something to you or someone does something that you don't approve of, you can choose how you react.

We do it all the time. I remember being a teenager walking the streets of my small hometown, Portlaoise, in the pelting rain one grey and dark evening. I was engaged in my usual rant inside my head, grumbling to myself, complaining about everything, and then I had a moment of realisation, an epiphany. It occurred to me that all of that internal ranting takes up too much time and energy. It is such a waste of what could be valuable thinking time so I said 'f**k it' and decided to stop doing it from that moment onward.

The Power of Negative Focus

Every time you send a negative thought through your mind you make yourself feel bad. That may sound obvious, but the reality is that what you are doing is building up toxic chemicals in your body. I'm sure you want to live longer, you want to be healthier and happier – well grumbling and moaning to yourself is not the way. Life's too important to be giving yourself a hard time.

If you stop for a moment and think about all the problems in your day, you might discover that many of them were built inside your head. Some of us approach our day negatively from the outset: everybody knows what I'm like if I haven't had my cornflakes, if I haven't had my coffee, if I don't get a good night's sleep, if I am woken up too early etc. In other words we get up in the morning with the contract pre-written and agreed. If this doesn't happen then I'm going to feel this way and if that does happen then I won't feel the other way. This chapter demonstrates how to end this damaging negative thought process for good.

The God Complex

We human beings like to feel that we're right. This is what I call our God Complex. Psychologists call this a 'self-serving bias'. Not only are we right but we believe that we can do no wrong either. We like this sense of certainty. It gives us a feeling of control over our world. However, your God Complex doesn't work in your favour all of the time.

Take the example of having an argument with someone – a partner, brother, sister, friend or work colleague. Whatever the outcome of the argument, whether or not you did the right thing and made up, the question is this: Did you in your heart of hearts believe that they were at least partially in the wrong? Of course you may not have thought that you were totally and completely in the right, but for the most part you did feel that you were right, if you really think about it deep down. That's the way it works. The self-serving bias kicks in before, during and even after the argument.

If done as a collective, an entire nation can do it and believe not only that they are right about their point of view, but that they are so right that they even have God on their side. I could never understand how humans ran with the thought that (1) they had exclusivity over God and (2) that their God would settle for and even approve of the total annihilation of part of his own creation in acts of war.

A visit to a local prison will confirm that the inmates have a justification for their criminal behaviour. Whether they see circumstances or provocation as the cause, they rarely see that they themselves are wholly responsible. Even when they say they were in the wrong, they usually add, 'But the reason I did it was because . . .' They are really saying what Tracey (the irreverent, slutty teenage girl in *Little Britain*) says when she has been reprimanded for doing something wrong, 'Yeah but no but yeah but no but, see like I was . . .' which is another way of saying 'I'm wrong but I'm really right.'

The God Complex runs something like this. 'I'm not really the type of person who hits people but he did deserve it, he got me so worked up and frustrated, he just kept going on and on . . . so he was just asking for it. I wouldn't normally do that, but he was asking for it.'

So you did something that you don't, as a rule, approve of and then you disassociate from it by saying that it wasn't the 'real you' because the 'real you' would never approve of such things. As if you are not responsible for the other you, the aggressive, unruly you. It was your opponent who unleashed him so it's all his fault! Then just to show how magnanimous you are, you will even take apparent responsibility and apologise for the 'not the real you' type of behaviour. While deep down you just know it wasn't your fault, you are always in the right.

This tendency for behavioural justification has deep ramifications, which I will return to in Chapter 8. For now I simply want to bring this aspect of human behaviour to light.

Reach the 'F**k it Factor' Faster

If you've been growling, muttering and barking at yourself you end up barking at someone else. If life has been good to you and you find yourself in a loving relationship it will result in you barking at your partner. Richard Bandler suggests that if you have a bad feeling you should avoid your loved ones until you get rid of it. He goes further to suggest that you find yourself a perfectly good stranger to walk up to and let them have it! Tell them how bad you feel and how life seems to be such a drag at the moment and how you just have to get this crap off your chest. Imagine how they are going to respond. They will look at you as if you're insane and they are unlikely to take you seriously – if they do you're in big trouble!

Rather than taking it out on the person that you love, it makes sense to treat your nearest and dearest like a stranger or an acquaintance when you are in a bad mood. In truth you would never go up to a stranger and give out to them the way that you do to your partner or your best friend. So wouldn't it make sense just to be a bit more stand-offish rather than just going off on one? Feeling free to attack, criticise or nag doesn't help you, it doesn't help your partner, it doesn't improve your relationship, it doesn't do anything constructive whatsoever. This is the time to say 'f**k it!' and just let it go. I call this the 'F**k it Factor' – the moment you decide to let negative thoughts go.

It's rarely that important, at least not as important as your love for one another. I always say reach the 'F**k it Factor' faster because you are going to get there anyway sometime. There will come a stage in your day, or some stage in your life, that you say, 'F**k it! The stress is just not worth it. All the giving out, all the moaning, all the complaining. F**k it, it's just a waste of time.' It really is such a waste of energy. It doesn't do anything for you.

Silence the Kangaroo Courts of Your Mind

Many of us spend too much time criticising ourselves, moaning at ourselves, complaining to ourselves and being down on ourselves. Then we ask ourselves why we are not happier. So you've been doing all of this self-abuse stuff and you wonder why you are still not happy . . . really? You know self-harm is not helpful and that's what you have been doing. Each and every time you put yourself down you are being cruel and violent to yourself. You wouldn't dare speak that way to your children or to your best friend because you know it just doesn't bode well. It takes you nowhere that you want to go. In fact it takes you exactly where you don't want to go.

One of the things most of us have little difficulty in doing is pointing out our shortcomings. Some of us do it silently through the mental chatter of self-deprecation that rants on and on in the kangaroo courts of our minds, incessantly judging ourselves with extreme prejudice and vitriol. Self-manufactured slogans are conjured up and fired at will – I'm useless, I'm an idiot, I'm not good enough, I'm not able for this – each one perfectly placed to sabotage our efforts.

Others take it a step further and announce to the world the findings of their own special court appearance, where they have been both judge and jury, tried and hung out to dry. Cloaked with false humour they announce they can't do this, they're not good at that or that's not the kind of person they are. These are the beliefs or decisions that produce restrictions in our lives. They place fences around our reality and prevent us using our natural ability to be flexible and produce the results we deserve.

The Richard Bandler Mantra

I want to demonstrate a simple meditation technique that will enable you to put an end to negative self-criticism. If you have meditated before (we all have to some extent), this is a separate meditation, you can compartmentalise it and still keep your sacred ones and continue to use them for what they are intended.

You may already be familiar with the lotus position in which you sit on the floor with just your shins overlapping; if not, don't worry. You do not have to do it exactly as I describe but it's the position that appears to work best for most people. If you are not in a place or a position where you can do this, perhaps you can imagine yourself doing it as clearly as you can. If you want, you can even wear a white robe and a medallion but I don't think it is necessary!

Assume a comfortable position, one in which you are sitting upright with your back straight, and cross your legs so that only the shins overlap. Then, with your arms held outwards by your side, make a V shape with each arm so that your hands are held in the same position as a priest at an altar raising thanks to his god. Next, create an O shape with each hand by joining your thumb and forefinger at the tips. Ideally now would be the time to close your eyes and follow my instructions but as you cannot read with your eyes closed please follow along as best you can.

I am now going to teach you a mantra. A mantra is a word or a sound or a symbol or an image that you use repetitively during your meditation. There is a guy called Sri Chim Noy and he meditates on a variety of things, on flowers, the sky, the earth. From his meditations he gets all sorts of good things and good feelings. I am going to show you how to meditate on something specifically.

Now I want you to set up the circuits. With true vitriol, disrespect and impatience I want you to say the things that you say to yourself when you've done something that you're not happy with, the words you use when you criticise yourself, when you moan to yourself, when you complain to yourself, when you give out to yourself and say f**k it I don't believe you've done that you f**ken idiot. I want you to run these types of criticisms through your mind in the way only you know how. I want you to talk to yourself the way you do when you criticise yourself, the way you moan at yourself, the way you give out to yourself, the way you belittle yourself.

What I am asking you to do is to really go after this and connect with it because you're going to do this for the last time. For example, I used to snipe at myself, in a tone full of cynicism and despondency, 'I don't believe you've done that you f**ken eejit. There you go again, you never get it right, whatever it is you say you idiot, you fool . . .' I know you are not familiar with consciously bringing up the negativity but I want you to do it now. Just for now.

As you are doing this, I'm going to give you a sound sequence, a mantra, and I want you to repeat it inside your mind as you talk to yourself in the usual negative, self-critical manner. To get you used to it I will give you the mantra in a few parts. I will break it down and then make it all one sequence for you to repeat until you have it mastered.

Ready? *(You might want to do this in private.)*

1. Think the negative thoughts and say them inside your mind (e.g. I'm useless, no good, a fool, an idiot, but use your own words).
2. Now interrupt the thoughts by saying the following word inside your mind in a low bass tone: *Shaaaaahhh.*
3. Think the negative thoughts again and continue to speak them silently in your mind.
4. Now say: *Shaaahhdaaa.*
5. Think the negative thoughts some more, hear yourself say them in your mind.
6. Now say: *Shaaahhdaaa Shaaahhdaaa.*
7. And now to complete the sound sequence and the mantra say to your internal voice:
    Shaaaaahhh
    Shaaahhdaaaa
    Shaahh daa fukup!

Shadafukup!
And again
Shadafukup!
Shadafukup!
Shadafukup!
Until you get the message.

Stop giving yourself such a hard time. Cut yourself some slack. Give yourself a break. You are doing the best that you can. You don't need the grief, in fact now is the time when you could do with a little compassion. Now is the time you could do with a little support. Get out of your own way and be kinder to yourself – it will do you a whole world of good. There is such a thing as a happy medium. You can get there if you are smart enough to offer yourself a helping hand, a kind gesture, a bit of practical support. After all, you would give that to almost anybody else so why not give it to yourself too?

What you're doing is actually quite scientific, in NLP terms it is called a 'Pattern Interrupt'. Our habits work as patterns, in fact there is a view that our very existence is one big pattern, from our cells to our body right up to our soul and even the earth itself. Candace Pert likens it to a ripple in a stream flowing against a rock; the pattern remains the same despite the fact that the water coming through the pattern is always changing. So even though the events you face may be different, the response you gave up until now remained pretty much the same. However, with the mantra you are changing all of that. As soon as you operate the mantra you're stopping a whole sequence of thought, a habitual pattern of thinking and when you do that everything becomes so much easier.

The Genesis of Evil

If you start out with a bad experience, follow it by a bad thought, enhance it with a bad image and then add a bad verbal suggestion, before long your thinking will be such that from one bad event you conclude that the whole day has gone bad too. That is a huge distortion. You get up in the morning and because you are not feeling in the best of form you think it's going to be a bad day and you say to yourself 'It's going to be one of those days I just feel it in my bones' – that's your neurons firing off. But what they are doing is what they are designed to do: they are connecting to each other, like connecting with like, as one set of neurons connects to another set of neurons that connects to another set of neurons, and before you know it, one statement is enough to give you a bad feeling that lasts all day.

ENOUGH IS ENOUGH. JUST SHUT IT DOWN!

If you decide right here, right now, that that's it, you've had enough, it's time to move on, then the mantra is for you. Look at it this way, you tried giving out to yourself but did it help? No. You complained at yourself but did that help? No. You criticised yourself, did that help? No. You moaned at yourself, did that help? No. None of those things ever really helped you, so what would be the point in continuing on that path. There's no benefit or use in it at all. Instead say to yourself, 'In future if I as much as say a bad word to myself then I'll say shut the f**k up.' Then you can prevent those negative, disempowering feelings. By introducing this mantra and by repeating the mantra in quick succession your mind gets flooded with the sound of it and this prevents the old neural net from being activated.

So decide from here on in that every time you criticise yourself, every time you try to moan at yourself, every time you try to give out to yourself, you will repeat the mantra 'Shut the f**k up, shut the f**k up, shut the f**k up, shut the f**k up' in order to shut down the old negative neural network. Once you hit it with a rate of speed, pace and constancy so that all that's in your head at that moment is the STFU mantra then the changes you are looking for will come about majestically.

A word of caution though, in case it is not obvious; the way NOT to do this is to say 'Shut the f**k up. Shut the f**k up. Shut the f**k up. Shut the f**k up you f**ken eejit.' That defeats the whole purpose.

You may be asking why the 'bad' language? I used 'bad' language because I have found that most of the people I work with use bad language in their heads themselves. I trained in the Bible belt in Texas and they preferred to use the mantra 'shut the hell up'. Really it's a matter of what works best for you. As long as there is strength and forcefulness in the words chosen that far outweigh the strength and force of the negativity that you are seeking to overcome, then they are fine.

If you have ever taken up the route to personal development before now, you will have come across the idea of using positive thoughts to overcome negative ones. Perhaps you have read the book, attended the seminar or watched the DVD. Perhaps you have even taken on board the concept of going to your quiet place inside your imagination. I was taught to visualise myself sitting in front of a magnificent sunset and to take in all the multitude of colours and that this would relax me. I tried this a few times when I was feeling stressed but it just didn't work for me. So I tried harder and then it worked less than before until one day I got the idea to change things. So I looked out on my sunset and I looked out on the sea beneath it and I even thought of a school of dolphins diving gracefully in and out of the water, I thought this might add to my experience and it did. It didn't relax me, but it gave me another idea. In the middle of my stress experience, frustrated and at my wits' end, I decided I needed someone to blame or someone to suffer because of my pain. And so it came to me. I reached into my imagination and took out a harpoon and one by one I harpooned each of the damn dolphins saying, 'Relax – me arse.' And then I felt better.

Every time you criticise yourself, you crush your spirit, you kill your sense of well-being, you wreak havoc on your self-confidence.

But the great news is that you now know you can stop it. I don't know anything else that works as powerfully as Richard Bandler's simple mantra.

I remember my Dad used to say jokingly, 'If you see a little kid walking past you, you might as well give him a smack across the back of the head with the palm of your hand because he is either walking away from trouble or walking towards it and either way he is the cause of it.' In this case it is the negative thoughts that are the trouble, so if you give them a smack across the back of the head when they are least expecting it, you can stop them dead in their tracks.

It is said that we have on average around eighty thousand thoughts in any one day. So that means that you have to use the mantra lots before it takes the full long-term effect and becomes habitual, at which point it will be automatic. Think about the amount of times you criticised and moaned at yourself – it never helped. You never got the message from it, so shut the f**k up. Now realise that when you say this you're not telling yourself to shut the f**k up, you're shutting down a program, an internal program. This is not who you are, this is not your better self; you are not at your best when you are criticising yourself and you deserve your better self to come through more often.

When you were a child your teacher corrected your homework. You showed it to her and she got a big red marker and said that's right, that's right and that's wrong and that's wrong. You looked at this method and thought, 'Ahhh that's it, I'm supposed to look for what's wrong with things.' So you went off and you looked for faults, problems and errors. But that's not useful in relation to your personality. It's better to look for what's right with things, for what's working, it's better to look for where you want to go, so that you can feel better about yourself. Do you get the idea? So any criticism, any sort of slamming down on yourself is just not good enough. Today needs to be the day when you decide you have had enough of that.

Yes, you can expect to be going around for the next week saying, 'Shut the f**k up. Shut the f**k up. Shut the f**k up!'

We had a lady at one of our Institute training sessions, a very prim and proper lady, whom we thought would never use bad language. So with caution we taught her the STFU mantra and when she heard it she laughed and her face lit up. She thought it was a wonderful tool that she could use to great effect in her daily routine. So off she went and started to use it. She came back to us a week later and said that the mantra was really great but it had got her into a spot of bother. I asked her what she meant and she said, 'Well, my internal voice sounds exactly like the voice of someone I know, so when I met that person after learning the mantra and she started speaking to me, I immediately said shut the f**k up. Not only that but wasn't I walking down the street the other day and I met her again and no sooner had she opened her mouth but I said shut the f**k up for a second time.'

We explained that the mantra is for your internal voice. Keep it inside, don't say it out loud. It's important to keep it inside and remember as soon as you decide to do this you're actually signing up to a contract with yourself, to be on your own side for the rest of your life. Have you tried to negotiate or reason with your internal voice? It doesn't work. So it's just 'Shut the f**k up. Shut the f**k up. Shut the f**k up.' Please remember you're going to have to do that for quite a bit until it becomes part of who you are. For me, nowadays it's just automatic. I don't criticise and demotivate myself in that way any more.

I know at times it feels like a good idea to tell some people to just shut the f**k up as well, but you can get into trouble for that. I know, I've done it far too often!

Instead of being down on yourself you can decide ahead of time what you want to have happen, rather than focusing on what should have happened but didn't. A lot of what you're going to be doing now for the next while will be about internalising that powerful little mental programme so that it stops all the negative debris and puts you in a position to fit something worthwhile in its place. This is not the only thing you do though. Because nature doesn't like a vacuum, once you remove the negative thoughts an opening occurs.

Once you create a space, nature will put something back into it unless you choose to do it first. So I'll show you how you can make positive, practical and constructive use of the mental space that you have freed up by ceasing to dismiss yourself any longer.

Consider all the thinking time you've cleared for yourself now that you've stopped giving yourself a hard time. At this point you need to consider what you will do once you've stopped all that crap. Imagine what your day could be like if you don't criticise yourself so much, if you don't moan at yourself and imagine how much freedom you will have when you decide you're done with all that, finished with it, you've had enough of it. Have you ever thought about what could happen to your brain if you give it a chance to do some worthwhile thinking for a change?

I remember one day Michael Connolly and I met up after a night out when we'd had too much to drink. To make it worse we broke our own rules as it was the morning before the beginning of one of our seminars. I had a bit of a hangover (which is never a great idea when you are training someone's brain) and Michael mischievously proceeded to tell me what a hangover was all about. He began to explain to me that 'the neuro-peptides in my brain were . . .' To which I responded, 'Shut the f**k up Michael. You know you're building something that I don't want to experience in my mind.' Most people with problems know a lot about the problem, the details of the problem and how the problem works, which presents its own set of problems. How you actually think about the problem often becomes the problem.

Talk to someone who wants to lose weight, someone that's overweight will very often know more about nutrition than you could ever know yourself. In fact oftentimes they know as much as the nutritionist or dietician that's working with them. This is because they have spent way too much time focusing on the problem and not on the solution. If you want to get thinner or slimmer or healthier why not model thin people? Wouldn't that make sense? But most people think they need to focus on following a low-calorie diet, which dictates that you deprive yourself of food.

This is not what the subconscious likes. The subconscious likes to keep you as you are but change requires that you do things differently. This book will teach you how to do that.

The Richard Bandler Mantra Summary
If you ever are tempted in the future to do what you previously were doing when you criticised, moaned, whinged, whined, complained, dismissed, insulted, demeaned, devalued or were otherwise down on yourself – just STFU! And ask yourself what is the most useful thing to do right now and so set yourself in a well-formed direction.

Richard's mantra mentions a 'well-formed direction'. We'll be looking at this in detail in Chapter 6.

CHAPTER 4

How to Get Past Your Twelve Psychic Guardians

A man should not strive to eliminate his complexes but to get in accord with them: they are legitimately what directs his conduct in the world.

Sigmund Freud

Unhappiness Habits

I f you woke up this morning and are having nothing more than an ordinary day, you are more fortunate than the one million people who will not survive to the end of this week. If you have never experienced the horrors of war, the agony of torture or the loneliness of imprisonment, you are better off than 500 million people on this planet. If you can put food on your table, clothes on your back and have a place to sleep safely, you are richer than 75 per cent of people in this world. If you have a few quid put away or even just a little money left over at the end of the week, you are among the wealthiest 8 per cent of the world's population. If this is the case, why is it that many of us are not as happy as we ought to be?

Research suggests that some of our happiness is down to our genes, but most of it is under our control. Our brain is designed to protect us, but sometimes the very mechanisms that it puts in place sabotage our efforts at achieving sustainable levels of happiness. The source of this is your psychic guardians. These are the defence mechanisms or self-deception devices and reality distortions that act as guardians of your God Complex. These are the pitfalls and traps that prevent you from reaching your full potential.

This field of psychology acknowledges that we human beings engage in certain behaviours designed to protect us. Often these behaviours are unknown to us but obvious to those around us. In NLP terms, these behaviours are neural nets that are only sustained by frequent use. If you make yourself aware of these patterns by looking at your daily behaviour you can choose whether to change them or not. Below is a list of typical behaviours in which people engage.

- *Compensation:* Making up for your own shortcomings.
- *Denial:* Ignoring or hiding from the unpleasant.
- *Displacement:* Shifting negative feelings to someone else.
- *Emotional insulation:* Detaching so you don't get disappointed.
- *Fantasy:* Imagining something better.
- *Introjection:* Putting other people's needs before your own.
- *Projection:* Blaming the other person.
- *Rationalisation:* Inventing excuses.
- *Reaction formation:* Feeling one way but behaving in another.
- *Regression:* Going back to behaving like a child.
- *Repression:* Burying or 'forgetting' the unpleasant.
- *Sublimation:* Substituting one goal for another.

Compensation/Bragging (making up for your shortcomings)

To recognise your achievements and be recognised for your efforts is an important part of building your self-esteem and improving your self-concept. It is healthy to be validated and to validate yourself, be it through reward or taking time to bask in the warm afterglow of a job well done. Indeed many people need to do this more often. However, if you notice yourself 'singing your own praises' a lot more often than those around you, it may be that you are seeking external validation for an unmet need of approval – generally your own.

Take the time to consider the motive for your actions and if there is an underlying need focus on that. To do this you need only focus on where you are at currently, the fact that the foundations may have been laid down in your earlier years means little and is not necessary for you to know what needs changing and how it needs changing. It doesn't have to be such a mystery, it won't take years of therapy, just ask yourself:

- How do you feel when you are 'pitching' for approval?
- How do you feel when you receive it?
- How long does that feeling last?
- Do you get your fill once you get the recognition or do you need to keep checking in?
- What is the most useful thing to do?
- What can you do in the future?
- What will you do in the future?
- Where is it possible and practical to get that approval from and once you get it how will that feel?

Put simply, if you still feel the need to go chasing approval like the addict chases the dragon, then you are compensating. Find out what you are compensating for and make your decision based on that. For example, if you are looking for your parents' approval and you know this is never going to happen, face up to that fact and let it go. If you don't know whose approval you are looking for, then just stop it and do something else.

Some habits lose their purpose over time so what you need to do is update your subconscious database. As a child you may crave your parents' approval, as an adult you do not have to be controlled by that youth-based impulse, it is time to build something new. The impulse is simply a bunch of neurons activated by previous associations and past rewards but time spent now on this outgrown need is time wasted and the decision you need to make now is to move forward. Yes, you 'need' approval and that is not a bad thing, so choose where else you will get the approval that will feel worthwhile to you rather than randomly and frantically searching for it from people that don't matter that much to you or that choose not to give it to you.

Denial (ignoring or hiding from the unpleasant)

Oftentimes, rather than losing face and squaring up to the fact that we are in trouble, we tend to soldier on defiantly and deny there is a problem.

If you are stuck you are stuck. It is not a crime. If you need help you need help and there are people out there that can help you. You can't get it right all of the time, so if you need help go get it. You will feel better and breathe more easily once you have. Denial is different from changing direction. If you deny something the brain keeps reminding you of it. You can choose to change direction, but to do that you may need help. You may need the all-essential part, the *how* to do that, and if that means calling on someone else who can show you, then go do it. Most behavioural change involves an element of skill, and desire by itself is simply not enough. So get the skill and be done with it, you will be so much happier once you have.

Displacement (shifting negative feelings somewhere else)

My son Dylan has a dog called Lassie. She is not nearly as tall as her famous namesake as she is part-collie and part-terrier. A very friendly dog with a white coat and a few tanned coloured patches on her ears and body, Lassie just loves attention, however, she does not like it when newcomers invade her space. So if Dylan has some friends around and they decide to go outside into the back garden, she rarely barks at them but instead makes a run at her stainless steel dog bowl, which she takes in her mouth and between her two front paws and attempts to rip apart. This never works out, so she ends up instead chasing after the bowl at high speed as it keeps popping out of her grip. This is an example of displacement. Lassie redirects her frustration (at having her space invaded) on to her feeding bowl rather than directing it at the real intruders who invaded her space. Humans do much the same thing but unfortunately they take their frustrations out not just on objects but on people too. Usually it is those that are nearest and dearest to them.

The child that is bullied at home takes it out on the children in school and bullies them. The shop steward who is frustrated at work barks at his wife for the least thing when he gets home. When we are frustrated or when we are unable to defend ourselves or simply when things are not going in accordance with the way we decide or expect they ought to, more often than not we vent our frustration or anger at those nearest to us or at those who we feel more powerful than.

Obviously there is a need to vent our anger and our frustrations as negative emotions left unexpressed build up as tension in the body. To help yourself deal with this, do something that requires physical effort (and does not mean beating the living daylights out of someone whom you think deserves it). Going for a walk, better still going for a run, taking a trip to the gym or ranting to someone who is not involved and knows you need to vent are all more useful ways of dealing with these things. A client of mine who got stuck in traffic in his car on the way home from work used the time to vent his frustrations. He told me how he would get all hot under the collar and would shout and scream and belt the steering wheel with his open palms and point and scowl out the front windscreen until the tension subsided. Or at least until he released enough tension that he became aware of the unusual glances he was getting from passers-by and other motorists.

I am sure most of them thought it was road rage or perhaps that he was using a hands-free phone. This was his way of letting off steam and he told me that as he ranted and raved he could see the people who were the source of his frustration and anger in front of him. He even had them answer him back and would eventually begin to see the logical or rational side of things. This helped him to meet with them the following day without the anger and frustration of earlier because, having vented it, he felt he had already had his say and now it was time to move forward. It's not something I choose to do because in my world that would only make me feel angrier but hey whatever works works and it's all about realising what works best for you in the short and long terms.

Emotional Insulation (detaching so you don't get disappointed)

When emotional involvement is not considered to be worth the risk, we lower the risks by detaching and by lowering our expectations. If you have lived for any length of time you will have had the experience of being 'let down' by people whom you considered to be close friends or even partners. The closer the friend the harder it hurt. You may have heard someone say during times of sickness or grief that it is then that you really find out who your friends are. These are just examples of this.

When we have friends we expect them to be there for us in times of need, we expect them to sympathise with us in times of hardship and we expect them to support us and be loyal to our cause in times of stress or vulnerability. If that doesn't happen, well then our bubble bursts. If they fail to live up to our expectations or if they break some of our deep-seated values we are driven into despair. Depending on how strong the bond was or how important the person was to our lives we run through an emotional rollercoaster cycle, similar to that of grieving, until we eventually 'bury' the person out of our future experience. Our view of the person changes profoundly and we look at him or her through different eyes. For the most part we sever all ties and connections with the person so as to avoid being hurt again. In extreme cases you will hear people say things to the effect of 'You are dead to me, you no longer exist, I no longer care about you. You can do what you like; you don't matter to me any more.' It's like a massive pendulum shift occurs and we swap one set of emotional distortions for another.

The familiar maxim that love is blind springs to mind. Just as with all of these psychic guardians there is an upside and a downside to them. It's great to fall head over heels in love with someone, to be swept off your feet and to see only good things; it is one of the many highlights of living. It is also an extreme example of the brain's capacity to distort things way beyond reality, similar to how depressed people look at the sum total of their life. They look back and claim none of it was real.

I had a young client recently who found out his girlfriend, whom he adored, was cheating on him. Once he realised this, he looked at everything in a completely different light and judged her every act, every gesture, every event, every behaviour in the light of her recent deception. If you have ever been in a similar situation his reaction will resonate with you. However, the reality could be that the deception was recent and that all the good experiences in the past held their integrity and so still remained true. From the moment he became aware of the situation, he tumbled through the cycle, reacting like a person in mourning until eventually he got to the point of severing all ties from her. He detached to avoid further disappointment, hurt or humiliation. The journey unfolds a little like this:

- *Shock:* How could she do such a thing?
- *Denial/disbelief:* I can't believe that she could do such a thing and especially to me.
- *Confusion:* I thought she loved me, you don't do that to someone you love, do you?
- *Disorientation:* My head is all over the place. I don't know what to think, or feel for that matter. It just doesn't make any sense. Why would anyone do that?
- *Anxiety:* She has made me look like a real prat. She has probably been laughing at me behind my back all the time and telling all her friends about what a fool I am.
- *Anger:* F**k her, she can go jump in a lake. I'll show her who the fool is. I'll let everyone know how much of a slag she is, see if she cares then. She thinks she can make a fool of me, well wait and see, I have a few little surprises lined up for her. Next time I see her I am simply going to ignore her, tell her to go jump in a lake,

she means nothing to me and I'll tell her she was pretty useless in bed anyway. That will mess her head up, yeah, stupid cow.

- *Optimism:* You know I am better off without her, just glad I found out before I married the bitch. Oh yeah, nice one, that was close.
- *Resignation:* You can't trust anybody these days, especially not women. Anyway I have been missing out on having the craic with the lads for ages. Time to get me glad rags on. Women, who needs them anyway?
- *Adjustment:* I know I will be cut up for a while but you've just got to get on with things, haven't you? I just have to accept that she is not the one for me. I think I will give the whole relationship thing a rest for a while so as I can get my house in order. Yeah, I think I will do that.

And so life goes on. Not every response will be that extreme, but they tend to go through the same cycle. Some of us get stuck at different stages of it and more of us go through it more quickly, at the end of it we tend to adjust and move forward.

I have had friends and work colleagues who let me down badly, who for whatever reason chose a different path than I expected or displayed different values than I had projected. As a result I picked up some seriously negative consequences. When I examined this, and you can be sure that I was forced to reach to the very depths of my soul for understanding, I usually came up with the following. Most people don't intentionally hurt their friends they do so out of self-preservation, self-gain or self-absorption.

- *Self-preservation:* It's either you or me and much and all as I hate to . . . it's going to have to be me.
- *Self-gain:* I want this and I want it badly and I want it now, I need it and there will always be other chances for 'everyone'.
- *Self-absorption:* Isn't life great? One great big universe and it's all mine. Aren't people great the way they help me get everything I want? It really is true that the universe always provides.

Now some people do renege on their friends, but when you think of it they are not really friends in the true sense of the word. Of course it can be understandably disappointing and devastating when people let us down from time to time and for a time we can be forced to lower our expectations, but we need always remember Don. E. Hamachek's words: 'When we dare not to hope, we cease to grow. When there is no risk, there is no loss; but there is no gain either.'

For when we do take the chance, life keeps its depth and richness and overall there tends to be more reward than hurt, so truly it is all worth the risk.

Fantasy (imagining something better)

Frustrated desires and unmet needs can give rise to fantasy. Fantasy is an excellent tool for solving problems and setting outcomes but can also be a trap for venting wish fulfilment and avoiding the reality of everyday life.

The Facebook pages of those of us who work in the field of personal development end up being full of people (usually trying to sell you something) telling us how ecstatically blissful their lives are 24/7. These are the snake oil merchants who live in the hope that *your belief* in them will take them out of their mental turmoil. They look for the one side to life, they seek out white knights on horses, heroes in golden armour, they live the fairy tale stories of their youth waiting for their Prince Charming to arrive to save them from their inner hell. This is fantasy in full flight. These are the people that when you ask them how they are doing will tell you that they are doing fantastically well. They are having large days and gigantic moments. Everything, and I mean everything, is rosy in their garden. Nothing is holding them back, they have it all nailed down. Their universe is responding like a submissive puppy to each and every one of their whims of fancy. If you have met them you will know them. Personally I wish they would f**k off and get real. Life is not like that. Life can be great but it is also challenging. Not everything goes to plan all of the time and to suggest that it does is plain bullshit.

I am all for daydreaming, I am all for fantasising and I am committed to the benefits that it can bring, but as with all things there is a limit. You need to check in with the real-term results that you are getting on a daily basis as a consequence of your dreams, otherwise all you are doing is inputting and what you need to be doing more of is outputting. Basically you need to do a daily reality check. The following questions can help you to do that.

Ten Reality Checking Questions
1. Where are you now with regard to your dreams, your desires and your life goals?
2. Where do you want to be?
3. What has to happen to get you there?
4. What has to be happening right now to ensure you achieve the best results?
5. What can you do now?
6. What will you do as soon you can?
7. What will you do if you can't?
8. What are you doing right now?
9. What could you be doing right now?
10. How important are your dreams, desires and goals anyhow? So get to it.

Introjection (putting other people's needs before your own)

Living in accordance with other people's values, generally a specific person's values such as a teacher or parent, is oppressive by nature and produces unhappy, disillusioned and often angry, bitter people. You can only walk your own path. You can only be your own person. As children we often get validated, recognised and rewarded for reflecting our parents' values or for conforming to social expectations. The 'look who is all grown-up now' effect. That may be temporarily okay when we are young but to follow through when we are older is far from ideal.

The feelings of guilt that we feel around our families are often a prime example of how we feel when we fail to put other people's needs before our own. We run through their expectations for us and if we don't meet them we feel bad, and to avoid feeling bad we may prioritise their needs above ours. The child that won't leave his parents' home because he can't bear to see them grow old alone will put his parents' needs before his own and justify his actions by 'knowing' he is doing the 'right thing'.

There are people that subscribe to a set of ideals, a religion or even a guru and then actively attempt to absorb all of that person's beliefs, values, persona and even dress sense (or the lack thereof) to the detriment of their own needs. These are the circumstances that give rise to fanatics. It's very simple really: you are who you are, you can't be anybody else so you've got to make do with what you have got and realise that it is not where you are but where you are going that counts when it comes to getting better. All the vehemence, vitriol and rage that pours out in defence of the realm (the parent, the leader, the guru, the religion, the god, the beliefs, the government, the country) is all displaced energy redirected from the self to those around you.

In my experience most inner conflict comes from expecting yourself to be other than you already are and being so tunnel-visioned that you forget to realise that all you ever are is a work in progress. You are not finished until you are dead and many would have you believe that even then you are not finished. So you might as well resign yourself to the fact that you are on one long journey of continuous self-improvement. Before you know it you will hardly recognise the person you thought you once were, which is a good thing because it means there is always hope and always room for improvement.

Now we are all responsible to some degree for a little introjection, if we weren't things would be different, life would be different and people would be a lot more selfish, in fact societies as we know them would not exist. So a little guilt can be a good thing and if that leads to a little self-sacrifice well that's good too. As long as the scales are tipped in your favour then things will flow all the more easily and everything will work out okay.

Knowing this, it is a good idea to check in on the habitual things that you do for others and to question your motivations:

- Are you doing what you are doing because you feel you have to?
- Are you doing what you are doing because you want to?
- Are you doing what you are doing out of guilt?
- Are you doing what you are doing for the recognition or validation that it will give you from a specific person?

If you have asked yourself these questions and are truly happy with your answers and your follow-through behaviours, then all is well and good. If you are not, however, there is another stage in your path to freedom waiting to be claimed.

Projection (blaming the other person)

Have you ever had an inexplicable dislike for someone, there is something about them that you can't quite put your finger on, something that makes you squirm or makes your blood boil, that gets on your wick? It may be that you are projecting on to them feelings that arise within you that make you uncomfortable, feelings that you would rather reject and you do so by assigning them to someone else. Perhaps you have found yourself getting hot under the collar during an argument and in a fit of rage blurting out, 'Who *me*? *I'm* okay, *I* don't have a problem. *I'm* not the one with the problem. It's *you* that has the problem; I don't see what the big deal is.' When someone over-reacts and protests inappropriately you can bet your bottom dollar that it involves an element of projection.

We often blame others for the very things we are guilty of and reject in ourselves. I remember with great fondness my little sister skipping into our sitting room at home holding a bag full of her favourite sweets in one hand. She had just paid a visit to the shop courtesy of an older brother who had bought her the goodies. She was greeted enthusiastically by her eldest sister, her mother and a few of her brothers including me. The sweets were greeted too. My sister said in jest, 'Oh lovely, sweets, can I have one?' and this was joined by a chorus of 'me too, me too'. Although we were joking, my little sister shouted, 'No.' With that she was met with, 'Ah ah aah – sharing is caring, don't you know?' This made her even more defensive and she repeated, 'No, you're not getting any, no one is getting any.' At that point the tone became a little more serious. 'How about one just for Mum?' This was an attempt to remind her as well as teach her the concept of sharing which as a family we held as a value. 'No, I'm not giving anyone any, they're mine.' A little cajoling ensued but she remained defiant until eventually she was told that she was being greedy keeping all the sweets to herself. Her mind was beginning to fill with a little guilt but not enough to change her decision, and she replied obstinately, 'It's not that I'm greedy, it's that you're all being mean.' This is projection. With that she gripped her bag of sweets, folded her arms and plonked down on the sofa hiding under her frown and only peering up occasionally to see what impact her words had on Mum, who couldn't help but smile inwardly but held the outward appearance of not being too pleased.

I like to view reality as a series of mirrors with pretty much most things in our experience simply being a reflection of who we are at some level. In business, professional interviewers are taught about the 'Halo Effect'. The Halo Effect is something that occurs during the interview process and can affect the outcome by distorting the perception of the interviewer. Basically what happens is that the interviewee speaks of or demonstrates a number of characteristics or attributes that remind the interviewer of his own personality. He then subconsciously distorts this perception by thinking that if the interviewee is like him in a good number of ways, then he must be like him in all ways. This can result in the wrong candidate being selected for the job. Now although the desired outcome may not be achieved, this is an example of positive projection or what psychologists refer to as complementary projection. It is the stuff that great relationships can be made of, it is also the stuff that can cause great disappointments.

Rationalisation (inventing excuses)

Human beings are meaning-seeking creatures so when things happen we apply meaning to them. When something happens that we find particularly difficult to accept we tend to rationalise it by coming up with a logical reason as to why it has happened.

This book is about giving your life meaning, because in essence I am no different from you in that I like to believe that life has meaning. There *must* be a reason, a cause, a purpose for the fact that you and I both occupy this space called earth, otherwise it makes no logical sense. Rather than accept the alternative – that we are here by chance or by anomaly and that all of this is just happenstance – we rationalise and come up with logical reasons to suggest that this is our purpose in life.

So rationalisation of this type can be useful. However, we also apply this mechanism when we have done things that we are not proud of, such as being unkind or unfair in our dealings with other people. We do this after arguments if we have lost our temper or said some nasty things. 'Well I wouldn't have done that normally but if I didn't she would have gone on and on, and then there would be no turning back, I mean you can't carry on a relationship in those circumstances, someone had to call a halt to it and it just so happened that it had to be me.' Such rationalisation is backed by logical deductions and conclusions that give it meaning and in turn 'justify' the instigator's actions, which would in normal circumstances be unacceptable. In short we are just creating false but credible justifications or excuses for our actions.

Rationalisation may also be used when something independent of us happens that causes us discomfort, such as when a friend is unkind to us. If a colleague is in a bad mood and arrives in late for work one day, you might rationalise and apply meaning to his actions by concluding that he is late because he is having relationship problems with his partner. Or you might rationalise and conclude that he is late so he obviously doesn't care about his job anymore.

Rationalisation makes us feel safe, makes us feel we know what is going on and that we have the answers. The problem is that some of those answers are not correct, so to avoid the negative consequences it is useful to question your deductions and conclusions about certain circumstances and events.

Even though as human beings we crave certainty, our world can be enhanced by questioning basic assumptions about things. For instance rather than making the deduction that the guy that was late in the above example was either having problems with his wife or didn't care about his job anymore, one could have asked:

- How do you know for certain?
- How does the fact that he is late mean that he doesn't care about his job?
- How does the fact that he is having a bad time at home cause him to be in a bad mood at work?

Assumptions can be dangerous. Remember just because the answers appear obvious, it does not mean that they are. You have got to examine all stages of the process, from your starting point and the point at which you begin your rationalisation. Remember too that once you apply specific meanings very often you build other meanings and if the foundation is not solid – well, need I go any further?

Reaction Formation (feeling one way but behaving in another)

Most people that are involved in therapy, counselling and coaching arrived to it through the doorway of seeking help themselves. As they make their discoveries and experience the benefits they then decide that they could help others do the same. This is healthy as long as they have dealt with the majority of their own issues. Unfortunately there are lots of examples where this is not the case. Now this does not necessarily mean they are unfit to do their job, some still do a very effective job. However, it is important that they are constantly working on themselves as this gives not only empathy but also real insight into behavioural modification and development, which is really what it is all about.

Other manifestations of this defence mechanism are the person who is super-nice to your face and bitches behind your back. Yet another is the religious zealot who harbours dark thoughts and denounces all evildoers other than himself. As Jesus wisely advised, 'Physician heal thyself.' Putting a Band-Aid on the world when really it is you who needs the plaster is a bit like putting the cart before the horse.

Regression (returning to younger behaviours)

Resorting to childlike responses to stressful situations or circumstances is not uncommon. They say when things get tough the tough get going, but that is true only some of the time. We all have our ways of dealing with the world and we all seek our version of the 'comfort blanket' at different times. Each of us needs to be able to retreat from the world occasionally so that we can lick our wounds and take the time to heal. Some of us do that by regression.

For example, the woman who doesn't want to do something so she pouts and acts helpless while the big strong man makes it all better. The factory worker who hates his job and so he regresses to playing pranks on his fellow workers or boss and hides chuckling and giggling at the mischief he gets up to. The man who claims he is sick when he is expected to do something he doesn't want to do and then exaggerates his illness by buying lots of remedies and making sure that his struggle is evident to everyone he comes into contact with. The girl who starts wetting her bed again as soon as the new arrival is brought home. These are all examples of regression.

Not all regression is bad, it has a valuable function and like all things as long as it is not used to excess it is fine as a coping mechanism. It's not necessary to be all grown-up all of the time, it's fun to do childlike things. My son Dylan put it brilliantly when he became a teenager and said, 'Dad, it looks like I'm getting older, but don't worry about it, I'm never growing up.'

Repression (burying or 'forgetting' the unpleasant)

When the truth is too painful we bury the experience, the problem is that we cannot bury it completely and so this has an impact on our behaviours through feelings of fear, guilt, embarrassment, insecurity etc.

I qualified as a hypno-analyst in 1996 and was taught always to look for the root cause of clients presenting challenges. This made perfect sense to me at the time. I was also led to believe that many of my clients would be in need of analysis and that if I could get them to release their repressed memories they would gain insight and ultimately be free from the 'free-floating anxieties' that were negatively impacting on their life. Furthermore I was given the tools of hypnosis and taught that if you combined the analytical techniques with the power of suggestion you could even further assist your clients in creating better and more fulfilling lives.

In my experience there was some merit in this approach, however, over time I found that repressions are not always easy to establish, identify or locate despite having the chutzpah to chase after them as we were taught resistance would occur. Then I noticed that when clients did release their subdued or buried memories, it gave them understanding and even a justification for their behaviour but it did not necessarily change them to the extent that I would have expected. On the other hand the hypnotic suggestions that I was giving them at the end of each session were producing huge dividends. As time went on I reached a number of conclusions:

- People are a lot more open to suggestion if they have undergone a painful experience, and the release of repressions is painful.

- A client's belief system has a direct impact on the result, so if a client believes analysis will work he or she will make it work.
- Perhaps the brain knows what it is doing when it represses a memory because every time you connected with it, it proved painful.

The way the brain actually works is really all down to neural maps. Every experience leaves an imprint on your mind and as a consequence of how the brain works each additional incoming experience is compared and contrasted with the original experience and stored in accordance with it. If there are enough similar experiences the brain becomes conditioned to respond in certain ways. This becomes a cyclical loop, the more you experience the more you are primed to respond in a particular way. If the experiences are good then the outcome is good, but if the experiences are bad then it is time to interact. It is time to take control and to build a new neural map, a map that will respond the way you want it to respond.

In time and with application the map that is most used will be your guiding influence. So then the need to release a repression becomes less significant than your ability to create new maps, build new responses and use the way the brain works to make your life get so much better.

Nowadays, I still have the tools of pinpoint analysis and even past-life regression to call upon. I rarely need to but if I do and especially if it fits in with the client's belief system I find it works well once combined with some useful replacement beliefs.

Sublimation (substituting one goal for another)

Emotions, be they positive or negative, create energy and energy needs expression. Research demonstrates that unexpressed negative emotions act like toxins in the system. Sublimation takes this negative energy and releases it in a less destructive way by turning it into something worthwhile. The athlete uses her fear of failure to spur her on. The entrepreneur uses his obsession for control to build a successful business empire. The nun carries out valuable social work to replace her maternal drives. The daily anxieties that people experience are often sublimated into creative outlets such as hobbies and pastimes. When you hear expressions like 'it keeps me on the straight and narrow' and 'it keeps me out of trouble', they refer to a redirection of unwanted impulses.

Often clients who come to me for business coaching use the mechanism of sublimation to keep themselves from dealing with the fear of pending failure. Rather than fully engaging with or denying it, they redirect their energies to a different or safer aspect of their business and then they say that the business is not as good as it could be.

If you have pent up energy you need to vent or express it. Take a moment to list some ways that you can do that safely.

_____

_____

_____

_____

_____

Try this little experiment as often as you like.

Exercise: Cutting the Cord

Think of someone in your life that has done you wrong and has been absorbing your energy in a disempowering way. Someone that you feel prevents you from being at your best. Someone that stirs up your darker side and perhaps triggers your negative qualities. It is okay if this is a family member. Someone with whom you have unfinished business or someone that you have been unable to finish business with up until now. A person that you are unwillingly still connected to through negative associations. The person may be gone from your environment or may even have left this world.

Once you've read through the following steps you can close your eyes for the exercise.

1. Bring the person to mind for this virtual meeting is about getting closure.
2. Start by telling this person how their behaviour has affected you.
3. Say what you need to say in order for you to move on. Release the full power of your emotions; it is your time to be heard. You are safe on this level of mind.
4. Notice this person's responses.
5. Tell the person that today is where it ends, that you have decided to move on.
6. Tell the person that the negativity belongs to them now and it is for them to choose to rid themselves of it. For you are now letting them go. (If you wish you can forgive them for their wrongdoing.)
7. Imagine that you are connected to the person through a cord of light.
8. Now cut this cord and let the person go. (If you wish you can send them some positive feelings through the cord before severing it. Not because they deserve it, but simply because you can.)
9. Let the image of the person fade from your mind.
10. Notice how it feels.

CHAPTER 5

Unveiling Your Personal Fountain of Bliss

The most powerful weapon on earth is the human soul on fire.

Ferdinand Foch

Working from the Inside Out

According to an article in a Japanese newspaper *The Mainichi Daily News* in June 2009, a growing number of companies are using the new Omron Smile Scan system for 'smile training' among their staff. More than five hundred customer service workers at Keihin Electric Express Railway are subjected to daily face scans. The smile scan software produces a sweeping analysis of a smile based on facial characteristics, from lip curves and eye movements to wrinkles. After scanning the face, the device produces a rating between zero and one hundred. If the smile is not up to standard, a number of smile-boosting messages will pop up on the computer screen. Statements like 'you still look too serious', 'lift up your mouth corners' etc. Now, I don't know about you, but being told to smile has the opposite effect on me. I have pictures in my head already of some customer service guy picking up the computer and smashing it for telling him to be happy once too often.

A better way to smile and be happy is to work from the inside out. If you have completed the previous exercises you will recognise that the words you use or the way that you talk to yourself and the images or pictures that you draw up from inside your mind, your memory or your imagination are going to shape how you feel at any given time. Those feelings in turn will strongly influence how you respond to any given situation.

If you examine that a little more closely you will see the golden opportunity that is at your fingertips. All of the above simply constitutes the act of thinking. So if your thoughts shape your feelings and your feelings influence your behaviours, then the question is: What happens when you take control of the thoughts you choose to pay attention to or focus on, on a moment by moment basis? Answer: You can feel bad or you can feel good more often. However, the real opportunity lies in the direction of your thinking.

We are all familiar with the concept of positive thinking, but few of us master the art of it. In the beginning when I happened upon the concept I tried to think positive thoughts as often as I could, but that's not easy when someone is breaking your rules or when you have been used to being so hard on yourself for such a long time. Back then if I made a mistake or if someone interrupted what I was doing the furthest I got to was to suggest the idea to myself, 'Be positive Brian. Think positive thoughts. Don't be grumpy. Don't be negative. Don't start giving out.' But that never worked and shortly afterwards I ended up having just another set of tools to criticise myself about. My 'positive' thinking strategy was in actual fact making me feel worse. Thankfully, I found ways around that too, which I will gladly share with you.

What it all boils down to is having the right response for the moment that you are in. For example, right now, assuming that you are in reflective mode, you could come up with all sorts of new, useful and creative ways of better responding to all sorts of challenging situations in the future. That is because you are more than likely presently in a detached state. While you are reading this, the outside world is held at bay for a time and your attention is more directed to the task at hand, so it all feels so much easier to do, doesn't it?

The situation would be very different if someone felt they needed your immediate attention right now and kept tugging at your sleeve, asking you a million-miles-an-hour questions in an urgently expectant tone. Those types of challenge require different types of response, which we will also look at.

For now, I would like you to take more of a global approach to feeling really good. One that you may not be used to doing, but one that once you engage in fully will get you moving in a better direction. This technique can act as one of the pivot points for the more evolved and powerful you.

In Search of Magic

My own relentless search for personal growth and sustainable happiness has led me from the reckless ingestion of the sacred plant ayahuasca (the shamans' psychedelic gateway to the other world) in the rainforests of Brazil to the sitting of employment psychometric tests in a recruitment agency in Ireland. It has found me as a disgruntled teenager listening to what the Jehovah's Witnesses had to say in my mother's home and led me to experiencing the hypnotic depths of the altered states of consciousness induced by the wizard of trance Dr Richard Bandler in Scotland.

I have done a lot and have still more to do. I am on a search for magic and I am finding it in the most ordinary of places. I look outside, I look inside and I always look for more. When I find it, I use it and get excited by what is left that I do not yet know. This journey appears to me to be endless and is bursting full of exquisite challenge and reward. Behind every challenge there is a treasure to behold and no sooner is it revealed but it gives way to the notion of how much more adventure you can venture into. How much pleasure can you stand? What more is there out there for you that you have not yet even imagined is possible?

As a young child I was intrigued by the mystical stories of the spiritual so eloquently delivered by my fifth-class teacher Br Ging. In college (with the help of the Jesuits) my mind was widened by the concept of Marxist consciousness. I found myself mesmerised by the apparent calmness and inner stillness exalted by my Transcendental Meditation teacher, whose name I never knew, and was lured to the lunatic fringe in a textiles factory through lack of sleep and smoking hash on the night shift. I believe evolution is about expanding consciousness and I know that all expanse is not a good thing. I have made what may appear to some as errors of judgment, but all of it has led to now. All of it has taught me something. I know for sure, thus far, that what you can create within your mind is still far more powerful than what you can create outside of it. It is with this in mind I would like to take you to your next experience. A simple internal journey to release your true nature.

Exercise: The Magpie Technique

The best way to get high, and by that I mean to get high on life, and the best way to indulge yourself is by drawing from your personal experiences, of which you have many. Often sheltered from the light of your present-day awareness, these 'mind bombs' are just waiting to warm you up as you quietly yet excitedly realise in your heart of hearts that you really have being doing well just to make it this far. May I be the first to congratulate you. Well done.

I will ask that you approach this exercise like a chemist would an experiment, the more you put into the mix the more you are likely to get from it. You have so many things to be proud of, so many reasons to hold your head high, so many obstacles you have overcome, both the little and the large, they all add up. It all amounts to a whole lot that is worth recognising. You deserve to feel good about this. You haven't even begun to discover what is there waiting for you because you forgot to keep reminding yourself of the things worth remembering.

What I ask of you this time is to take a little wander through your thoughts, through your memory, to bring to mind the things that you have achieved to date that are worthwhile. You can start from anywhere, it can be the recent or distant past, it can be whatever pops into your head. It doesn't have to be in chronological order because that is not how your mind works. All that is important is that you open up your memory to the possibility of locating as many situations as you can. The times when you did what it took to get the job done. Whether you knuckled down to improve your school grades or whether you plucked up the courage to face off an opponent. Whether you went beyond the call of duty for a friend in need or whether you dared to say hello to someone you were interested in. Remember all of this is private, no one need ever see it. You can even use secret words or cue words to remind you of each significant event.

Look for the things in your life that defined you, that shaped you, that determined who you are today. Those magical moments that propelled your life into a particularly good direction. Recollect examples and times that made you say words to the effect of 'I've done that, I'm proud of it and I'm happy that I've done it. I'm delighted and I feel good because of it.' Approach this as though you are a newspaper reporter looking back into your past. You are looking only for the good times. This is the essence of the Magpie Technique. You are looking to find only the parts that sparkle; just like a magpie you are collecting these shiny things. Just gather the good feelings, the good ideas, the good accomplishments, the things you've done, the things that define you and shape you. This is the better you. This is the you that you want to be. This is the you that you want to remind yourself to continue to be in the future. Imagine at the end of it you are about to do a party political broadcast of the life and accomplishments of you. Do it to impress your audience. Do it as if it is a sales pitch. You are the product so make it so that only the best of you comes through.

The first thing that comes to my mind when I think of these things is the memory of producing my first hypnotic CD, *The Rest of Your Life*. The hours spent writing the script and learning how to use the software to design the cover. I remember getting it printed and produced and finally collecting it from the studio. I remember how proud and yet anxious I felt, wondering if it was good enough. I think of it now and feel proud every time I hear the feedback from it.

I also remember getting my degree and the feeling that goes with that. Five years of perseverance and dedication, of long hours in work, in college and at home all leading up to that point. I recall the pride, the fun and the laughter as I and my college buddies graced the college grounds in the beautiful May sunshine, our hats being blown off and our gowns being tossed about with the wind. We had finally made it.

I remember deciding to put a suit on and going to a job interview that secured me a 100 per cent wage increase in one conversation. I remember walking barefoot across red hot burning coals saying, 'Cool moss. Cool moss.' I remember being handed my Master Trainer of NLP Certificate and sitting with Richard Bandler as he conferred it in a way that only he could. I remember at fourteen years of age taking on Martin Giles, the kid that had bullied me once too often. I remember chasing him up a hill, taking off my jacket, punching him in the face and watching him fall back down the hill again. I remember seeing him cry and run away. I remember as a shop steward getting the female workforce parity with the male workforce. I remember how loyal the workers were to me after that. I remember sitting my trade union exams and scoring the highest but being refused a position because of my individuality. I remember being on the very edge of my ayahuasca experience, facing off all of my fears and surviving them. I remember, despite the vomiting, the shaking, the sweating and the hallucinations, knowing that all things come to pass and knowing that if you can survive this you can survive anything.

I remember the birth of both my children. I look at how they make it all worthwhile, how all that effort and input keeps giving that return. I am sitting in my office which I remember vividly creating in my mind. I remember the expression on my wife Theresa's face on her fortieth birthday when she was overwhelmed in a hotel in Paris by what we had done for her. I feel proud to have been a part of that; I know I helped put that feeling there.

I remember my first client who had irritable bowel syndrome and I remember when she opened her eyes having come from a deep hypnotic trance with a confused look on her face. I remember asking her was everything okay and after what seemed like forever she said, 'I have never in twenty years sat down without pain and with such comfort for such a long time.' That day her symptoms disappeared forever. I remember my first interview by a journalist for a newspaper, my first radio interview, my first TV appearance. I remember setting up my own business. I remember hooking up with my friend Owen Fitzpatrick and us both setting up the Institute.

I remember each and every one of these examples as a challenge overcome and as an achievement that fills me with pride, something I can use to spur myself on, something that helps me to feel good more often and more of the time.

I want to invite you now to travel your own road and see what you can come up with. To do as I just did, to spend some time reflecting back, sorting for the positive accomplishments that you have achieved, maybe that you are secretly proud of. You can keep them secret but just not hidden from yourself. It's time to be like a magpie and look for the bits of your life experience that sparkle, to gather up as many of them as you can and to weave them together so that they make you shine from the inside out, to be filled with that warm, fulfilled feeling that makes life wonderful.

Whether you choose to take a few moments and close your eyes as if to rest deeply as you do this and then write it all down at the time or later is not important. What is important is that you give yourself permission to awaken the better side of you, to bring the stronger you to the surface, the you full of courage and hope, the you filled with the determination to succeed, the you full of compassion and care, the you that makes you proud to be you.

Haven't you had enough of pain already? This is time to get serious about having fun. Just imagine if you like that the love train has pulled into town and it's your turn to hop on board, to lighten up and find out what good fortune awaits you when you dare to take this mental adventure into your personal well-being. After all, this is why you are reading this book – right?

This is an exercise in positivity, it is not meant to be therapy, we are not looking for pain we are looking for pleasure, for good feelings, happy feelings, victorious feelings, sunny feelings, shiny bright feelings, lovely luminous heart-warming tremendously inspiring feelings. Do you get the picture?

Please do it now and once you have done it let me take you further than you may have ever been. With closed eyes you could imagine yourself stepping right into your experiences and begin to immerse yourself, looking through your own eyes, feeling your feelings, embracing your accomplishments, your awards, your personal victories, your greater achievements. Give yourself permission to step right in and to take a deep breath and pull the experiences towards you so that they can fill and flow right through you. Allow yourself to walk through each and every accomplishment, each and every achievement, each and everything that was worth doing, the nice things that people said about you during or afterwards, the things that make you feel really good about you. Just give yourself permission to sail right through it and to enjoy it.

This is your time to open up and let yourself go for it. Really feel what it feels like, there are certain things that you did and you're so happy that you've done them, you're so happy that you've accomplished them, you put in the effort, you got the results. Begin to get the feeling of that glowing sense of achievement, and as you envelop yourself in the experience, think about all the other things that are there too that you've not yet visited, that are ready and waiting for you to claim the wonderful feelings that go with them. Just indulge yourself, enjoy yourself and you might be surprised to know how truly worthwhile you are and how much more capable you've yet to become.

In the quietness of your own mind only you know what else needs doing to complete the process so that after some time you can find yourself back to the here and now feeling better because of it.

Now – if I even need to say this – if you haven't done it already there is no time like the present. Go ahead, give it a go. Here's a summary of the Magpie Technique.

Step 1

Sift through your memory and gather some of those key and critical defining moments. Moments that set your life in a particular direction. A point in time when you said to yourself 'that's who I really am, that's what I am all about'. It might have been a time when you won an award for a special achievement, perhaps a time when you were singled out for your efforts, a time in your life when you got to shine and the true you came bursting forth. Whatever it is for you, identify as many accomplishments as you can (and no less than five), one at a time, no matter how long ago, that happened to you and that still make you feel very proud when you recall them now.

Step 2
Take a few moments to reflect on each one. As you do so allow yourself to re-live the experience in your mind. Feel what you felt then, see what you saw and hear what you heard. Run it through in your mind and bathe yourself in your own glory for a few moments.

Step 3
Once you have the experience captured in as much detail as possible, write down the sights, the sounds and the sensations that you experienced; write down where you were and who was there with you or around you. Above all, capture in writing how it felt to feel those feelings. Keep one rule only in mind as you write: do so in the present tense as if it were happening all over again.

Step 4
Read and rewrite it until you've got it all and then put it down here for you to review at a later time.

_____

_____

_____

_____

_____

_____

_____

————————————————————————
————————————————————————
————————————————————————
————————————————————————
————————————————————————
————————————————————————
————————————————————————

Step 5

Now that you have brought these experiences to mind it is time to use the energy released from them to propel you to a brighter future. Run through the experiences fully once more and then think about a future challenge. Using your imagination and the feelings that are now running, begin to visualise how you want things to turn out and draw on whatever visual, auditory or kinaesthetic stimulants you can think of, real or imagined, to accelerate your momentum.

Let me tell you if that doesn't make you feel good you have either not done what I have asked you to do in the way that I asked you to it, or you're dead. Now remember if you've done this before it's still worth doing it again and repeating it again and again. This is about getting good at this stuff, it's not about doing it once, it's about finding out how you can run good feelings on demand, and how you can build the skill and practice of making your own body a temple of bliss.

Your Natural Self

I am no longer the grumpy sod that my mother had to endure for years, I am no longer angry at everything and everyone including myself. I am no longer down on myself all of the time. Unlike many of us I have managed to establish a healthy working relationship with myself (at least most of the time). I have my moments, but they are few and far between. Now I am no tree hugger or cloud muncher (as my friend Owen Fitzpatrick would say) but I am a whole lot happier than I could have been because of what I have learned to do. And if I can do it, you most certainly can too.

Does it take courage? Well if shedding your ego takes courage then it does. Does it require change? Absolutely, we are talking a major overhaul but not in a way you might think. You will still be who you have always been, only better in that your brighter side will come through more often. Am I asking you to get out the medallion and the white robe? Well only if you intend to scare people.

What I am hoping is that you will become more natural and when I say natural I would ask you to take a look around at what being natural means. Nature is not all peace and tranquillity. It is ferocious and determined. It is creative and powerful. It is capable of great and astonishing beauty and it continues relentlessly despite adversity. That is the type of natural I am talking about. The one that makes you look at life as a rare and unprecedented opportunity to grow, to evolve, to create, to survive, to thrive and to become all that you can in ways that only you know how. To express yourself as a pulsating current of energy and to light up your life and the lives of those you meet.

Marking out your accomplishments, your victories and your positive achievements acts as a stimulant and a reminder of what the better side of living is all about. That's what this is about, remember this is you, this is the real you, this is the stuff that you are made of too. This is the fire that's in you when you're at your best. When you run through your experiences like this and when you give yourself permission to step in and begin to enjoy them. When you think about what it is you've accomplished, what it is you've achieved, and draw on these experiences, each and every one, and completely drink them up by drawing them towards you. You remind yourself of who you truly are as you give yourself permission to do more, achieve more and accelerate forward.

Exercise: Building Your Magnetic Future
This process becomes your opportunity, your time, your fuel to propel you into more opportunity. Something you can do inside

your own mind, nobody need know that you're doing it, so you get to do whatever you choose. If there are accomplishments or achievements that you've already had there that you did not yet revisit, you can now. If there are things on your mind that you want to do but haven't yet done, now is the time to imagine them being done from this place of strength, tenacity and vitality. You can imagine becoming more victorious and let yourself step right in as though to a celebratory fanfare of your achievements. This is your time to blow your trumpet inside your own mind, this is your time to proudly march in and claim your victory. This is your time to really feel it like there's a group of people around you, giving you a round of applause, patting you on the back and saying well done, and giving you the credit that you truly deserve. Just imagine stepping right into it and feel that feeling of well done, just go for it. You know that now you're unstoppable, everything's happening for you, you're beginning to build an unstoppable confidence.

Imagine each and every event and allow yourself to sail right through it with that deep sense of appreciation and sense of knowing that you're worth more than you ever give yourself credit for, that there's so much more that you can do. I want you to step right in and crank it up, really begin to feel what it feels like and to do what you need to do inside your own mind to enjoy the experience at its maximum.

Some people as they do this exercise can imagine drum rolls and people bellowing and whistling, 'Yo. Way to go!' Your job is to do what you want to enhance your experience of things. Add to your experience whatever you want, imagine a whole choir of gospel singers promoting you and sending you forward, imagine you're doing the best that you can as people rally behind you and you feel more supported than ever before. Hear the recognition, see the approval and feel the drive. If you've got guardian angels you can use them as well. Imagine them giving you a round of applause. If you've got a spirit guide you can bring that in as well. You can bring your ancestors in and imagine them all spurring you on, imagine them all giving you that shape and that enthusiasm, just really backing you up and saying, 'Well done. You're really worth this and you're capable of so much more.'

Give yourself permission to really begin to play with this. Imagine being at your best and in everything that you do people are out there batting for you, they're looking for you to do well. Hear yourself talk to yourself with words of encouragement and inspiration, begin to be able to promote yourself in a much more positive light, imagine everything going well from now on, imagine that's the best thing you've ever done so far and it's going to be even better the next time. Imagine there's so much more that you can do and will do as you are now developing the thirst for it. Give yourself permission, play with it inside your mind, do it the way you want to do it, it's all about how you choose to enjoy and brighten up on the inside of your mind, for we know what the mind can conceive the mind can achieve and by doing this you are laying the foundations for greatness, your own personal chemical army that can fuel your momentum to much greater heights.

By now I imagine that you are getting the idea of what this is about. Did you find you could do it? Did you learn something about yourself? Did you learn that you're a lot better than you thought maybe? Have you realised that you've a lot more to offer and that you have achieved a lot more than you've ever given yourself credit for? Doesn't it make sense to mark what you've achieved? It's worth paying attention to and it's not bragging or boasting it's just enjoying and celebrating the fact that you've accomplished things. In order to be successful it's what you need to do more of. You wouldn't have gotten this far if you weren't successful in many different things. Richard Bandler says you were born a success; imagine it, you were the only sperm that survived. So you're conditioned from the beginning to be a success; you have a head start.

Tapping into Your Personal Resources

Now I want you to think about the things you know about yourself, your characteristics, your abilities, your qualities, your personality, the things that you are strong at, the things that you are good at, the things that basically define you and shape you as a person. The things that people would say about you – the good things. I'm sure there are a few people that might say some not so great things, but we're only interested in the good stuff, that's all we're here for, because you're already an expert in the bad stuff.

I want you to approach it in layers and ask yourself what you know about you, what do you know about your skills, your abilities, your qualities, your personality, the type of person you are. Are you happy, humorous, fun loving, decisive, focused? Are you very achievement-oriented? What's good about you? How do people describe you? Are you a bit of a laugh? Are you a creative, insightful person? Are you friendly? What stuff are you made of? What is it that makes you you?

Now I know some of you squirm or shrink a little bit at the mention of the word 'family' and you think perhaps your family only see what's wrong with you, or perhaps that's what you listen to and you don't take notice of the good things they may say about you. Whatever the case is, it is the way it is and that's okay too, because remember we don't all present the same face to the same people. We may have a different face for our family than we have for our close friends. Very often we have a different face again for our work colleagues. What we're looking at here is what you already know about what people know about you. It's not always what is, but it's what they know. I want you to realise that maybe you are not drawing from all that you can. When you begin to pay attention to these things it becomes easy.

Exercise: Personal Resources

You have at your disposal a number of resources, some of which you are aware of and others you are not yet aware of. Some you identify as your natural gifts, talents, strengths, abilities and special qualities and some are unknown to you but others attribute them to you as natural characteristics. Things that you do so automatically and spontaneously that you no longer take cognisance of. These are learned habits that are so frequently employed by you that they feel as natural as riding a bicycle or driving your car. You no longer think about them, you simply do them. Now is your opportunity to uncover these hidden resources and to employ them in even more productive ways. To complete this exercise you will need to call upon your family, friends and work colleagues.

A useful way of approaching your family, friends and work colleagues would be with the following question: 'If you were to describe my strong points to a stranger or to someone who was enquiring about me how would you describe me?'

In the boxes below:

1. List in detail *what you know* of your natural gifts, talents, strengths, abilities and special qualities, those positive characteristics that you choose to use to define your personality. In other words the things that you are really good at.

You	Partner/Family/ Friends	Work Colleagues

2. List in detail *what you believe your partner/family and friends know* of your natural gifts, talents, strengths, abilities and special qualities, those positive characteristics that they would use to define your personality. If you can, ask your friends the same question, this will provide you with even better quality information and perhaps reveal positive aspects about yourself that you were not aware of.

3. List in detail *what you believe your work colleagues know* of your natural gifts, talents, strengths, abilities and special qualities.

Exercise: Appreciation

Science has proven that the action of noticing what we have and subsequently expressing gratitude for it is a fundamental source for developing the habit of happiness.

Appreciation: A short story by a grandson about his grandmother

I admire my Nanny because she got cancer but she never ever complained or moaned or sulked. She was never sad either. She was always happy. She had to undergo loads of treatment. But she was still happy. Her body was in a really bad state but her mood was in an excellent state. I admire her because she never gave up. Everybody associates cancer with death; that's why so many people die from it. To cure an illness you have to stay happy. That is better than any medicine. She is now cured and healthy. She defeated cancer in the battle for her life. She is a wonderful person that's why I admire her.

By Dylan Colbert, aged 9

This story was written by my son about my mother. I feel very fortunate to have both of them in my life. Each of us is blessed in some way. What are the things in life that you are most grateful for right now? It might be your health, your family, your job or your wealth. It might be your ability to stay in the moment or to take the time to catch a sunset.

Whatever it is, find it, note it and write it down and remember that the state of appreciation is a great place to start the process of manifestation.

Example 1

_____

_____

_____

_____

_____

_____

_____

Example 2

_____

_____

_____

_____

_____

_____

Exercise: Inspiration

Just as there are moments that define us, there are situations that serve to inspire us. It may be a movie, a book, an individual, an incident or an event in history. These moments teach us how to view the world from an empowering perspective. The power of these experiences leaves such a strong impact on us that we use them as metaphors for living and they act as filters through which we channel much of our life experiences. Select five of the most inspirational experiences and give them life through writing a synopsis of the situation and its meaning to you.

Inspiration 1

_____

_____

_____

_____

_____

_____

Inspiration 2

_____

_____

_____

_____

_____

Inspiration 3

_____

_____

_____

_____

_____

_____

_____

Inspiration 4

_____

_____

_____

_____

_____

_____

Inspiration 5

_____

_____

_____

_____

_____

_____

Exercise: Quotations
Select three quotes, maxims or sayings that sum up your philosophy
of life.

Quote 1

_____

_____

Quote 2

_____

_____

Quote 3

_____

_____

Exercise: Reflection Chamber

We all need quiet time to take the opportunity to reflect or meditate on the challenges we are facing or upon the events that are influencing the direction of our lives. I invite you to think now of how you can construct time and situations that allow for this. Personally, I like to take time out by listening to a relaxation CD or sometimes I just go to my room and lie on the bed in the quietness and reflect. I know of many mums who choose to 'steal' a few minutes quiet time in the bath. Your preference might be to go for a walk or to go to church. The more choices you select the more likely you are to avail of the opportunity. There have been times in the past that you have used to reflect, how could you introduce them now into your daily life?

_____

_____

_____

_____

_____

Exercise: Happiness Chest

There are times in the face of adversity, challenge and worry when we need to remind ourselves that we still have plenty of resources that can keep us sane. It's no secret, but it is something that we forget to remind ourselves of very often. So list out as many things as you can that make you happy and be prepared to use them as part remedies to your stresses and worries.

_____

_____

_____

_____

_____

_____

_____

_____

_____

_____

_____

_____

CHAPTER 6

Always Keep Your Focus on the End Result

Certain things catch your eye, but pursue only those that capture your heart.

Native American Indian saying

Well-Formed Outcomes

One very helpful habit to learn is how to ask more useful questions. Questions that not only direct your mind, but free up your consciousness to move in more creative ways. This brings us to the concept of building 'well-formed outcomes'. Many of you may already write down your goals and if you are in employment you could even have had someone determine and write them down for you, at least the professional ones anyhow.

Research consistently demonstrates that if you write down your goals you are more likely to achieve them. I have a theory about how to do that, which we will talk about in time. My wife writes down her goals at the beginning of the year, but she is one of the few that achieves them all. She does this because she has an approach that works brilliantly. I have asked her to add some things on to her list and each time I have she has always achieved them. Theresa is a rare breed, once she puts her mind to something she makes it happen and it happens because she doesn't just put her mind to it, she rarely takes it off it, which means that time and time again I see her checking in on her diary, checking in on her progress, making adjustments if need be but never letting up. She does this without stress because in her mind once you put your mind to something it is going to happen, in fact it already has, and she is simply waiting for the universe to catch up with her. Rather than trying to force the universe into her way of thinking, she stays patient in the pursuit and facilitates the universe to do her bidding. Now I think that is a cool way to work with reality, but not only is it cool, it is practical, hugely effective and always produces the results.

Theresa is not like me and she could take or leave NLP, but she does have an unshakeable confidence in what can be achieved and her goals are never too extravagant. She doesn't want for the sake of wanting; she doesn't input her order and expect not to play an active part in creating it. She sees it all as a two-way process and believes you can have what you want as long as what you want harms no one. As she says, 'You will get what you want as long as you are pre-pared to do what it takes and prepared to adjust in the light of new circumstances.'

To me the universe has its rules about the order of things, individuals have their own rules about how that order should be, but in my opinion the quality and even the content of the reality you create is brought about by the intertwining of the two. In NLP there are certain 'rules' or considerations that when taken into account are more likely to ensure you successfully achieve what you have set your mind upon.

Making Sense of Things

The more senses you activate and connect to the creation and pursuit of your goals, the more likely it is that you are going to achieve them. This is a point that is too often under-emphasised in the abundance of literature on the subject. For example, some approaches emphasise the fact that you've got to visualise your goals to make them happen. But that's not all true, although it is partly true. Some people say you've got to write down your goals to achieve them. That's also partly true, because by writing down each goal you are doing two things: you are thinking about it and you are writing about it.

Really what it all boils down to is a question of intensity. The more you do in the direction of achieving your goal, the more likely you are to get it. So if you see yourself vividly and clearly in your mind's eye achieving your goal you are more likely to achieve it. If you sound out your goal, by hearing what you will hear, what you will say, the sounds that will be there, you are more likely to achieve your goal. Just as if you generate the feeling of what it will feel like as you achieve your goal, and you access the various blends of emotions and sensations that go with that, you are more likely to achieve your goal. If you capture all of this down on paper you get to become closer to achieving your goal.

The secret behind all of this is to begin to build and connect *all* of your senses towards achieving your goals. When you ask yourself the questions – What will I see? What will I hear? What will I feel? What will I smell? What will I taste once I have achieved my goal? – then you get closer to achieving what you want. But that is not all that needs to be taken into account. You need also to become aware of the impact that your goal will have on yourself and others. To help you with all of this there is a little process in NLP called 'well-formed outcomes'. I will demonstrate how you put this into proper effect.

Earlier I discussed how nature abhors a vacuum and that if you create a vacuum you need to put something in its place. In this case what is needed is a well-formed outcome or what you might know as a goal or a series of goals. Otherwise your brain will fill it in with what you used to be doing. So rather than giving yourself a hard time, you need to start to ask useful and resourceful questions: What do I want to experience right now? What do I want to see? What do I want to hear? What do I want to feel? From there you can look at the whole process of actually setting up your goal.

Be Specific

First of all when setting your well-formed outcome you have to be specific. You must set it up so that you know specifically what it is that you want. For example, if you decide that one of your goals is to improve your standard of living and part of that involves the purchase of a house, there is little point in calling into an auctioneer and just telling her that you want a house. You know that if you offer such a vague description she is going to ask you about the kind of house you want. So you decide to become more specific and say, 'I want a house by the sea.' Once she has that piece of information, she will ask even more questions about what the house should look like, how many bedrooms you need etc. So then you'll hear her summarise what you want, 'So you are looking for a three-bedroomed detached house by the sea.' Music to your ears.

Off you go, happy as Larry that you have given her 'the specifics' and that she knows what to do. Shortly afterwards you take her call and to your extreme delight she tells you that she has the very property for you and wants you to meet up so that you can view it. As you excitedly make your way there you are impressed by the sea view to your right, the beautiful blue ocean flanked by golden sandy beaches, it's absolute paradise. As you journey some more up the incline, the beach goes out of view but you can still hear the gentle rise and fall of the surf on the shore. The weather is beautiful and your spirits soar as high as the seagulls overhead. Your journey continues onwards and upwards a little longer than you expected but that's okay. You can no longer hear the sea as the auctioneer turns to you and says, 'Here we are.' The car comes to a halt, the handbrake is pulled and you open the door and get out. There in front of you is your house exactly as you described it, but not as you imagined it. The house has three bedrooms and is detached as you requested, it is by the sea as you requested, but it sits on the edge of a cliff. You failed to specify that what you meant to say was: *by a beach* by the sea. As the truth sinks in, you seek to place blame elsewhere and say, 'Now hang on a minute, the house is beside a cliff for God's sake.' To which the auctioneer replies, 'Yes and it is beside the sea. You did ask for a house beside the sea, didn't you?'

Your brain works the very same way: if you're not clear enough, if you're not specific enough, you cannot expect your brain to know what to do. Your brain has to have precise instructions of where to go, what to do and how to get there. Your brain needs to know exactly what it has to do, because it will do what you tell it to do.

Now because of the way language works, every time you talk to yourself (and every time someone else talks to you) you're actually setting up instructions for your brain to respond. So if you're saying to yourself 'I just want to be happy', then you need to ask yourself if that is detailed enough for your brain to track. Your brain doesn't necessarily know what 'happy' looks like, sounds like or even feels like. You're not giving it the detail it needs to bring about the thing you desire. You're not putting in the detail that it needs in order for it to draw you towards it in the way that works best.

Be Positive

This lack of attention to language often leads people to attract exactly what they don't want rather than what they do. When I ask clients what they want to achieve from the session, they sink lower into their unhappiness and say to me, 'Well *I don't want* to be sad anymore, and *I don't want* to be upset all of the time, and *I don't want* to be depressed, and *I don't want* to be . . .' and the list keeps getting longer. All of this stuff that they *don't want* to be.

> We know that our brain cannot process a negative so if I tell you *not* to think of a big pink elephant running down your stairs wearing a little Barbie dress, opening the door of your fridge and squeezing itself into it, that's exactly what you will see. You were forced to do exactly what I asked you not to do.

Most clients don't even pay attention to the power of their language. Most clients aren't even aware of what they are saying. What they are saying is what they *don't want* and in so doing they are attracting to themselves the very thing that they want to avoid. You need to state in positive terms what you do want. Your language needs to be phrased in a positive way. So 'I don't want to be stressed out' is not phrased positively in terms of what it is you do want. 'I don't want to be stressed out' needs to be replaced by 'I want to be calm' or 'I want to be relaxed'.

If you woke up this morning and said to yourself 'I don't want to be so stressed today', your brain went up into its stress file, opened it up and said, 'You don't want to be how stressed?' As it did that it had to connect with the stress and so release part of the experience that you were trying to avoid, thereby leaving the remainder of your attention primed to sort for stress for the rest of the day. You've got to decide what it is that you *do* want and you need to be positive and set it up in a way that it is actually achievable.

Ignite Your Senses

It is not enough just to say that you can see yourself achieving your goals. You need to hear yourself and you need to connect with the feelings that it will give you when you have. Tom, a former client, phones me and says,

> 'Brian, I'm ready to take it to the next level. This is my time, and I want to make it happen for me.'
> 'Okay, well you've been here before, you know this stuff works Tom so let's get started.'
> 'Well I want the million euro house now.'
> 'Fair enough.'
> 'Actually I want to become a billionaire.'
> 'Okay . . . that's a big leap.'
> 'This is what I want, right. I have done what you suggested previously. I've been up in the house that I want to buy and I've seen it. It's absolutely magnificent. It's a fantastic house, absolutely gorgeous. It has magnificent oak doors on it, huge living and recreational spaces and they've got a pool table there and they've got a swimming pool and there's a gigantic multi-media room on the other side, soft leather seats, subdued lighting, the entire works.

Absolutely fantastic. It looks the way I want it to look. It has got the ideal design, the perfect location, a superb finish and all of the rest. I've been in it, I sat down in it, I walked through the place, and I've felt it. I've as good as tried on the experience. I know what it feels like and I'm loving every bit of it.'

To which I say with apparent empathy, 'That's cool, that's no bother at all Tom.'

The last time Tom had visited me he wanted a Camero sports car. He got his car and this is how he brought about the circumstances that led his dream to become a reality. At first we identified specifically the type, year, make and even the colour of his new Camero sports car. I told him that in order to get what you want, what you need to do is to begin to get a sensory experience of it. So I told him to go and take a test drive in his imagination in his brand new, state-of-the-art, sleek and stylish, black Camero road-eating machine. To imagine the open road in front of him and experience the sudden tug of the six second acceleration from nought to sixty. I asked him to get the feel of the car, to get the smell of the leather and the feel of the seats, to turn on the CD player and blast out his favourite driving music (he was the type).

I suggested that he engage fully with the experience so that if he closed his eyes he could hold his hands on the steering wheel, he could slide down the window and feel the breeze in his hair and hear the sporadic purr of the engine revving as it feeds on the road in front of it. I got him to tap into the feeling of excitement of pulling into his driveway, to hear the crunch of the gravel underneath the rubber of those alloy wheels. I got him to see his reflection in the window of his house as his Camero glided into vision. I got him to do the whole lot, nothing was left out. We put in as much detail as we could think of and in as many situations as we could place both he and the car that would generate even more desire. This is the type of stuff you need to do because this is what juices up your feelings so you actually go for it. You need to keep it on a sensory basis.

Check for Ecology

The next thing you can do to make your goal more effortlessly achievable is to ensure that it is ecological. Look again at the conversation with Tom:

'I want to take it to the next level and I want to become a
   billionaire.'
'Okay no problem.'
'And you know me Brian I can work and I know how to work
   hard and I'll go for it with everything I've got.'
'What is it that you are prepared to do?'
'Oh I'm prepared to work 24/7 for this and as a matter of fact
   Brian it needs to be 24/7.'
'So for how long?'
'For the next five years.'
'Okay so, for the next five years, yeah no problem. By the way
   how are the wife and kids?'
'What do you mean?'
'Just what I said, how's the wife and kids? And what age are
   your kids now? Mark is five and Shannon is three am I
   right? Okay yeah so that's 24/7 for five years. So you're not
   going to see them for the next five years really are you?'
'Yeah, well yeah, but like I will be giving them everything they
   want afterwards.'

Now any of you who have children will know that five minutes in a child's life is pretty much a major deal. My little fella comes into me one day and said, 'Dad you never play with me anymore.' I said, 'Cian I was playing with you a half an hour ago.' 'Yeah,' he agreed, 'but you never play with me anymore.' That's how time works for most kids. Perhaps you remember how long your school holidays lasted when you were that age. Or how long it took for teatime to come when you were ravenous with hunger after playing all day with your friends. Wouldn't it be good if all the good things just took forever?

Let's look at this model even more closely. I want to win the four million euro in the lotto for this weekend. I know it's four million exactly – so that's **specific** isn't it? And **positive**, it's pretty positive as an outcome. I know I'm going to feel great. I know I am going to feel fantastic because I'm going to be in the money, I will be rolling in it.

So now to **activate the sensory experience**: What will I see, what will I hear and what will I feel when I've achieved this goal? I won't be seeing the usual people that I see every other day because I'll be off sipping beer on a sun-drenched beach somewhere on the Mediterranean. What will I feel? I will feel fantastic. What will I hear? I will hear the sound of 'chi-ching' and that's the interest clocking up in my bank account by the second thanks to my new-found wealth. So I've got the sensory thing going on.

Is it **ecological**? Or in other words does this goal fit in with the rest of my life? Will it mean I can achieve all of my other goals? Will I be able to do the things that I want to do now? Will I be able to relax and pay the butler and the maids? Will I have enough money to keep my new Lamborghini *and* my Dodge Viper? Will I be able to afford my new home with the gigantic swimming pool and the media room? Of course I will, this goal will fit in with all of what I have: my family, my friends and my job and if my friends don't like it, well with all that dosh I can always go out there and buy more friends, can't I? Can't I?

Be in Control

There is just one minor detail left to examine, without which the goal will not be well formed: Is this goal under my control? And the answer in the lotto example is one big huge gigantic resounding, 'No. Nada. Afraid not. Sorry. Well it's not your day today perhaps the questions didn't suit you . . . Next.'

It absolutely has to be under your control. No negotiation, no questions asked. For a goal to be well formed you have to be in control of it. The next best thing to that is for it to be under your influence – well Bob Geldof, Midge Ure and Bono all have bucket loads of influence – and yeah influence can take you to some cool places but does it get the job done the way you want it? Now I wouldn't for a second suggest for the guys to surrender their influence because with it you can move mountains and they are living proof of that. However, in your world and in terms of what you want to ensure gets done, you know your goals are unlikely to happen if you have no control over them. Wishful thinking is all well and good, but there is nothing like action to produce the results that you want in your life.

Remember this is about looking at your life and finding out what you are in control of so you can change it. A lot of stress is about not being in control of things. But the reality is that in order for you to create an effective change you need to have it under your control. If you can't put external things under your control, for example the moods and behaviours of others, then you have to control the elements you can influence, which is what you feel or how you choose to respond to what happens at any given moment.

Get Moving Straight Away

Let's look at what people do when they're setting up their goals. Okay so if my goal is to complete this book, I need first to calculate what stage I am at right at this moment. Quite simply I need to take stock of what is already done and what is left to do. In NLP terms, this is called being in the present state while focusing on the future state. So rather than concern myself with *why* it has taken me this long or *why* I haven't this much done or *why* I am not finished yet, I simply take stock of where I am now. What have I got done and what have I left to do?

This makes for an easier transition. This makes for a steadier and more productive flow of energy. This will get me to my goal in the quickest and most efficient way possible. No dragging up the past, no drudging through my shortcomings, no self-deprecating rants, no self-blame, none of that. Just looking forward from the present and supporting myself as I go. It feels much healthier that way. So here's to a longer-lasting, health-enhancing, adventure-filled life. There's a lot to be done, more fun to be had, so let's get this party started.

My goal is this, I want to complete this book, I want to go from my present position of typing this page to my desired position of walking into the bookstore and experiencing the moment when I see my book, with my name on it, sitting there on a bookshelf amongst the other published authors. That is where I want to be. That is my desired state. That is the moment that I want to experience. That is the fuel that keeps me focused. That is the sensation that spurs me on. That is what drives me in the direction of my goal. That is de facto my desired state.

Begin with the End in Mind

One of life's major problems is that of approach, and many dreams get hijacked by focus rather than by circumstance. One of the essential governing rules for your continued success will be your ability not only to begin with the end in mind but to continue keeping the end in mind until you have satisfactorily achieved your outcome.

The problem for most people is that they start out right but lose sight of their goal under the pressure of the obstacles. They are hypnotised by disillusionment and sucked into focusing on what is in their way rather than how they will create headway. That's how we end up looking at our problems rather than our solutions and as a result allowing the universe to give us more and more of what we focus on. If you focus on the problem, the problem will only get bigger; if you focus on the solution, your opportunities will become greater and your success becomes easier. Let me explain the nature of this, which persuasion engineer John La Valle calls 'Crystal Ball Gazing'.

Crystal Ball Gazing

So now I am going to ask you to give me permission to be chauvinistic and to use some stereotypical concepts, but as I will be equally offensive to both sexes I am sure you will find it in your heart to forgive me.

Women have two true gods, two reasons for complete adulation and submission. The religions I speak of, which can only be truly understood and appreciated by you if you are female, are the religions of the Shoe and the Handbag. Most women love bags and shoes; whereas for men, it's cars, fast cars, the faster the better. A woman's eyes may light up at the sight of a designer handbag or a pair of high heels. With her heart rate increasing she looks excitedly at the shoes as the dutiful shop assistant slips over and says teasingly, like the serpent on the branch, 'Would you like to try them on?' At which point, fashion takes hold and she looks and she thinks and she looks at the price and she thinks again about her credit card already reeling from overspend and as she looks again the image of her wearing the shoes becomes much brighter and delightful and she says, 'Go on then, I'll be a bit naughty.'

She picks up the shoes and her foot glides in, fitting as neatly as a pair of favourite gloves. Delight overwhelms her as she finds the perfect matching handbag. She is seduced and knows she looks gorgeous with them on. As she sees her reflection in the mirror and looks back at her credit card, she asks herself how such a small little thing could present such a huge obstacle. In fact the more she looks at it the smaller it becomes, and the smaller it becomes the less resistance it offers, until moments later it's just not a problem at all. The thoughts of not eating for a month seem so much more bearable and even desirable, it's all possible in the light of a not-to-be-missed opportunity like this.

When the woman buys the shoes and/or handbag the money for it gets found too. (I am not suggesting you go out and buy whatever you want without the resources to back it up!) The lady in the story moved forward in her mind to the future. She imagined herself wearing the shoes with matching handbag. She fully connected with the idea of it and even got the sensory experience of it. It was from that mental movie, from that internal imaginary experience as she looked from her dream to her credit card and back again and again that she was able to think differently around her challenge. She was able to look back at the 'problem' from a resourceful state, from a state of feeling good, and it was from there that she was able to see a way to her goal and a solution to the obstacle. This is an approach that lends itself to success much more often than one that focuses on the problem or problems all of the time. It is an approach that works most of the time, which makes it worth doing.

So putting the shoe on the other foot, so to speak, the bloke walks into a car dealership, casually strolls up to his preferred choice of car, pretending he is loaded and not in the least bit fazed, when in truth he is as close to penniless as makes no difference and so excited that his pounding heart is practically bursting through his chest. Acting as if he knows all about the car, he casually shoves his hands in his pockets, leans back and looks down on it, his head tilted sideways as if to measure it up. The truth of it being if he were to lift up the hood he may as well be looking into a field. With that he is greeted by a fellow male and they swap ego stances. Now there are two of them: the salesman knows even less than the customer, except for the price tag and the urge to get it off his hands.

To confirm their mutual empathy the conversation opens midstream and continues as casually as the potential buyer's John Wayne-type entrance. 'She practically drives herself that one,' says the salesman. Thinking thank God for that, he responds, 'Yeah,' as if he already knew, rubbing his chin or scratching his head for added effect. You see for this type of man it is all about the label, all about the image and all about who he thinks will think that he is great. When the salesman enquires, 'Do you want to give her a spin?', it is no sooner said than done, in all of two seconds flat that boy's straight into it. Catching himself off guard, mid-flow, he slows down into his macho stance, frowns heavily and utters in a slightly subdued voice, ever so nonchalantly, 'Mmmhhh.' He struggles a tad before he settles into the squeaky leather seats.

The salesman joins him on the other side and they drive out of the showrooms and into delight. Once the open road is in front of them, excitement gets the better of him and he lets down his guard a little. The movies in his mind take over, he is centre stage, heading the bill and has even upgraded to Paul Newman or Steve McQueen. Michael Schumacher will be saved for when the salesman isn't around. Outwardly he does his best to hold on to that stoic image, slipping on his Matrix shades for that 'ice cool' effect, which has the added benefit of hiding the childlike delight sparkling through his eyes. 'This is bleeding great,' he thinks to himself and chuckles secretly. Now that the movie has been rolled out, opportunities present themselves to him. 'You know I think I could afford this. Maybe if I gave up the drink for the next four thousand years!' Well a slight exaggeration but you get the idea. The finance is easily arranged. Absolutely. And what does he think: he thinks, 'Who's yer mama?' And what does he do: the very same thing as his female counterpart in the department store, he looks back at the 'problem', and he doesn't see it so much anymore. He has got the good feelings, he has got the sensory experience of it and now he even has hindsight and we all know that hindsight is a great thing. He has jumped forward to the future (i.e. a time when he owns the car) and from the future he has looked past the 'obstacle', which becomes smaller and less of an obstacle when the taste of the solution is still fresh in your mind.

Action Is King

Now some people believe that you can send out for anything into the universe and you'll get it. There is another philosophy too that if you have a goal and you put it out to the universe, it will become manifest and if you don't collect it then someone else will. Some say if you want that Mercedes or that Ferrari or you want those Jimmy Choo shoes and matching handbag, if you want this happy life or this brilliant relationship, it requires that you be prepared to do something to get it. It doesn't just come to you, you have got to show up and play your part.

A guy called Joe Keaney was my first hypnosis teacher in the 1990s. One of the last exercises he taught me involved getting the attention of the students in his class by having them form a circle with their chairs and placing a candle on a desk in the centre of the room. He then asked one of the students to light the candle and as the student sat down, he addressed his attentive audience saying, 'Right guys you are all hypno-therapists now, you've worked hard, you've got your results and you know what you are capable of. You are ready to go out there and start your new business, your new profession. You are familiar with and know how to use the power of the mind to help people, to facilitate healing and well-being. What I want you to do now is to use that power, to use your phenomenal, unconscious power to will out the flame on that candle in the centre of the room.' Full of anticipation and resolve, everybody used their new-found powers and drove themselves into the deepest of trances as they focused on making the impossible possible. As loyal students they followed their master's lead and really went for it.

Seconds passed and nothing happened, minutes passed and still nothing, until the concentrated silence was broken by the sound of a chair being shuffled as one student got up from where he was sitting. He made his way across the floor to the centre of the room wherethe candle was standing. When he arrived he placed his thumb and forefinger in his mouth to wet them and then used them to squeeze the flame out. He turned on his heels casually, and without saying anything, returned to his place and sat down again. To which Joe said, 'This is exactly what it's all about. Sometimes you've got to do something to make things happen, it just doesn't happen by itself.'

You know you have to be there, you have to show up. So one of the rules for your life goals is that you have to show up.

Getting down to Business

So it's time to do a little exercise. I want you to select a goal that will improve your life. Previously you talked about the things that stopped you achieving your goals. For example, you may have said not having enough time. The question now is what do you want and the answer is 'I want to make better use of my time. I want to have more time.' What specifically do you mean by that? 'Well I want to have more time to do what I want to do.' What is it specifically that you mean by that? 'I want more time to do such and such a project.' What specifically do you mean by that? And so on until you are as focused as a laser beam. If in your head you've had muddy visions then that's not good enough. You've got to be clear and precise and focused to get where you want to go. It's time to decide what you want to achieve.

The following questions are well thought out and very specific. They are exacting questions, each with its own precise function. Select at least one goal and send it through this process. You are going to be asked particular types of questions that may at first seem peculiar to you and may not even make grammatical sense. They are written in a way that suits the mechanics of your brain and ultimately this is the tool that you will use when achieving your goals. There are some questions in there that will cause you to think in unfamiliar ways, this is intentional and this is checking for ecology. By answering these questions you are ensuring that your goal is worthwhile and that it can be achieved without upsetting the other good things that you need to keep going in your life.

These are the questions that can be the difference that makes the difference. If you are used to goal setting these are the questions that may have been omitted in the past. Please try each one on and realise each one has a different function and each one produces a different response. Be patient with the process and take your time as you try on each question by running it through that phenomenal wizard of a mental computer that you have residing between your ears.

Keep the following principles in mind:

- Decide what you want.
- Take consistent and deliberate action.
- Notice what is happening.
- Be flexible, if something is not working, change your approach, not the goal.

- Be sure to work within your capabilities. If your goal is too small it will not hold your interest, if it is too big you may be too scared to do anything.
- Remember write your details in terms of positive outcomes.
- As soon as you achieve one goal, go back to your list of Big Picture goals and select another goal.
- Feed the goal into your subconscious daily until it is achieved by using the image-streaming technique outlined towards the end of this chapter.

Exercise: Know Your Goal by Using Well-Formed Outcomes

1   What do you want specifically?

_____

_____

_____

_____

2   When, where and with whom do you want it?

_____

_____

_____

_____

3   What resources do you have to accomplish this?

_____

_____

_____

_____

4   How will you know when you have it?

_____

_____

_____

_____

5   What will you see/hear/feel/smell/taste?

_____

_____

_____

_____

6   What will it look like/sound like etc?

_____

_____

_____

_____

7   What will happen if you get this result?

_____

_____

_____

_____

8   What won't happen if you get it?

_____

_____

_____

_____

9   What will happen if you don't get it?

_____

_____

_____

_____

10   What won't happen if you don't get it?

_____

_____

_____

_____

11   What do you get to have or keep by not achieving your goal?

_____

_____

_____

_____

12   How do you know it's worth getting?

_____

_____

_____

_____

13   When, where and with whom does not having your goal work for you?

_____

_____

_____

_____

14 How will getting your goal affect your life? Family? Business? Job? Friends?

_____

_____

_____

_____

15 What will be different as a result of having this?

_____

_____

_____

_____

What if it doesn't work? If you found that you completed the well-formed outcome exercise only to discover halfway through that what you thought you wanted is not really what you want at all, that most likely means that you have hit upon a value issue. Generally if you can't settle on it, it is because there's a deeper value in competition with your overall goal. I will show you later how to get to the deeper values so that you will truly know what you want and be clear about that.

The beauty of the well-formed outcome system is that it flushes out inconsistencies and incongruities. It's designed to do that so that when you do settle on a goal it is worthwhile doing.

There will be times where you do not have the luxury of applying the above process due to circumstances or time constraints. The following exercise is for those situations.

Exercise: Everyday Goal Setting
This technique is suitable for locking your focus on successfully reaching your goal, particularly when time is against you. This is for goal setting in the moment. So if you have to make a decision, make

a sale or negotiate a deal and you need to clear your head of negative, disempowering thoughts and get motivated, try this.

1. *Begin with the end in mind:* Imagine things working out well instead of the opposite. Keep in mind that you get more of what you focus on.
2. *Remind yourself of your past successes:* Have you ever been in a similar situation in the past? Have you ever been successful in the past? What did you do then? How did you walk, talk and feel? What could you see? What did you do then that you could do now?
3. *Focus on the solution not the obstacles:* Project yourself into the future by using your imagination. Imagine what things would look like, feel like and be like if they all worked out wonderfully well. Soak up the good feelings that go with that. (It makes you smarter.)
4. *Assist your brain by asking particular questions:* What *would* happen if you *could* only succeed? What has to happen for that to have already happened now? How good will it feel when you have? What will be different as a result of this?
5. Keep repeating this process until you become unstoppable.

Write out a goal that you have right now using this process:

_____

_____

_____

_____

_____

_____

_____

CHAPTER 7

Don't Worry Be Happy

Every evening I turn my worries over to God. He's going to be up all night anyway.

Mary C. Crowley

The Mechanics of Worry

Some people claim that worry is in their make-up. I suggest if that is the case they ought to change their make-up to a different brand. Worrying is behaviour – it is not who you are and because it is behaviour you can change it so that you can gain more control. Sometimes it is appropriate to be concerned about how things are or could work out and for that you can do what we call 'Constructive Worrying'. Mostly, however, worrying is a waste of your time. I worried a lot for a long time, like most people, but there is a point when you get to a threshold and you just have got to say f**k it. Whatever comes you will make it through. You've just got to keep a clear head, adjust your thinking and trust that you can, and you do.

Some people use the excuse that they are not worried for themselves but they are worried about others, for example their kids. Ultimately what parents want is for their kids to know that they love them and for them to be safe and happy. The one thing that kids want is your love, and your love flows more freely when you are worry-free. Your children worry when you worry. They worry about you. They are upset when you are upset, they are upset for you. They read from your demeanour what you are trying to hide from them.

Children don't just pick up on the good stuff. They see and learn from the bad stuff too. If you are working flat out every day to get ahead or to keep food on the table, a roof over your head and all that comes with that, chances are that either your Mum or your Dad worked their asses off as well and you are just doing the same thing, repeating the same learned pattern.

Working hard is one thing and working flat out is another, while working smarter is the real deal. What your partner and your children want is the best of you and the best of you is when you get down and you play with them, be with them, are there for them in the here and now, fully present and fully engaged. That's what they want to see, that's where they will learn so well, that is the skill that they need to learn.

Remember, worry has to exist in a mind that is focused on it. You can only be worried if you are spending the time thinking about it. Now which would be more valuable, thinking about what could go wrong or worrying about the future or hugging your child? Sure, this could go wrong and that could go wrong, but it could also go right and it makes a lot more sense to think about how it could go right, doesn't it? It makes much more sense to think about things working out in general.

If you are a good person doing a good job as best you can, why worry about what could go wrong? Of course you will make mistakes, guaranteed, because the person that never made a mistake never made anything anyway. If you think about it, all the worrying you've done to date was all done in advance of things which you predicted would be much worse than they actually were. Doesn't this give you an indication that this type of worrying is more a waste of time than anything else? How much better it would be if you decided to plan for things to work out for the better and filled your mind with those type of thoughts instead of the other. All that good quality thinking time you can free up – just imagine how much more creative space you can draw from and it's all so much healthier.

The Worrier's Questionnaire

Let me ask you some questions:

- How many mistakes do you think you have made to date in your life?
- Did you manage to get over them?
- Did you get through them?
- Did you fix them?
- Did you manage to deal with the consequences of them?

My guess is that you got through most of them and even if it wasn't to your satisfaction, you actually survived them. You will always get through, that's part of being human, that's why you have succeeded thus far.

We often put conditions on our success. People say, 'If I could just relax then I could think clearly and I'd be able to get through.' Being relaxed does mean that you can think more clearly, you can go after what you want much more easily that way. But trying to adapt this into your life by imposing a set of rules on it is just as bad as worrying itself. Saying to yourself 'I shouldn't be worrying, I really shouldn't be worrying' is not a good thing if you keep repeating it. This is where the STFU mantra needs to come in. It is important simply to shut that down immediately: say it once, get the message, take the learning and shut it down straight away. Redirect your consciousness to a more productive route by asking yourself, 'What do I want to have happen instead?' Tell your inner critic to STFU. And rather than worrying about it think what you can do about it.

Constructive Worrying

For those of you who still believe that you have to worry over some things, make a commitment to yourself to schedule in some quality worrying, say a half an hour a day. You don't have to give up worrying altogether. You can always decide on a set time when you are going to do it. So you can agree that you are going to worry between the time of half nine and ten. So rather than say I don't have time to worry about it now, you can say I'll worry about that later. Is that not reasonable? You don't have to give it up, but if you are going to worry do it properly, just pencil it in.

It's not quality worrying if you are plodding around all day semi-conscious of the worry, letting it hover in the background of your mind while you try to get on with other more important things. You are not really worrying properly at that stage because your attention is divided. You want to do good, proper worrying. You want to sit down and ask yourself 'What have I got to worry about?'

How much time do you think you should spend worrying a day? How much is adequate given the importance you place on your life and the things you have to do? When it's done you've got to get a plan. Proper worrying is all about adequate planning, you plan before it's done, you plan during it and you plan after it, but you've also got to decide where the best place to worry is and when is the best time to do it so that you can do it without interruption. Eventually I suppose you could actually change the word from worrying to productive thinking, but that of course is up to you, isn't it?

When life presents us with particularly uncomfortable dilemmas or challenges and if we feel unprepared or unable to deal with them it is natural for most of us to experience feelings of fear, anxiety and worry around the area of the solar plexus in our bodies. Some of us may interpret this as a feeling in our stomach or a little bit lower than that. Once that sensation kicks in, it is telling you to be aware, to be alert. If you try to ignore it, which most of us also do, then your brain will just keep turning up the energy.

You don't get away with *not* worrying if you are not acting on what you were worrying about. Your emotional brain will keep pushing the same buttons over and over again resulting in ever-increasing intensity. Think of it like a red light on a machine, when the light goes on you are supposed to do something and if you don't it will have a knock-on effect. Before you know it all sorts of things fail to work properly and ultimately become dysfunctional. So the red light is a good thing, not necessarily a welcome thing but overall a good thing. Emotions are just like that.

The red light often just flickers at first and then stays on until you do something about it. Because you have a conscious mind, you can choose to heed these signals and respond appropriately *or not*. So worry is a good thing, it's a good emotion because it's a signal; the thing about emotions is they keep knocking at the door if you don't address them. That's what worry is all about.

What you need to do is to give the feeling recognition, perhaps by saying simple words to the effect of 'Got you, I know what you are doing okay, and this is what I'm going to do about it.' Most of us fail to do that for a myriad of reasons. We may think that now is not the time, or if I do what I know I need to do and get it wrong I could make a fool of myself, or if I do what I ought to do what would people think. We let social conditioning take precedence over common sense.

You have also got to understand that your emotions are only a part-response to an event, situation or stimulus. They do not always represent the truth of a situation. They are not always accurate because they don't give you full information. What they do is they respond and how they respond is real and undeniable. No amount of saying that you are not afraid or you are not worried or you are not anxious is going to change that.

These signals come from the reptilian brain or the amygdala. This is the part of your brain that alerts you to danger. The part that produces the flight, freeze or fight response. The part that pushes blood to your legs when threatened so that you can run to safety. The part that sends blood to your arms so that you can defend yourself from danger and the part that when over-stimulated can freeze you right to the spot and make everything dreamlike and you get the feeling of becoming detached from your own body while you endure whatever extreme situation you have to experience.

I learned as a production supervisor in a textiles firm very early on in my career that if there is a feeling of tension, worry or upset in your stomach you must get it out by using your mouth, by verbalising it. Psychologists call this 'venting'.

Unfortunately many people when they get the worry signal remain focused on the problem or the reason for the signal instead of accepting the positive intention of that message and from there starting to work on the solution. Albert Einstein said you can't make a good decision out of a bad emotional state. If you are thinking that everything will go wrong, that produces the wrong type of brain chemicals to produce good decisions. Your job is to get yourself into a good emotional state as soon as you can so that you can overcome whatever obstacles are in your way. One of the quick ones is the mantra: STFU. STFU. STFU. STFU. STFU. That is what is called a breaker state, and it can immediately serve to put a stop to your negative hallucinations and distorted assumptions and make way for the next and vital step in this process, which is to ask yourself what is the most useful thing to do right now.

Exercise: Constructive Worrying

1. *Stop and engage with the feeling:* When worry, stress, fear or anxiety surfaces, ask yourself 'Can I sit with this feeling a little while and recognise its true purpose?'

2. *Label it and give it cause:* Instead of immediately trying to dispel the feeling, which is understandable, it can be very useful to identify the specific feeling and label it. 'I am feeling this way because . . .' Generally you will find the cause is both recent and evident. If you don't know the cause that's also okay just recognise that. As mentioned earlier, many of us experience anxiety, fear and stress in the stomach area and because of this some of us react to these feelings by feeding or suppressing them with food – that just dulls the sensation and overrides its function, you are not actually hungry at that point. This is a bit like getting a nosebleed and wrapping your entire head in a cast. It is not necessary and the consequences are catastrophic.

3. *Open yourself up to positive solutions:* The third step in this process is to create a well-formed outcome. You can begin redirecting your thinking and creating better chemicals and more resourceful feelings by asking yourself the following questions:

- What do I want to have happen now?
- How do I want to feel?
- What do I want to be experiencing?
- What has to happen for that to happen?
- What can I do now?
- What do I have control over?
- What is possible?

With these questions your brain begins looking for solutions and looking in a good way because they are clinical questions: How do I want to feel? That gives your brain permission to feel good, it is not saying what it is already feeling but it is not denying it either, instead it is giving you permission to feel good. So you can respond in those trying moments in ways that will generate the feelings that you want to produce: I want to feel strong, I want to feel powerful, I want to feel assertive, I want to feel in control, I want to feel confident, I want to get through this, I want to be able to be relaxed, I want to be successful, I want to excel, I want everything to turn out great etc.

4. *If practical action is possible, commit yourself to a timeframe and do it:* In other words, 'I will solve this problem by . . .' Now you are setting your brain up in that direction, your brain looks after you once you allow it; your subconscious mind, your imagination mind and your emotional mind look after you all of the time. Your brain doesn't always get the signals right, it doesn't always get the information right, but it always serves your better interests and you can complete the process by behavioural follow-through.

Get the Good Feelings Flowing Fast

When it comes to developing more useful responses around worrying not everybody knows what to do all of the time and even when you show them they can still be a little stuck. This is because of the impact the worry has on their self-confidence, which in turn can have a knock-on effect on their self-esteem. The following exercise works wonders on self-esteem.

Exercise: Looking through the Eyes of Love

1. Think of someone who loves you and makes you feel good. (This could be a friend, a partner, a young child etc.)
2. Close your eyes and imagine that person looking at you with a great big smile on their face. Imagine what they feel and say to themselves whenever they look at you. (Perhaps they say things like *you're such fun, you're a great friend, you're the best in the world.*)
3. Imagine how they think about your personality, your qualities, your special characteristics, the things you do for them etc.
4. Now imagine transferring your awareness into them and looking from their position, i.e. looking at you through their eyes. Gather up their feelings, their thoughts about this wonderful person in front of them. Notice how good that feels. Notice how good you really are. Soak up those feelings.
5. Open your eyes and have a wonderful day.

The Socratic Method

You can talk yourself into success by asking yourself useful questions. If you ask yourself useful questions, your brain will come up with useful responses. When worry, fear or anxiety hits you can ask yourself:

- What can I do?
- How will this strengthen me?
- How will this empower me?
- What can I learn from this experience?
- What will happen if it goes right?
- How good will it feel if it begins to work out for me?

Now all of the above are great questions to put you in the right emotional state for clean and clear decision-making. As you ask questions of yourself you begin the process of bridging your feelings and that allows you to move from fear to inquisitiveness, which is an altogether easier and smoother ride than going from fear to calm. Because of the way your emotions work, shifting from one emotion to another tends to be more gradual than sudden in most situations. Think of a time when you were angry or upset or were having a heated debate over something, even if you won the argument, the feelings of tension rarely leave straight away. There is a natural wind-down period before your body matches where your head is at.

Asking questions not only directs but occupies your consciousness so that your mind is not subjected to the usual old patterned response. A response that may go something like: 'Oh man I just know what's going to happen now I am going to freeze, I am going to fumble, I am going to make mistakes, I will look like a complete fool. What will they think of me?' Crowning it all off with a less than useful question just digs you deeper into the toxicity of your thinking. You may even add to your terror by stating what you don't want to have happen. 'I don't want my legs to start sweating, I don't want my throat to start trembling, I don't want my hands to start shaking and I don't want to feel like everybody's looking at me, staring at me . . .'

What's Wrong with Your Thinking?

Because of the way we have been conditioned as children most of us tend to look for what is wrong with things or what could go wrong with things before setting out on any project. As a result we limit ourselves by not just getting on with things.

So now when you decide to go for something – say do a course, make a speech, take up a hobby, learn how to use the computer – you cripple your efforts with mental movies and critical statements of what will more than likely go wrong, how you will make a fool of yourself etc. All of this being the fuel itself that is most likely to produce the very result you are trying to avoid. You work yourself into such a state, that all it takes is one look, one comment, one mistake and you give up. You decide you are not that type of person. You are not a computer person, you are not a confident person, you are not a . . . and the list goes on and on. Let me ask you this: Would you treat your children as badly as you treat yourself and if you did what would be the result?

The following exercise has wide and varied applications, the primary one being to build or boost your confidence level (which we all know tends to be absent when we are worrying). You can use this to help you make that brilliant presentation or if you want to come across really well at a particular meeting or to a particular person.

Exercise: Beam with Confidence

1. Think of a time in your future when you would like to come across as being very confident. (It could be a job interview, an important conversation, a public presentation, whatever.) Now think of three different ideal emotions that you would like to be experiencing in that situation when it comes about (i.e. *confidence*, *relaxation* and *determination* – you can replace these with other emotions of your choice).

2. Next think of your favourite colour. (If you don't have a favourite colour think of a vibrant bright colour that you really like.)

3. Using your imagination, create a circular beam of radiant light (about two feet/sixty centimetres in diameter) of the colour you have picked and see it shooting up from the ground at a step's distance from you.

4. Now imagine that you are standing in the middle of this beautiful, glowing beam of light, full of *confidence*, filled with a wonderful sense of *relaxation* and a strong look of *determination* written all over your face.

5. Keeping that in mind now close your eyes and take a real step forward as though you are stepping into your imaginary self in that beautiful circular beam of light in front of you.

6. Take a deep breath in and begin to embrace the experience, imagine the light from the beam rising up and surrounding you, let it run right through you as you are bathed in it and as you do so imagine those feelings of *confidence*, that flow of deep and calm *relaxation*, the sense of *determination* beginning to build with each and every moment, with each and every breath you take.

7. Take another deep breath in and feel the entire experience get stronger, feel a surge of *confidence* rising, bringing with it a wonderful, *relaxed*, collected sense of *determination* and a feeling that everything is going to work out wonderfully well this time.

8. Taking your time, transport yourself through to the future situation in your mind. Imagine that now is then and then is now; imagine yourself sailing through that future situation stronger, more *determined*, more *confident*, more powerfully *relaxed* than ever. See what you'd see, hear what you'd hear, feel what you'd feel, take a deep breath in and intensify the emotions. Imagine the looks on their faces, as you move with grace, talk with conviction and put across your points so eloquently. You are saying the right word at the right time in the right sequence and you can feel it as you unleash that reservoir of confidence that is in you in a way that is appropriate to you and those around you. Take some more moments and let your imagination run away with itself.

9. Now bring the situation to a successful conclusion and see yourself signing off and signing out with a smile on your face. You've done it. You've cracked it. Well done. Take a step back to your original position and open your eyes.

You are now primed for success. Each time you think of your future situation do this. You are conditioning your mind through mental rehearsal to program yourself for success.

Do this every time you think of it. It only takes seconds and it is far better than worrying, isn't it? The more you do it, the stronger it becomes and after the first few times you don't even need to do the physical part (stepping forward) just the mental rehearsal itself will fire off the feelings. You do not have to feel all the feelings 100 per cent for it to work. You just have to feel better and keep practising – that will get you there.

If you're finding it difficult to visualise, you are probably trying too hard. Rather than trying, just remember instead. Your pictures do not have to be perfect . . . your mind just needs to get the message. You can talk yourself into confidence too.

The Importance of Relaxation

We instinctively know that perpetual worrying is not useful and that relaxation produces better quality thinking. As wonderful and all as it is, not all of us remember or take enough time to relax and simply be. Most of us are too busy running from pillar to post getting the next thing done that's on our 'to do' list so that once everything is done and the worrying is over then we can relax. The truth of the matter is that the list never gets done, life is full of things to do and there will be things that worry us from time to time and that is as it is. But just because there are things to do and problems still unsolved or worries to be dealt with that doesn't mean that we have to do them or that they have to be dealt with right now. Everyone needs to relax sometime and the more you learn how to relax the more you can get through the bigger trials and tribulations more easily. Here are a few tips that will help you to do just that.

Relaxation Reminders – A Summary
1 Breathing
By taking control of your breathing you can automatically bring about a pleasant feeling of relaxation.
2 Exercise
Whether that is going to the gym, doing yoga or Pilates or going for a walk or a run, studies show that half an hour of high-intensity

exercise helps lower stress. You can do this as a way of getting rid of any pent-up energy that is preventing you from relaxing too. High-intensity exercise is more effective at lowering stress levels than working out at a moderate pace. What's more, the benefits last for as long as ninety minutes afterwards.

3 Stop trying to be perfect

Perfectionism often leads to disappointment and procrastination. It is unrealistic to expect everything to be perfect so instead ensure that you keep your goal but be prepared to know when enough is enough, when to let go and realise you have done your best, which means you are going in a perfectly good direction. Quit saying things would be better 'if only . . .' Quit saying things will never be as good as they used to be.

4 Ask for help if you need it

Realise that you may not get it all done and delay your decisions if you are stressed.

5 Hold hands with your loved one

It is a simple act but studies have shown that loving contact such as holding hands lowers blood pressure and heart-rate responses in stressful situations. Studies have shown that those who experienced contact were nearly twice as relaxed as the unloved, untouched group.

6 Write it all down

Reduce your stress and free up your mind by writing it all down. This is your 'to do' list so check and re-check it often and tick off your achievements as you go. This will give you an increasing sense of accomplishment, which will keep the good feelings going for longer.

7 Hypnosis/meditation

Hypnosis, meditation, prayer and reflection are all methods that develop an inner stillness, are easy to learn and hugely powerful at relaxing you and bringing about additional positive health benefits. You can easily purchase relaxation CDs nowadays.

Exercise: Calm Body, Calm Mind

1. Find a comfortable place to lie down and close your eyes.

2. Now imagine your body as a series of rubber balloons filled with air.

3. Imagine that you have two valves in your feet, two in your hands and one on the very top of your head.

4. Imagine first that the valves in your feet begin to open up and as they do air gushes through from your legs and the lower part of your body.

5. You feel your legs and lower body collapsing until they are empty and lie flat against the surface where you rest.

6. As that happens begin to notice the valves in both hands opening too as the air pours forth and the vessel of your body releases the air and also collapses in on itself gently.

7. Now imagine the valve opening at the top of your head, as the air is released the upper part of your body collapses into itself as it empties of air.

8. As you lie there bring your awareness outside of your restful body and look at yourself from above; see a calm look on your face as your furrows smooth over.

9. Take a deep breath and sink deeper into your 'bed' becoming aware of your breathing that is now slowing down and the tingling sensation building on your skin.

10. Repeat inside your mind the word 'soften' over and over again: soften soften soften . . .

11. Ease further into this pleasant state of rest that you are learning to take with you wherever you go.

12. Rest some more now and when you feel refreshed bring yourself back to the here and now.

13. Gently, softly counting inside your mind 1 . . . 2 . . . 3 . . . 4 . . . 5, eyes open and have a good day.

And Finally

Here are some simple steps that will help you to raise your self-esteem, improve your self-image and work wonders on your self-confidence.

- Stop criticising yourself.
- Stop criticising others.
- Stop comparing yourself with others.
- Treat yourself as you would your best friend.
- Always see yourself at your very best.

CHAPTER 8

The Keys to Overcoming Obstacles

Obstacles are things a person sees when he takes his eyes off his goal.

E. Joseph Cossman

Knowledge Isn't Always Enough

A lot of people think that knowledge is sufficient to solve problems and overcome obstacles. But knowing how something got broken or why something is wrong doesn't automatically teach you how to fix it. Therefore when faced with a problem or an obstacle, it makes sense to direct appropriate 'how' questions first and by that I mean, you must point your 'how' questions in the right direction. If you say 'how' did I get myself into this mess that is as bad as saying 'why' did I get myself into this mess. Both questions will only drive you further into where it is you want to leave. You have got to focus on where you are, where you want to be and *how* to get there. So the first question to ask is:

- How can I get to where I want to go?

Next you can ask questions like:

- Have I ever been in a similar situation in the past?
- Have I ever been successful in the past?
- What did I do then?
- What could I do now?
- How could I do that?
- What has to happen for that to happen?

What's Not Right about Asking What's Wrong?

People occasionally find themselves in challenging situations and ask themselves questions like 'What's wrong?' For example, a person having problems in a relationship is likely to ask what's wrong with the relationship, assuming that because the relationship has got challenges there must be something wrong with it. Looking for what's wrong with something is not always the best starting point, especially if your overall goal is to have the relationship develop and grow stronger.

A more useful approach is to start by working on the basis of what's right, what's working, what's good about the relationship, or even what would you like to have go right with it or what would you like to improve with it, rather than reducing the entire relationship down to something as narrow as being broken. It is not always necessary to fix everything head on or as soon as it arises. Bad feelings are only made up of neurons. Neurons weaken when left unused and from the point of view of the brain, if you want to get rid of them, it's better to leave them alone for a time.

Anybody that's been in a relationship for any length of time will relate to this. This is one of the things you begin to realise as you go through time. I have been in a relationship with my wife, Theresa, for more than twenty years. The fact of the matter is that we have what you could describe as a vivacious relationship. We argue about some things, generally unimportant things, but that happens when you love someone and that's healthy because it means that our needs get met. But the thing about it is a lot of the time these problems simply need to be let go. You don't have to address every issue, let it off by itself. Now most people think you've got to sit down and go head to head and deal with things. But actually a lot of the time you just say to yourself 'get over it' and it sorts itself out. It is about letting things slide, because most of the time these arguments are more about ego than the actual issues that are being discussed.

The 7 Steps . . . the Secret of . . . and the Key to . . .

The reason why a lot of change management programmes fail is because they say this is *the* solution and they only give you one or maybe two solutions. The trick to getting past problems and obstacles is to ask yourself how many different ways you can achieve your goal. Keep moving beyond the problem in the direction of the solution. Entertain no obstacles, focus solely on the solutions. When an obstacle is offered think about what else you could do. What else is possible? What would happen if that happened? How would you do that? Just keep jumping past the problems.

Human beings have a lovely capacity to weave you into their own reality. We do it every single day. Rather than focusing on the solutions to our problems we claim we have tried everything. When you claim to have tried everything, that presupposes there aren't any other things that you could try or that are worth trying. In my experience to date I have always been able to find other things. Most of the time it is not that you haven't tried many things, it is just that you think you have tried everything and that is a little like a goldfish believing his bowl is the world and the room he can see is the rest of the universe.

The God Complex

As discussed in Chapter 3, psychological literature and research refers to the 'self-serving bias' that comes from our tendency to assume that we can do no wrong. In other words we can only be right, which is what I like to call our innate God Complex.

We don't like to prove ourselves wrong because that makes us feel stupid and no one likes to feel or look stupid. We like to feel smart. We like to be smart and in fact we are smart, but not all of the time. Unfortunately we sometimes believe that there is no other person as smart as we are so the chances of someone coming up with a solution that we have worked flat out on for ages appears ridiculous and threatens our self-esteem. From there our natural reaction is defensive, 'You are hardly going to come up with the solution, because I'm a smart person and I've thought it all through.' With that type of background thinking the shutters come down and cynicism or exasperation takes centre stage. Then when we get offered any solutions we announce, 'No, no there's no point, I tried that. No that won't work either. I am telling you, no. I've tried that, that won't work. I tried that too, it won't work.'

Very often other people can come up with the solution more easily as they are not as emotionally attached to it as you are. But you've got to get out of your own way for them to do that. The trick is to really listen and find out stuff that you have you not tried yet, but that you can and will try. Look at things and ask yourself who can help you. Who has been there before? Who can advise me? How can I guarantee my success? How can I be successful, no matter what? There's a gazillion ways of doing that.

Here are some common excuses and suggested ways to challenge them:

- *I have tried everything.* Everything? Every single thing, there isn't anything you haven't tried – not one thing?
- *It will never work.* Never ever, so you are a clairvoyant and can see into the future?
- *I can't.* What would happen if you could?
- *It's pointless trying.* How do you know?
- *It won't work.* What will happen if it does?
- *I don't see the point?* What would be different if you could?

Exercise: Problem Solving

Here is a simple technique to unblock problem thinking. It is a little exercise that you can use if you are faced with a problem that you have not yet solved or that your self-esteem would prefer to think is unsolvable.

Bring the problem to mind and ask yourself the following questions, not just once but continuously, until you begin to come up with useful solutions or with potential solutions. This exercise will be much more effective if you get someone else to ask you the questions. Avoid justifying your problem, just tell the person that you have a problem and could he or she ask you the following questions as you both attempt to find a solution to it:

- What is stopping you from solving your problem?
- List three of the most critical parts of your problem that need to be dealt with for you to find the solution?
- Describe what a successful solution would look like, feel like, sound like and be like for each of those parts?
- What parts of the problem are reliant on knowledge, skill, resources, time, politics or opportunity?
- How many of these elements can you influence positively now?
- What has to happen for that to happen?
- What specifically do you want in place of what you have got thus far?
- Are there any other ways of getting this?
- How will you know that you have achieved what you want?
- When will you know that you have achieved what you want?

Think of a problem you have that you would like to solve now and answer all of the questions above. Fill out the section below as you do.

_____

_____

_____

_____

_____

_____

_____

_____

_____

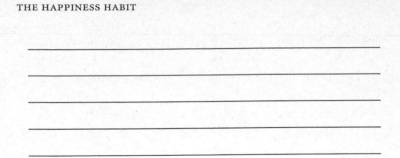

Exercise: Abductive Reasoning

Now if the deductive (logical) approach has not produced the desired result then it is time to use what is called the abductive (analogical) approach. This was a favourite of Albert Einstein and of Thomas Edison so you are in good company.

1. Bring your problem to mind.
2. Recall yourself experiencing something totally unrelated that you are already really good at. (It could be football, selling, building websites, public speaking – we are all good at something.)
3. See your chosen activity as a metaphor that contains the solution to your problem.
4. Now ask yourself how you overcome problems within your chosen activity. (For example, how you handle it if someone asks you an unexpected question at a speaking engagement.)
5. Translate this metaphorically to the problem you are currently faced with.
6. How could you now handle it differently?

Well-Formed Solutions

When faced with a problem, an obstacle or a dilemma, whenever you are unsure of what to do, when faced with any of life's glorious challenges, the formula to use each and every time is the well-formed outcome formula, as described in Chapter 6. This applies in this context too. As the process in its entirety is quite substantial, and rightly so, you are not always going to have the time, opportunity or patience to sit down and think it all the way through. The questions below are for those times. These questions serve all the principles of 'well-formedness' and can be called upon when you need to get to where you want in a hurry.

The quickest way that I know to change a negative emotional state is by asking yourself (or others for that matter) these few simple questions. When faced with challenge most of us try to be positive but it doesn't always work out. For example, when we are in conflict with someone else our attempts tend only to escalate the issue rather than solve it. This is because we get more and more frustrated at ourselves for not being positive as well as with the other person for not meeting our rules. More about that later, first here are the questions that will help you to get moving when you have that 'stuck' feeling.

Six Core Questions for Becoming 'Unstuck'

1. What do you want to have happen right now?
2. What's the most useful thing to do right now?
3. What will you see, hear and feel when that is happening?
4. What can you do, say or change to make that happen?
5. What will happen if that happens?
6. Is there a win–win outcome?

Tips to Improve Your Concentration

On a larger level what you are beginning to do is to set your life in an entirely new direction and this requires concentration. Many people complain about not being able to focus long enough in order to work out what they want from life. Here are a few guidelines to help you to do that.

Concentration is about your ability to focus on one thing, to the exclusion of all else. Total concentration is that feeling you get when time seems to fly by or even disappear. You have experienced it many times before and can learn how to bring it about again as it is a skill like anything else. Whatever you are doing, your results will be greatly enhanced if you give all of your focus and attention solely to the activity at hand. Concentration is often hampered when we get distracted by a number of things at the same time.

- *'One-pointedness'*: To improve your concentration you must become single-minded. This involves ridding your mind of all thoughts and concerns other than what you are about to attend to. This means refusing to get caught up in anything other than what you are doing. This will not only permit you to concentrate more but will get the job done more quickly too.
- *Cut off any disruptive noise:* Noise can interfere with your concentration levels so be sure that you reduce or cut off any noise sources so you can keep your mind clear. And that includes your own internal dialogue.
- *One task at a time:* Focus on one thing at a time, one task at a time, one result at a time until such time as you become competent. After a while you will be able to multi-task as the individual tasks become habituated, take no conscious effort and feel natural to you.
- *Mix up your activities:* You have heard the expression 'a change is as good as a rest'. If you are studying a number of things at once, it is often better to mix and match: spending small amounts of time on each area so that it feels easier to concentrate on the overall project.
- *Stop quibbling and start doing:* Talking about it is not going to get the job done, questioning whether you are up to it or not won't either. The quicker you start, the easier it will become and the less time it will take to get it done. Stop procrastinating.
- *Clean your environment:* Ensure you have space to concentrate. Put the phone out of view. Turn off the e-mail alert; if you are not using the computer, turn it off. Keep your desk clean so you can take notes. Have all you need within reach. Have a supply of water to keep your brain hydrated, and drink a little often.

- *The five more rule:* When your concentration is about to whittle away, you can recommit by using the five more rule. Promise yourself just five more minutes, five more pages, five more exercises etc. and, of course, stick to your promise otherwise the quality of your concentration will suffer.

- *Understand the process:* Get clear on what it is you want to do or what it is that is being asked of you. Get clear on the instructions for what is required, the standards you need to follow, the restrictions that are there etc. If you're writing an essay, for example, find out how many pages, how many words, what topic specifically you are being asked to discuss and what style is required. Ask questions until you are clear – this will free up your mind to concentrate fully.

- *Set a deadline:* The brain works best when given a deadline, provided that your plan of action leaves it within your abilities to reach. So if you can, set your own deadline, back it up with a tangible and practical plan and adjust as you go if necessary to avoid the tension of not reaching the deadline. Realise it is actually better to shift the deadline if the quality of your concentration is being affected by it. Deadlines focus the mind and eliminate wastage, but for some a deadline is like walking a tightrope and if it is not realistic you can fall off.

- *Brainstorm:* If you don't know where to start it is a good idea to brainstorm. Brainstorming is a little like mind mapping and works through free association. Basically you let whatever ideas come to mind, no matter how illogical or nonsensical, to be captured on paper. When you have run out of ideas have a look at what you have written and see what can be used.

- *Relax and be patient:* Set everything up so that you can relax. Use the tips provided in Chapter 7 and be patient with yourself, know that it will all get done in time, it is not a race and it can be done. Practice makes perfect, so be prepared to put in the practice.

- *Physical alertness:* You have also heard the expression 'a healthy body a healthy mind'. Getting sufficient sleep, staying physically

fit and undertaking exercise will help develop your concentration. Eating the right type of brain foods, for example
tuna, also helps.
*   *Brain games:* Brain games are widely available and are an
    excellent means to sharpen your concentration and have fun at
    the same time.

Reap the Countless Benefits of Sleep

Although it is easier said than done when you have things on your
mind, bringing your problems to bed can be a really good thing to
do as long as you commit to handing the challenge or problem over
to your subconscious to take charge of and commit to picking it
back up in the morning. The human brain is a fantastic problem-
solving instrument so at night time, before you retire for sleep, think
of your problem, worry or concern and then say to yourself that you
are handing this over to your subconscious to sort out for you. You
can do this by simply imagining what the solution would look like
if there were absolutely no obstacles. Once you do this you are in
effect instructing the brain to solve it. After you have done it then
redirect your thinking to more pleasant things and refuse to
entertain the problem until the morning. You may find that by the
morning or at some point in the following day a solution to your
problem will 'magically appear out of nowhere'. It has in fact come
from the program that you ran in your mind the previous night,
just before you went to sleep when you were in a daydream state,
what is called the Alpha state. This state of consciousness is a hugely
resourceful state that facilitates subconscious programming.

Your brain operates at different frequencies throughout the day
and night. These frequency shifts result in different states of
consciousness. You could think of them as bandwidths similar to
what you get from a radio transmission. Each bandwidth means that
something different is going on and this difference is reflected by
the waves that are being emitted:

- The Alpha wave range occurs when a person is relaxed, but alert. During this state, a person is awake but resting.
- The Beta wave range occurs when a person is focused, alert or engaged in any form of physical activity.
- The Delta wave range is associated with deep sleep. Delta waves are known for triggering the release of hormones that provide healing; this is why sleep is so important during the healing process.
- The Theta wave range is known as the twilight state and it occurs fleetingly, mainly as we drift off to sleep or as we are rising from it. Theta is a state characterised by vivid imagery flashes and heightened sensory acuity, it is a free-flowing state of inward focus where you are deeply relaxed.

Routine thinking occurs in Beta consciousness and this is the state that most of us are more familiar with. Beta consciousness is just a faster frequency than Alpha consciousness, and Alpha consciousness is the state where you can actually learn more easily and quickly. You are also more open to suggestion in Alpha state, so when you are in that state you can make suggestions to yourself to help yourself sleep, to be confident, to be happy, in fact to do and become whatever you want.

So if you have had trouble sleeping well you could say to yourself 'I enjoy being more comfortable, I enjoy feeling drowsy and I enjoy feeling the weight of the blankets on my body, I enjoy breathing slowly' – and then breathe slowly. 'I enjoy feeling the tingling sensation in my hands' – as you do it notice what happens, you can change how you feel and you are now setting yourself up in a well-formed direction for sleep or for confidence, for happiness, for success, whatever you choose. Remember the rule is to set you up for well-formed outcomes or to go in well-formed directions. Say to yourself what you want to do – 'I want to sleep, I want to sleep comfortably, I want to drift into sleep effortlessly, I want to sleep deeply and well' – because the more you say that the more you are likely to bring it about.

Most people bring their problems to bed and then run commentary on the fact that they really need to get sleep, that they just have to sleep urgently because if they don't sleep, they know that they are in trouble, they just know they will be wrecked in the morning. They say they will be tired, they say it will be hell, they run a movie of everything going wrong in the morning and then they wonder why they wake up and they're feeling frazzled. It's because they've been programming the wrong suggestions into their minds. Remember you are supposed to match up what you want, so if you want to be sleepy go into a sleepy state. If you talk real slow to yourself and say I really want to fall asleep, then you are doing the right things. If you want to have a good day tomorrow it's a good idea before you go asleep tonight to say I'm just wondering what it would feel like if tomorrow was much better than today. Then program yourself to do it by thinking about it, by saying it to yourself and by imagining how you want it to look, sound and feel. You need to begin to focus on what feels good rather than on what doesn't and the more you do that, the more that you will get. Focus on what's working and when you focus on what's working, it will work more of the time.

Tips for Improved Sleep

First things first, whatever your thoughts and feelings are about sleep understand that it is a totally natural process, just as night follows day and dark shades the light, your body is designed for sleep. You cannot bring it about through force (unless you medicate yourself which is not ideal) but you can facilitate and dramatically improve the quality of your sleep by creating the right environment and by reducing any interruptions and obstacles that get in the way of your enjoyment of it. Sleep restores and revitalises your body, making you fit for the day ahead.

Poor sleep habits may be caused by different factors. From staying up too late at night or getting up too early in the morning. From insufficient daylight exposure to bringing our worries to bed.

From use and abuse of food, drink and drugs and even from exercising too late in the evening. Whatever your situation, you will find some useful pointers below. Obviously, in the unlikely event that the situation persists, it is always wise to seek professional help on the matter.

- *Develop your pre-sleep ritual.* First, relax your mind. Life can be hectic so give your body the opportunity to ready itself for sleep by using as much time as you can to wind down in advance of it. An hour or two should be more than sufficient. Going straight to bed after a rock concert is unlikely to induce sleep, so close off your day gradually by reducing the high octane activities and replacing them with more calming activities. Gather some quiet time, sit down and read the paper, read a book, have a conversation with your partner, friend or a family member, listen to some soothing background music, watch a 'feel good' movie on the TV, have a warm bath, burn some lavender oils, take a breather and reflect on just how much you got done today and give yourself a clap on the back for surviving it.

  Then relax your body. Certain habits that we associate with relaxation are stimulants. The late night cup of tea or coffee or perhaps the alcoholic drink and the final cigarette all speed up the nervous system so it makes sense to keep as much time as you can between them and your scheduled sleep time. If you must have a snack, warm milk and toast or perhaps some cereal can aid relaxation because of the chemicals contained in the food. Condition your body by going to bed at a set time each night. That being said, go to bed earlier if you are feeling sleepy.
- *Set the scene:* The atmosphere in your bedroom should be peaceful and calm and the decor should reflect this. Block out as much light as possible from the room with blackout blinds, heavy curtains etc. If you have a digital clock, cover the screen with a card or something. Make sure your bed, your bed linen and your pillow are comfortable and that your back and neck are supported while you sleep. Keep in mind that your bed

should be reserved for two activities only – sleeping and making love – and that may mean removing the TV from the room. If your partner is restless, get a bigger bed. Make sure also that the room is well ventilated and the temperature consistent. Keep it as quiet as possible, even if that means using a fan or a 'white noise' machine to help block outside noises such as traffic and loud neighbours.

- *Bedtime stories:* Once you are in your bed, it is time to build upon what you have already created. It is now time to wind down completely. If your mind is racing, get control of your thoughts by slowing down the pictures and your internal dialogue to a pace and tone that you would use if you were really drowsy, open your mouth wide and take a huge breath in as if to yawn. Do this a few times and you will begin to yawn for real. This will help convince your mind that it is sleep time. If there are things in the day that remain undone, imagine them being completed successfully and then let out a sigh of relief with each accomplishment. If you have problems on your mind, acknowledge them and promise yourself that you are going to sleep on it and will return to it more refreshed in the morning. Most problems are sorted that way anyhow. Stop moaning at yourself and suggest in soft tones inside your mind how you want to go asleep. Now make up images of yourself so deeply relaxed that you nod off effortlessly.

As you work on relaxing your mind you can help by progressively relaxing your body. First become aware of your body in the bed. Wriggle your toes and curl them up as you take a gentle but deep breath inwards, as you exhale repeat the word 'soften' like you mean it. Next work your way systematically up your body, tightening first and then loosening each and every muscle, repeating the word 'soften' every time you do this. Indulge in the feelings and enjoy being awake while you do. Once you're done and totally relaxed, turn to your favourite sleep position, close your eyes if they are not already shut and let your imagination conjure up some really fun and pleasurable fantasies.

- *When all else fails:* Try to stay awake. Keep your eyes wide open and refuse to close them. Or listen to a specially prepared hypnotic CD for sleep. Or get out of bed, leave the bedroom and do some quiet activity like those in your pre-sleep ritual until you are tired again and then return to bed. If necessary, seek professional help.

- *Post-sleep rituals:* Expose yourself to bright light or sunlight soon after awakening; this will help to regulate your body's natural biological clock. Exercise daily, if possible in the morning but otherwise no later than three hours before sleep time. Twenty to thirty minutes of this daily exercise can help you sleep. Avoid catching twenty winks during the day as this can also interfere with your natural biorhythms; if you absolutely have to, be sure to sleep for no more than thirty minutes in the day. You could try meditation or hypnosis as an alternative. Write down your 'to do' list for the coming day and use your imagination to view how it will look when everything is done and dusted to your satisfaction.

CHAPTER 9

How to Talk Yourself into Doing Anything

---

*The most important action to take is the work within you.
When that is done, you will be moved in the outside world to
receive what you asked for.*

Rhonda Byrne

Dreams and Goals and Wishes

People have all sorts of hopes and dreams and goals. They run movies in their minds and see themselves as they would like to be. However, they sometimes fail to run the movie fully. A distinctive set of processes is needed to make things happen. There is also a distinction between reality and fantasy. No doubt many of our fantasies would get us into a spot of bother if they became real.

The dilemma is this, seeing yourself doing something in your mind is only part of the process – it gives your mind a target. What actually sells it to your mind and translates it into behaviour is when you step into the experience as fully as possible, when you live, breathe and feel the experience so that you are engaging all your senses. That is the stuff that makes things happen and convinces your mind that this is real. That is the stuff that converts the fantasies into realities and makes behaviour follow.

At first it is just a thought, a fantasy of sorts. You then have to draw down your goal from the realm of fantasy and make it a reality. This requires your action, intention, focus and behaviours all to be in alignment so that it gets done on the physical plane where you are now. Setting well-formed outcomes and continuously programming them into your subconscious by the process of mental rehearsal is undoubtedly an extremely effective and time-proven tool for making things happen. For most, both of these processes are enough to ensure that you follow up with consistent action in order to achieve your goals.

Imagineering: The Life of Your Dreams

Imagineering is just a word I have made up for the process of setting your imagination to work on achieving your goals and then writing down what you have come up with to activate the process. This is a tried and trusted way to create the life of your dreams. If you take the time to sit and just imagine, you can create pretty much whatever you want from life. In fact the room that I am writing this book in is a room that was built first in my imagination. The Shootfrom-thehyp CDs that I produced with my good friend Deirdre Robinson were the product of a daydream. Just a few moments that I spent being curious about what it would be like to sit in a state-of-the-art studio at my leisure without incurring any cost and to produce a CD that could include my own unique brand of hypnosis. In September 2004 that daydream became a reality when I began the process of recording in the same studio the boy band Take That had used and produced the *Trance Tripping* CD, something which I am both proud of and grateful for.

Imagine for the next fifteen to twenty minutes that there are no restrictions preventing you from having whatever it is that you truly want. All you have to do is to write it down and it will be yours. With this in mind, I would like you to consider the things that you want to have, the person you would like to be, the stuff you would like to do and with whom you would like to share it. Think of the skills you would like to develop, the contribution you would like to make. Think also in terms of what you would like to have accomplished at the end of your life.

If it helps, you could imagine what the most perfect day in your life would be like. What would you be doing? Who would you be with? Where would you be? What would you see? What would you hear? What would you feel? What would you taste? And what would you smell? Let yourself get swept away by your imagination. Imagine that it has already happened, that you are there, as you record your experience using the present tense. You might want to refer to the Circle of Life exercise and your Big Picture goals to ensure that no stone is left unturned, that you have everything included in your list.

This is not an exercise in grammar so just put your pen to paper, get your head into gear and keep writing non-stop until you have exhausted all eventualities. Do not concern yourself about how it looks or sounds; write it down as you think it, as it comes to your mind; do not censor anything even if you feel it makes no sense, you can tidy it all up later. Right now all I want you to do is to browse through the sample starting points listed below and when that is done just go for it.

There may be a time when you appear to run out of ideas. If that happens, simply turn to this section and check whether you have answered each and every single question in as much detail as you can generate. Right now you are about to direct your mind towards a specific set of directions so ensure that you provide it with as much detail as possible so that there can be no room for error.

Below are some of those possible starting points to help you get into the flow of this.

I want to be . . .
I want to go . . .
I want to do . . .
I want to get . . .
I want to give . . .
I want to find . . .
I want to have . . .
I want to know . . .
I want to learn . . .
I want to share . . .
I want to show . . .
I want to make . . .

I want to develop . . .
I want to experience . . .
I want to be known as . . .
I want to succeed in . . .

So now it's time to begin:

_____

_____

_____

_____

_____

_____

_____

_____

_____

_____

_____

_____

_____

Talk Yourself into Success

Self-talk has been shown in research by medical and communication professionals to affect health states. Studies have shown that people can begin to harness the power in their minds by taking an active role in deciding what to think, enhancing the positive messages they send themselves. By doing so, people can face challenges – health related or otherwise – with the knowledge they can succeed if they literally 'put their minds to it'.

155

When you do this often, and if you also alter your state of consciousness while you do, you begin to get the results you've been looking for much faster. Altering your state of consciousness is something you do more often than you might imagine. Activities such as meditation, prayer, hypnosis, reflection, deep thinking – indeed any of the meditative states – are all altered states of consciousness. These are the states where you become highly suggestible.

What we're going to do now is to learn how to program your mind, and put in the right ideas and the right feelings, to get the right images running, to get the right states running. But you need to be able to do it in a proper way which I will now demonstrate.

You can do this by using affirmations. An affirmation is a deliberate, purposeful thought created by you and repeated several times over a number of days with the intention of creating the conditions for achieving something that you want. This works on the basis of repetition, the more you suggest something to your mind the more likely it is to respond to it. You can have as many affirmations as you want, however, with a little thought you will find that using a handful at a time will set you on your way in a more focused manner. Here are some examples of affirmations:

- I enjoy achieving.
- I love feeling confident.
- I can forgive.
- I can improve.
- I can enjoy change.
- I can enjoy the feeling of being healthy.
- Being slim and trim fills me with pride.
- Everyday brings me closer to my goals.
- Being positive makes me happier.

It is important that your chosen affirmations are worded in a manner that fits or suits your unconscious mind because that is the mind, the behavioural, the imagination mind that you are attempting to influence.

Once these thoughts take root in your unconscious they influence your physical, emotional, psychological and even spiritual well-being. Each day you already run thousands of thoughts spontaneously, the content of which often goes unnoticed by you as they operate below your everyday level of awareness. These thoughts give rise to your feelings and beliefs about who you are and what you can and can't do. The creation of affirmations is another more conscious method designed to give you more control over this process and therefore bring more success and happiness into your life.

Your Inner BS Detector

One of the pitfalls to making effective affirmations is the following internal process. Let's say your goal is to get into shape. You are currently overweight and you say to yourself 'I am slim, trim and healthy.' Your mind is likely to say, *No you are not*, and it might add, *Not only are you not slim, trim and healthy but now you are just stupid for even thinking that you are.* A few attempts at this and a lot of us give up, saying these affirmations don't work. However, if you say it this way: 'I *enjoy being* slim, trim and healthy.' Then your mind will ask *Am I slim, trim and healthy now?* and answer *No* (the present). *Have I ever experienced the feeling of being slim, trim and healthy before?* The answer is more likely to be *Yes* (the past). *Do I like that feeling? Yes. Can I imagine what that would/could be like in time? Yes* (the future). Now you are moving in the right direction, because your mind has the liberty of taking a remembered feeling from the past, bringing it into the present and imagining what it could be like in the future.

As the above example illustrates, the wording of your affirmations will determine their effectiveness. With each and every word you say or think your mind responds literally to what is being projected outwards. With affirmations the same rule applies. So let's imagine that your goal is to be more confident. You have already run it through the well-formed outcome process and you have also been doing your mental rehearsal technique, now you have decided to stick in a few affirmations to strengthen your resolve.

Let's imagine that one of the affirmations you have chosen is 'I enjoy being confident and relaxed.' You know now that when you speak, whether it is out loud or silently, your mind responds literally to what you say. From there your mind will take three basic directions: the present, the past and the future, and will pose the following questions to verify your experience. About the present, it will ask, *What's happening now?* About the past, it will ask, *Have I ever experienced that before?* About the future, it will ask, *Can I imagine what that would/could be like?* Now if you are not feeling confident when you state your affirmation, for example if at that particular moment you have a public presentation to make then your mind, having heard the affirmation 'I enjoy being confident and relaxed', will check in with the present to see what's happening. So when it asks, *Am I confident and calm now?* the answer is *No*. Then when it sorts for the past and asks, *Have I ever experienced being calm and relaxed before?* the answer will undoubtedly be *Yes*. No matter how briefly, everyone has experienced confidence and relaxation at some point even if both feelings were only experienced separately. Finally when the mind asks, *Can you imagine what it would or could be like in the future?* the answer will also be *Yes*.

These 'yes' responses produce the threads of the experience that you are after, because in its search to find out whether you have had or could have such an experience in the past or the future, the brain has to access the memory or imprint of the experience. When it accesses that it does so by releasing the feeling connected with it. This is called synaesthesia. When you see something you get a feeling response, and when you hear something you get a feeling response. The beauty in this is that the brain can access these experiences so quickly that you may have no surface conscious recollection of the experience but are left with the residual confident, relaxed feeling, which puts you chemically in a better state to build from. In a nutshell, this gets the ball rolling.

Remember one affirmation stated once is unlikely to be enough. The more you repeat it the more the mind can re-access it, the more it can re-access it the stronger the feeling will become and the more you can build upon it, draw from it and ultimately make it so that it becomes true for you, that you become that confident and relaxed person when circumstances call for it.

So now that you know how, remember that repetition is the key. If you imagine one picture of yourself being confident in the future, then that is precisely what you have programmed – one picture. So to make it an ongoing thing, turn your pictures into movies, step into them and crank up all your senses. What will you see, hear, feel, smell and taste when you have achieved your outcome? That way all of your neurology can direct itself towards your goal. Do this often and notice the difference.

Exercise: How to Create Perfect Affirmations

1. Describe in detail what you want to see, hear and feel.
2. Write it down in the present tense.
3. Use the continuous present and create movement in your mind by adding –*ing* to the end of your verbs. For example, I enjoy be*ing* confident and relaxed.
4. Write it down several times.
5. Be sure that is within your control.
6. Be specific.
7. Be positive.
8. Be realistic.
9. Read it out morning, noon and night.
10. Put it somewhere where you will see it often.
11. Express gratitude to your god when you achieve it.

Create your own affirmations now:

_____

_____

_____

_____

You can create an affirmation at any time; however, the most ideal times to activate them are just before you go to sleep at night or just as you awaken from sleep in the morning. Your mind is generally in the Alpha state during these times. The Alpha state is the accelerated learning state, it is in this state that your mind is at its most impressionable, and this is the state that hypnotists use to install suggestions to bring about behavioural change. You will recognise it as it is accompanied by feelings of relaxation and it has a dreamy feel to it, a feeling of not being fully present, as though you are in between two worlds. In fact you are, you are neither fast asleep nor fully awake.

I have set up a company that can help you do this called Myownaffirmations, you can visit us on the web at www.myownaffirmations.com. There you can have your own affirmations recorded and combined with a hypnotic script, produced and delivered by myself, to help guide you into that state of Alpha consciousness where your brain becomes more suggestible and you can get access to its enormous potential.

Words that Motivate

Now it's time to learn another distinctive process that is responsible for you learning how to become and stay motivated. When you use this to good effect life can be wonderful, when left unchecked, well, that's a totally different story. NLP helps you to become more aware of your unconscious processes so that you can get a hold of them and begin to work on improving that which already works well and on eliminating that which doesn't. What follows is a little experiment to give you the tools of control.

What I want you to do now is to think about one of your goals, whatever your goal is, whatever you want to achieve. Bring the goal into mind: to be fit and to be healthy, to be happy, to be confident, to be focused, to be decisive or whatever it is that you want. Maybe it is to be in a better relationship, to be calm, to be fun filled, to be relaxed, just select one goal for now and then you can apply the process to the rest of them in time.

When you think of your goal, it is usually followed or accompanied by an internal commentary. If you are not accustomed to hearing it or being aware of it, that's okay, you soon will be. Typically when we think of a goal we say such things to ourselves as 'I *want* to do this', 'I *must* get that done', 'I *need* to get it started', 'You know what I *am going* to do now' and so on. These commentaries determine our focus and levels of motivation. These specific commentaries run repeatedly, although we are not always aware of them, and often determine what does and doesn't get done.

Now that you have selected your goal I want you to modify the commentary in the way that I am proposing. I want you to repeat inside your mind the words that I'm giving you, rather than the words you typically use. So when I suggest a sentence, once you read it I want you to notice what you see, what you hear, what you feel as you 'try on' the sentence. I want you to take stock in a way that perhaps you are not accustomed to doing, and to notice exactly what happens as you run that through in your mind.

Now I know normally you don't really think so consciously but today you are beginning to do that. You are beginning to notice what happens when you use certain words on yourself. There are certain things that you are doing or not doing for very specific reasons, and very often this is because of what you are saying to yourself. So first I want you to say (silently inside your mind is okay): 'I want to achieve' and state whatever your goal is immediately after you say that. So if your goal is to make a successful presentation in your job next Monday, you will say, 'I want to make a successful presentation on Monday.' So then, on to your goal: 'I want to (your goal).' Notice what you saw, what you heard and what you felt as you said it. 'I want to . . .' – notice what happens; the pictures, the feelings, the sensations and the likelihood of it happening. The likelihood of you following through based on the experience.

Now instead of saying I *want* to achieve my goal, say instead 'I *need* to achieve (your goal)'. Whatever it is, you fill in the goal, whether you need to be fit, or you need to be trim, you need to be healthy, you need to be happy, you need to be decisive, whatever your thing is, whatever it is that you need. Notice what you saw, what you heard and what you felt as you did that. 'I need to achieve . . .' – notice what happens to the pictures inside your mind, and the feelings, your response to them, the sensations that go with it, and the likelihood of it happening. The likelihood of you following through based on your experience a moment ago.

Now repeat the same process and try on 'I *can* . . .'. You can achieve your goal, you can. 'I can achieve . . .' – notice what happens the pictures, the feelings, the sensations, and the likelihood of it happening. The likelihood of you following through based on the experience.

Now try 'I *will* . . .'. You will achieve your goal. Now try 'I *should* . . .', 'I should achieve my goal'. Now try 'I *must* . . .', 'I must achieve my goal'. Now try 'I *have to* . . .', 'I have to achieve my goal'. Now try 'I *am* achieving my goal, I *am* achieving my goal'. Now try 'I *am going* to achieve my goal'. And now try 'I'd *like* to achieve my goal'.

At this point you will have noticed that you have different emotional associations attached to different words. For some, the more ways you talk about achieving your goal the more you feel like doing it. For others, certain words turn you off and certain words fire you up. Certain words create a sense of urgency or pressure and certain words open up a world of possibilities inside your imagination.

Whatever your own specific responses, your target is to find out which ones made you feel as if you were moving in the right direction. These are the words that turned your pictures into movies inside your head, the others produced the opposite or were like slides/stills or snapshots, they were flat, not in 3D. You can recognise these by your response or lack thereof in terms of translating your response to the possibility of action.

These are the words that work like the 'could' and 'would' words did earlier but they have far greater precision. They not only open you up to the possibility of getting to where you want to be, but they put your foot on the accelerator and propel you into action. They are the stronger force within you. These are the words that make the difference between doing and procrastinating. These are the words that form those sentence sequences, the mantras that repetitively run and hover (oftentimes below your everyday awareness) and act like an unconscious impulse driving you towards or away from your dreams.

It makes sense that you grab control of them and you do this by paying more attention to how you talk to yourself on a daily basis. So the next time you find yourself not doing what it is that you really want to be doing, listen to how your commentary is running. Are you saying you really *need* to go to the gym, or are you saying you really *have* to get the job done. Notice how you are talking to yourself and change the words until it feels nice, knowing that this is a better way for getting things done. Now like many things this will require a bit of practice, I am still practising and I have known about this stuff for years. The difference is I know now from experience that as I change the old mantras and replace them with better suggestions I get better results quicker.

Although we were all taught language in more or less the same way, each of us responds neurologically in different ways to many words. For example, while 'want' may work for one person, the very sound of the word for another person could actually produce resistance. The way you respond to language is as unique as your fingerprints, so what is important here is not that one word works better than the other, it is that *you* respond better to particular words in particular sequences. No one can teach you this; you can only learn it by doing. Do the detective work on yourself and find out how you respond best and work on that.

Although I have already told you that feeling nice is a better way to get things done, it is not the only way. Through my own exploration and personal detective work I have discovered what works really powerfully for me is when I say to myself 'I had better do such and such a thing'. How I got to there I don't know, but then again my own personal neuroses never cease to amaze me. If I have a goal that I am slacking on, it generally means that I am talking crap to myself about it. My most frequently used procrastination mantras are: 'I have all this stuff to do', 'I have a lot on my plate at the minute' and 'I will never get through this stuff. I am just too busy.' Eventually when I waken from that unproductive trance and change the program by saying, 'I had better do this', 'I had better get this done' or 'I had better get going', this gets me up and moving. I follow it up with, 'Okay what has to be done? What do I need to do now? What can I do to make some inroads into this project?' All of these statements work for me. They may or may not work for you, but they are the unique cocktails that make me produce the goods when called for.

Of course, there are words that a lot of us respond similarly too. Tony Robbins says people that keep saying that they 'should' all of the time end up shuddering all over themselves, they get nothing done apart from a rant of self-abuse. Most of us do not like doing our 'shoulds'. In Ireland, for most people, this sounds too much like a command, which produces an automatic negative response. Most, but not all of us, do not do our 'shoulds'. We will take great pleasure in doing our 'should nots' but not our 'shoulds'.

As there are different levels of emotional intensity attached to each of the words, you may have found that one word opened your mind to the possibility of doing something, which led to another word that meant you were definitely going to do it. For example, you may have said to yourself in the first instance 'I'd *like* to do such and such', which made you entertain the possibility of doing it without any pressure attached to it. Once you got this far then you may have said, 'You know I would like to do it, so I think I *will* do it. No, guess what, I *am* doing it.' What happened there is that the option of like or liking gave permission to the will – as in 'I *will* do it' – which led to the 'I *am* doing it' and the certainty of doing it.

My mother runs the *must* mantra, she tells me, 'Brian, I must come up and visit you.' She's been saying that for twenty years, so my guess is either she hates me or she just doesn't do her 'musts' and I know which option works best for my self-esteem. (She is a mum and like all mums her good points far outweigh her minor short-comings and she makes up for the fact in a multitude of other ways.)

So Mum simply doesn't do her 'musts', when she says to herself she must do this and she must do that, it is highly unlikely it will get done and if it does it is only after a lot of hesitation.

The process of exploring the way you motivate yourself is a worthwhile journey of discovery, however, it doesn't end there. There is often a difference in the way you motivate yourself and the way that someone else motivates you. So there are words that you will accept from yourself to motivate yourself and there are words that you will accept from others as a way of becoming motivated. So you might say to yourself 'I have to achieve my goal' and they may be the very words that work for you as long as it is you saying it to yourself. If I come along and say to you that you *have* to do this for me, that very word may produce resistance and be the cause of your refusal.

You may have heard the expression that 'it is not what you ask for but how you ask for it that gets results'. This is a case in point. Part of the response will have to do with the task that is being requested, but the point here is that the likelihood of a positive reception to the request is dependent on the words that are chosen and these words can be the very reason that a task is accepted or rejected. Basically, if you use words that make me feel uncomfortable then I am less likely to be co-operative.

Did you ever get the sense that when someone talked to you, you just didn't like the way they came across, you didn't like the cut of them or there was something odd about them that you just couldn't quite put your finger on. Very often it was down to the language that they were using.

Let's assume that I'm a team leader, a business manager or a company supervisor. How am I going to get my staff motivated, knowing that one word could put them off? Even if it is a very reasonable request, these guys may not be as co-operative as they could be because I may not hit on the right words for them. I have an order which *must* go out; I have been told by my boss that it *has* to go out. She has said to me, 'You *have* to get this done.' So if I repeat her words exactly and some member of my staff goes inside his head and says I don't like the sound of that and ends up dragging his heels on it there will be hell to pay for it. One way that I could handle this is:

> Right guys. We've got this order that *needs* to go out by five o'clock, I'm hoping you *can* help me out on this one, because it *has* to go okay and I know it *should* have gone out yesterday, but if you *could* help me, I *will* be very grateful, so if we *get going* on this as soon as possible we *will have* it *done* in no time.

This may sound like I'm babbling, but what I am really doing is going through a list, checking with each output the expressions on the group's faces to see that I have them all on board. Thankfully when people hear the word that works best for them they are inclined to ignore what came before and after, which is helpful. As usual this is about generating good feelings. Just as much as you do for yourself, you need to generate good feelings for others too. If you find out what you can say to a person that opens them up and makes them feel good on the inside then that tends to make them more co-operative and they feel good in your presence or while they are working with or co-operating with you. That's a win–win situation.

I was delivering a seminar a few years ago and one of the delegates, also named Brian, a fascinating, light-hearted, curiosity-filled, open-minded man, was engaged in an exercise with one of the other delegates but it was clear to see he was slightly distracted. I walked over in his direction and as soon as he noticed me he said, 'Brian do you know those modal operator thingies?' I smiled at the 'thingies' reference and said 'Yes?' raising my tone upwards to provoke a follow-up response. To which he replied, 'Do they *actually* work?'

Questions like that are not unusual in this trade. I get asked this often by radio and TV presenters and it always brings a smile to my face. 'Does such and such a thing *really* work?' As if my answer is going to be, 'No, as a matter of fact none of it works I am just a charlatan and it's all made up. I was just pretending but now that you asked me that question I just had to tell you the real truth and thanks for that.' Of course it works. It all works if you use it properly and if you practise it until you have got it working perfectly.

I asked Brian, 'What do you mean?' Knowing that his question pointed to the fact that he had something on his mind that he wanted to change or get done. He said, 'Well I really need to give up the cigarettes and was wondering whether this could help with that? To which I replied. 'Sure you *need to* give up the cigarettes and that may be true but do you also *want to* give up the cigarettes too?' He raised his eyebrows suddenly, as his jaw dropped slightly and his face opened up in amazement. He had just tried on what I had said and the feeling was dramatically different and the reply that I got was the one you often get in a situation like this. 'I never thought of it like that before. Yes, I *want to* give them up, but I'm always telling myself I *need to* and it felt yuck so I said I couldn't be bothered.'

To which I replied, 'Just because you need to do something doesn't mean that you can't want to do it too. So now each time you hear yourself say that you need to give up the cigarettes add in "Yes, I know I need to but I also want to" and build on from there.' That was the last time Brian smoked.

Now that is a dramatic example of how one word can make you change things around for the better. It doesn't work in that instantaneous way for everyone all of the time, but it does work over time. So this is a matter of you catching yourself talking to yourself and changing the words until you find the ones that work for you and then making a habit of speaking to yourself in that way so that life gets to be so much more pleasant and you get so much more done of what you want to be doing.

Exercise: Modal Operators

Think of something you have on your 'to do' list, listen closely to how you tell yourself what has to be done and while you are speaking to yourself notice what happens to the pictures or images inside your head and the feelings that follow. Are they good feelings or are they bad feelings? Are you more or less likely to do the task when you speak to yourself in that way?

Now you can try out a little exercise. Think of the same task and replace what you say to yourself with the words listed below – notice how you respond and the likelihood of the task getting done. For example, if you usually say, 'I *must* go to the gym this evening' and you have been promising yourself to get around to that forever at this stage, then try using the other words on the list, 'I *want* to go to the gym this evening' etc., to see what works best for you. Here are the phrases to try:

- I want to . . .
- I need to . . .
- I can . . .
- I will . . .
- I should . . .
- I must . . .
- I could . . .
- I have to . . .
- I'd like to . . .
- I am . . .
- I am going to . . .

Write down the ones that work for you and the ones that don't so you can remember which to avoid and which to use more often.

Phrases that work for me

_____

_____

_____

_____

Phrases that don't work for me

_____

_____

_____

_____

Exercise: Motivation

Certain things just fire you up. This is the stuff that gets you going, that juices you up for the challenges ahead. The things that get you in the mood to take it on, to work it out and to put your foot on the accelerator of change. What happens when you become unstoppable, when your focus is as sharp as a razor blade and your concentration as directed as a laser beam? Think now of the times when you get into a state of determined conviction, of absolute certainty, when you know what is to be done, how it is to be done and who is going to do it. When you have moved beyond the thinking state and are now in the doing state and it will only be a matter of time until it is all done and dusted, already a part of your history.

So think now of a time when you were at your most motivated. What did you do just moments before you were driven to action? What could you hear? What did you say to yourself? What could you see in your mind's eye? Who was around? How did it feel? Once again write this down in the present tense as if you were getting ready to begin again this moment. Then repeat the exercise for another time when you were highly motivated.

Situation 1

_____

_____

_____

_____

_____

_____

_____

Situation 2

_____

_____

_____

_____

_____

_____

Exercise: Bringing It All Together

Motivation is the fuel that gets things done. That fuel is activated by desire. It can be the desire to avoid the hassle of not doing what you are asked by doing something else instead, or it can be the desire to attract the rewards that doing the task can give you. The questions most likely to run through your mind before you become motivated are: What will I get to have or keep by doing this? What will I lose or avoid by not doing this? How you answer these questions will determine your levels of motivation to begin with.

But once that happens oftentimes there is more left to be done. The following principles will assist you in becoming more motivated:

1. Decide what it is that you want to do and ask yourself 'What will I get to have or keep by doing this?' and/or 'What will I get to lose or avoid by not doing this?' Give your mind some time to fully conjure up the answers to these questions.
2. Write down all the reasons for doing it that make it worthwhile and all the consequences of not getting it done.

3. Next set your goal. Again, write it down and make sure it is brain friendly. You can do this by being very specific about what you want to achieve and by keeping your language positive. You will need to engage all of your senses in the achievement of your goal, so write down what you will see, what you will hear and what you will feel once you have achieved it. This way the brain will have a clear target to aim at and this makes it easier for it to deliver what you have asked of it.

4. Mentally rehearse every detail of your goal continuously. This will activate the feelings that you will achieve once you have accomplished your goal and likewise build your motivation towards making it happen for you.

5. Set a completion date and work out what has to happen for that to happen. Organise your timetable and place it somewhere you can see it daily. Ask for help if you need it.

6. Break down your goal into manageable chunks and work on each chunk a little at a time. Set dates for completing each chunk. Do the bits that are easy first as when you see your progress it will build your motivation.

7. Reward yourself each time you make progress and remind yourself how much better you are getting.

8. Focus on what is accomplished, not on what's left to complete.

9. Compete to better your best and stop comparing yourself with how others are doing.

10. Think of who you will become and what you will have achieved once you get this done.

Exercise: Imagineering

1. Now find somewhere to relax, where you will remain undisturbed for the next ten to twenty minutes.

2. Sit down or lie down, whichever suits.

3. If you have some relaxing background music (without lyrics) that will help, although it is not necessary.

4. Close your eyes and imagine that you are already achieving your goals.

5. Take your time and let your imagination run away with itself.
6. Engage all your senses and bathe yourself in the experience.
7. Run your goal like a movie through your mind, using the details from the exercise you have just completed.
8. This is the language of your unconscious, the habit-forming part of your brain.

By doing this each day you are programming yourself for success.

CHAPTER 10

Staying on Track despite Adversity

People are like stained-glass windows. They sparkle and shine when the sun is out, but when the darkness sets in their true beauty is revealed only if there is a light from within.

Elizabeth Kubler-Ross

Circle of Influence

Every so often I get to hear from a client that I worked with previously. Sometimes years pass and I don't hear from them until one day out of the blue I receive an e-mail or a phone call from them to tell me how they are doing. Stephen was one such client. Stephen was a young man in his early thirties who worked as a team leader for a large firm. He prided himself on being an honest, hardworking, no-nonsense type of guy. (He was quite opinionated and outspoken, but well meaning.) Stephen was a rising star who held back no punches when it came to identifying what needed to be done and who needed to do it. Despite his direct manner, he got on well with his team because they knew where they stood with him at all times. Stephen knew instinctively that most people want respect and admire honesty. He was not conventional, but his ability to get results through people commanded the attention and affection of most of his peers. At one stage it looked as if Stephen could do no wrong. Production was on the up and up, project deadlines were being met ahead of time and staff morale was at an all-time high.

Stephen was a fully fledged company man and such were his achievements that he was invited by management to assist in bringing other departments up to the same level. This was the beginning of his demise. From then on his strong opinions and no-nonsense approach got him into difficulty with other departmental managers who were not performing as well. Stephen naively believed that departmental results were on everyone's agenda and that if someone's toes were walked on then that would be forgiven as long as the company improved overall. Stephen came to me for help as he was suffering from extreme stress. He had stated his opinion one too many times and had aggrieved the wrong people. After a company restructuring based on his own recommendations, he found himself reporting to a different manager. Stephen had previously high-lighted this manager's departmental shortcomings and this man had taken it personally. His ego was bruised and now it was time for him to get even. A meeting was being scheduled and Stephen knew his job was on the line. I had only one hour before Stephen had to face the music so I needed to teach him some rapid survival techniques before I could get him to improve his overall communication skills.

This is the story Stephen related to me all those years later:

One of the most challenging times of my life was when I was brought into that meeting. It seemed to me at that stage that if you voiced your opinion or pointed out deficiencies you were marked as a moan or fired for insubordination. So if you did as I did, the guns got pointed in your direction. This happened to me many times, but I had always survived it. I was targeted, not because of incompetence, but because I was a threat. I know I was extremely competent and that was one of the problems. I showed up the wrong people, I made them look incompetent. I was just doing my job but in their heads the better I did the worse they looked.

That was the day when they brought me in to tell me that they were restructuring my section and disbanding my team. I knew this was simply a ruse. My manager had the ear of the powers that be and had made his case under the guise of cost-reduction and insubordination. I have to admit though he did get it right on the insubordination aspect. I knew I was in deep water here. My job was on the line and he had done his homework well. I had little defence against a decision to restructure the department and disband my team; he was the manager after all so it was his call. I knew this was all rubbish. It was just a way of putting me in my place.

As I stood in the office and listened to the lies I could feel my head race and my blood boil. I knew that I had to maintain my composure. You told me I had to hold my state no matter what. But really at that point all I wanted was to reach over and belt him one. He had applied this same tactic to others that got in his way before and I knew he needed to be shocked back into the reality of the harm he was causing. But now was not the time and I was not going to be the person to do it. It was one of those moments where this guy was just being bad. There were no grounds for doing what he was doing, his grounds were not solid, they weren't ethical, they weren't good and they weren't fair. I wasn't at fault, he was just being nasty. Then I remembered what you had told me, Brian, you said if I needed to change my emotional state very fast I was to use my Circle of Influence.

To start off first by bringing someone into my mind, into my imagination to reduce the stress a little, I brought my two daughters. I imagined their pretty little faces and that helped me catch my breath. You said this would help free up my thinking a little from my stressed and agitated state and it did. At that point I desperately needed help because my body was in turmoil. It was in a haze of emotions, ranging from feelings of hurt to feelings of confusion to feelings of rage. I was anxious and I was angry and I was stuck. I didn't know where to go with what was happening to me. There was a very real danger that I could have leaned over and I could have lashed out and that would have been the end of me. It would have all been over for me.

175

Can you imagine if I had done that? That's just unthink-able. That's the 'you'll never work again' type of thing. Thankfully, because of what you taught me, I asked to take a breather for a few moments and left for the loo to gather my composure. I used the Circle of Influence technique and when I went back in I found a way through without anyone getting killed in the process. Well maybe they were harmed a little but only in my imagination. I left the company shortly afterwards and I have never looked back. But that technique really did save the day and for that I want to say thank you. Thank You!

Exercise: Circle of Influence

I want to help you develop a resource like this to get you through challenging times. The first step is to think of someone, someone in your life that is just a funny person. A person who when you think about them it brings a smile to your face. You know one of those guys or girls that is a joker or a prankster. When you think of them, they make you smile. I want you to write down or memorise their name. See their face, imagine how they normally look at you and hold the thought for later. Just select one person. If need be you can update all of your choices at a later date, for now choose one and stick with it until the process is complete.

Next what I want you to do is to think of someone that is a lovable rogue. Someone you know or know of. I use Jack Nicholson, he's a lovable rogue, he's a good guy to have, someone that you respect and that is a bit mischievous with the world. I don't know Jack personally, only through his movies, but that is enough for me. The idea is to choose an essentially good person, mischievous but good. A person whose ethics are good but who is a bit roguish about stuff and who doesn't take life so seriously.

Your next person is a person in your life that is very real and that you would describe as being a positive person. You could choose the motivational guru Tony Robbins or even the Dalai Lama. He's a positive guy; you can't imagine him being depressed. So if you've seen him, or if you've listened to his speeches or read his books, and in your assessment he's a powerful and a positive person, then select him. It could even be your friend, your parent, your child – anyone who is positive.

Next I want you to select someone that you say is important to you, someone that you know, a very special person to you. I want you to have the freedom to pick that person without my parameters on it.

Next I want you to pick a fictional character: Superman, Spiderman, Wolverine, Homer Simpson anyone like that. Someone that's inspirational will work really well here. It can be a character from a movie, it can be a person, it could be Sean Connery as 007 Bond, James Bond. It could be Pamela Anderson as C.J. in Baywatch if that's what does it for you.

Later, after you have read this, I want you to close your eyes and imagine yourself sitting in a chair and in your mind see that there are five more vacant chairs set out in front of you in the shape of a semi-circle. I want you to imagine the five people that you have chosen are making their way into the scene before you. Bring in your funny person and let that character sit down so that you have full sight of the expression on their face. Invite in your lovable rogue and see the smirk on their face, up to mischief as usual, while your funny person is just grinning from ear to ear like a Cheshire cat. Next comes your positive person, the one that it lifts your heart to see. Now for the next person, the one of your own choosing, whoever that person is, that's a special person. Invite them in and ask them to take a seat. Finally bring in your chosen fictional character.

Now I want you to think of a challenge that you've got, something that's been getting in the way. It might be becoming more confident, it might be making more decisions, it might be being too analytical, it might be searching for instant gratification. Whatever it is, I want you to present your problem to the five people sitting in front of you. Now these five people are completely on your side, they have your back. They want you to do well, to excel and to be at your very best.

Now talk with each of them in turn and get them to give you their advice, and if one of them is Winnie the Pooh or Yogi Bear maybe he's got advice too. I want you to ask those questions and get them to answer back. Let them do it the way you would imagine they would do it. The funny person is going to look at your problem in a different way. The lovable rogue is going to have some unique ideas, right? Just imagine how they would respond to you. Tell them this is your problem and let them give you their responses to it. If you chose Tony Robbins what would Tony Robbins say about this? Whatever your challenge is, whatever your dilemma is, just get them to offer input. Say to them, 'This is my dilemma what do you think?' And imagine how they'd talk back to you. Now if you want, if you've not already done it, you can choose your own angel or your own spirit guide, it's up to yourself. Talk to each of them in turn and see what light they shed on your solution. Take your time. Remember they are all on your side. Present your problems and let them present their solutions. How would they handle the situation themselves? What would they do in that situation?

Do all of this with closed eyes and once you have got their answers, give yourself an extra few minutes of deliberation before opening your eyes and bringing back your new perspective.

Once you get into the habit of this it's hard to worry any more, on account of all those helpers in there. For some of you this will prove to be a strange experience and that is perfectly okay as long as it puts you in a different space and in a better place to present your solutions from.

Now you might say that's just my imagination, yes but it presents your challenges in a different way. If you've got Winnie the Pooh advising you on your problem you just can't take it so seriously can you? If you've got Winnie the Pooh sitting in that chair and you are trying to face the biggest dilemma in your life, you can't help but lighten up, it's as simple as that. If that little exercise made you think differently about things, that's exactly what it was supposed to do. You want to be able to think differently about those things.

The idea is to lighten up on your problems, lighten up on your challenges. To begin to think about it and begin to look at life and say okay, whatever it is you've got a filter inside your head. It doesn't matter that that was an imagination exercise. If you chose someone from the spirit world some people will say that they were actually there right? One thing we do know is we do have assistance in some form or shape, it might be just your emotional mind but you definitely do have support. There are people there, things there or ideas, there are feelings there supporting you all the time and at the very least your unconscious is on your side, which is a brilliant, brilliant thing.

CIRCLE OF INFLUENCE
Funny Person
Lovable Rogue
Positive Person
You choose
Fictional Character

Now I might be accused of simplifying this, which is fair to say, but I'm not over-simplifying it. It needs to be simple. One of the things we do is worry and over-complicate things. Worry is rarely about one thing going wrong, we usually factor in a gazillion things going belly up and this is a result of distorted thinking.

Personal Rules

Distorted thinking leads to all sorts of silly rules such as the 'just in case' rules. Operating from a worried, stressed or pressured state, people decide it is time to create rules so as to prevent any future occurrences of the problem they've just encountered. This is just not the best time. If you are in a fearful state that will mostly lead to fear-based decisions and exclude other rational possibilities. In school nowadays if a child falls, a teacher is not allowed to reach out and physically help the child up from the ground. That's a prime example of where the rule makers have lost the plot. Better safe than sorry I hear you say. Well, it is a very sorry thing when you remove caring human contact from a child's life because of the tiny marginal minority that are screwed up.

Some organisations get so big that they put their rules above their people, so that the entire working experience loses most of its positive social aspects and becomes dehumanised. That way it is easier to hurt people because you can say 'it's just business' when in fact it is unjust. Many businesses cause unhappiness in this way. Obviously not all organisations are the same, not all rules are the same and many rules were devised to make the organisation survive and thrive. The rules are just the mechanics that allow for this to happen. Unfortunately, however, what people sometimes do is place too much emphasis on the importance of rules and forget about their intended function. When you buy into the company rules you need to remember those rules are supposed to make the business survive (and profit) not to make you perish in the process. If your esteem, your motivation or your sense of happiness is being crushed then you have got to ask yourself 'Is it my rules causing this or is it the company rules or is it my interpretation of the purpose of the rules?' One thing's for sure: something needs to change.

Having said all that, we all need rules and we all live by rules, some are obvious and overt and some only become evident when they are broken. Whether in work or in our interpersonal relations there are rules; these rules are reflections of the decisions around what we feel is important to us – in essence our values and beliefs – and as such any breach can be met with strong emotional reactions at times. These rules can be broken down into two categories:

1. The rules you hold for yourself.
2. The rules you hold for others.

We all live by a set of rules, for most of us these rules are outside our everyday awareness. These rules are your beliefs and your values about what is right and what is wrong, what is good and what is bad, what type of person you are, what sort of standards you hold yourself to, how you expect the world to see you etc. If you break these rules or do not live up to them then you feel guilty. If someone else breaks your rules you feel angry. Guilt is necessary, without it you earn the official title of being a psychopath! It only becomes bad if you fail to act on it or if you dwell in it for more time than is necessary.

Why You Feel Guilty

The purpose of your guilt is to act as a message from your unconscious to let you know that you are better than that and that you can do better than that. If you take this on board you will be fine. Unfortunately, because of the way we have been conditioned, most of us take the feeling and use it to beat ourselves up, which is not useful.

When faced with a dilemma, we respond. For example, Helen's four-year-old son pushes her buttons one day (or messes with her rules) and she shouts at him. Startled, her little boy looks at her in total disbelief, his eyes fill up and he whimpers and buries his face into the back of the sofa in an attempt to disappear from her sight. Helen's heart immediately sinks and she thinks to herself 'I've blown it. I'm a monster, a bully, a heartless, worthless . . . call yourself a mum do you? I'm just not good enough.' And she's off, her guilt feelings are now in full swing. Heartbroken, she kneels down, reaches out to her little boy and cuddles him lovingly as she seeks his forgiveness. 'Mummy's sorry, Jamie, Mummy shouldn't have shouted at you. Sorry Honey. Will you make up with Mummy? Are we back friends? Who is Mummy's best little boy in the whole wide world?' Jamie holds himself with a tiny hesitation at first and then puts his arms around her neck, still upset from the attack, and nods his saddened face to let his Mummy know that everything is okay again.

Afterwards Helen reviews the event in the kangaroo court of her mind, over and over again. She thinks about what she could've, would've, should've done and she runs mental movies of it to further humiliate herself, adding her own special soundtracks of accusation, blame and self-deprecation.

Here are some guilt-built expressions or thoughts: I am not a good enough. I don't do enough. I don't give enough. I am not there enough. I don't know how much is enough. Those of us who are really good at it, make the leap and say, 'Well if I did this then I must be a bad person.' This is destructive thinking and smacks of self-indulgence. You saying to yourself 'I shouldn't have shouted at him. I could have been more patient. It was wrong to lose my temper' etc. doesn't alter the fact that you did. Quite simply, once is enough to make you feel miserable so get the message, STFU about it and decide what you can do from here.

Tips to Deal with Guilt

- *Accept your role:* Whether you are a partner, a son, a daughter or as in Helen's case a parent, realise that every role produces a set of rules. You cannot exist without these rules and you can be sure that there will be times that you will fail to reach the standards you set for yourself. When this happens, realise that you are human and – rather than beating yourself up about what you failed to do – decide in the moment what you can do. It is never too late to change and it is never too late to build new rules. For example, being a parent brings with it its own set of rules. It means having ultimate responsibility for your child's well-being and this involves the good and the bad, the rewards and the punishments.
- *Know you will get it wrong sometimes:* Getting it wrong is a natural thing, accepting responsibility for it requires courage.
- *Stop criticising yourself:* You are not your behaviour. You are not a bad person because you did a bad thing. If you have made a mistake, ask yourself how you can do better the next time.
- *Stop comparing yourself:* Instead of feeling guilty about how someone else appears to be doing so well, ask yourself how much better you are getting.
- *Shift your focus to the present:* If you have messed up, ask yourself what you can do now to improve the situation.

- *Change your mental movies:* Instead of running negative, incriminating movies in your mind, use the time to work out ways in which you can improve the situation.
- *Find out what matters most to the people that matter in your life:* Knowing what matters means knowing their rules. Their rules are merely a reflection of their values, the things they place importance on. Adult values remain reasonably static, however, children's values shift regularly and their personalities are building, so keep in touch with their needs, wants and desires by having a weekly family meeting (see below). This will help you stay on track.
- *Meet your own personal needs (or rules) constantly:* Meeting your own rules means that you retain your identity as an individual. That way you remain happy as it will raise your self-esteem. If you keep putting others first all of the time, you will only end up feeling guilty and not be at your best as often as you can be.

The Weekly Family Meeting

For those of you who have children a simple way to stay connected with and informed about the changing dynamics of a growing family and to keep on top of the evolving rules is to have a little check-in once a week. Below is a system I have used and which works well most of the time. The family meeting can be held anywhere, anytime. In our home it tends to happen on a Sunday morning: the children come into the bedroom, we have a chat and set up what we are doing for the day. So it is no big deal, it is natural, ordinary and organic. It is something we like to do and it doesn't feel like something we have to do. The idea behind this is to keep it that way. No pressure, no theatrics, no heavy-handedness, just the members of a family sharing the same space and enjoying each other's company as a family. The key rules are to: keep it informal, keep it simple, stick to the specific questions and keep it positive.

There are five core questions:

1. What was your week like?
2. How are things going?
3. What did the other person(s) do this week that was good and that you appreciated?
4. What did you do that is worthwhile and that you are proud of?
5. What would you like to see improved in this coming week?

The rules in detail are:

1. Any member can call a family meeting but ideally only hold one meeting a week for effectiveness.
2. Each person must be allowed to speak uninterrupted while they express their experience.
3. The tone of the meeting must be kept at an ordinary level (no raised voices or shouting).
4. Keep focusing on the experience, i.e. how the person felt or responded to the actions or behaviours of the other family members, and avoid the blame game or finger pointing.
5. Any member can suggest or ask to be treated in a particular manner by any other member of the group while the entire group get to decide whether this is fair and acceptable.
6. All traditional roles – parent, child etc. – are excluded from the meeting as all members are equal and must have equal input.
7. Each person is responsible for controlling the flow of the meeting.
8. Meetings should be kept as brief as possible and talking time should ideally be limited to three to five minutes per input at an absolute maximum.
9. No one is allowed to leave the meeting without an issue being fully resolved to the satisfaction/agreement of all members.
10. All meetings must end on a good note (see points 3 and 4).
11. Detailed input is expected from all members.
12. Brevity is the order of the day. Keep the meeting effective, not rushed but short.

CHAPTER 11

Golden Rules for Dealing with Difference

To know when to go away and when to come closer is the key to any lasting relationship.

Doménico Cieri Estrada

Relationship Rules

In Chapter 10 I wrote about the fact that we feel guilty if we fail to adhere to our personal rules. We get angry or feel disappointed in ourselves when this happens. If someone else breaks our rules, we tend to get angry or disappointed with them too.

Relationship rules are the rules about how you expect the world to see you. They are about how you expect the world to treat you and about how you expect the world to be. We tend to react negatively when these rules are either broken or come under threat. We do this by getting irritated, frustrated or angry, or by expressing our disappointment by moaning, whining or sulking. When that happens we tend to attempt to restore order by imposing our rules yet again and oftentimes more emphatically or forcefully. However we do it, we do so in a way that lashes out or snipes at the 'offender', thereby breaking that person's rules and so the conflict exists and the argument begins.

The fact of the matter is that when you enter into relationships with other people, whether it's your family, your life partner, your friend, your boss, your work colleague or whomever, there will inevitably be at some stage some degree of conflict. It is how you handle the conflict that matters. Arguments occur when someone fails to live up to your expectations of what should be done or should not be done. Or in other words they break your rules.

Behind every argument there is either a should or a shouldn't.

Conflict is often a sign that something is wrong or that someone is unhappy. Avoiding conflict or ignoring the problems could mean that you are choosing to avoid talking through important issues or exploring the underlying reasons that have caused the conflict. Conflict can be healthy and often leads to improvement if handled sensitively and correctly, that is the upside. The downside is that we can get entrenched in our camps of self-righteousness and we dig our feet in so that it all becomes a lose–lose situation.

Often our arguments come down to our mental sorting patterns (or meta programs) and have little to do with the issue itself. We will deal with this in Chapter 12.

Solutions to Conflicting Rule Sets between Individuals

- *Acknowledge where you are at emotionally first.* If you are fuming with rage, you know this is not the best way to get a resolution to your problem. Give yourself a chance, take some time out, change your state, go for a walk, go for a run, and work off some steam. Do the washing or something physical before you end up working it off on your loved ones. That being said, it is important that you state how the problem makes you feel, remembering that you get to choose your feelings even if your partner's actions initially gave rise to them.
- *Look before you jump.* Acknowledge where the other person is at too. In general, people tend not to be malicious, oftentimes they do things because they are so wrapped up in their own world that they forget they belong in yours too. There are other times when their reasons are valid too. Wayne Dyer tells the story of two children on a train. They are being noisy and boisterous running about banging and bashing into the other passengers,

who are visibly getting annoyed. Eventually one of the passengers pipes up at the children's father and asks if he is not embarrassed by the behaviour of his children. Does he not expect them to behave better around others? The man answers, 'I suppose. But I don't know how they are supposed to behave when they just got news their mother died.'

- *Ask yourself whether it has to be dealt with right now.* Most things can wait until you are in a better mood and most things work out better that way too. Put it out of your mind for now. If you keep thinking about the problem you are most likely to magnify it and with it your responses to it. Sometimes it is simply better to direct your focus elsewhere until you are better capable of coming at the problem with a level head and an easy stomach.

- *Keep the bigger picture in mind.* We tend not to argue with people we don't care about. Work out if the issue is worth fighting over. If this person is important to you then . . . how important is it that the lid is on the toothpaste? Will the world end if her room is not tidy? Is it more important that he arrives home safely than that he is later than he said? If you look back on some of the things you have fought about, you realise they are silly, funny even. So rather than wait until the future, do what the comedians do and find the funny part to it now.

- *Separate the problem from the person.* Arguments lead to criticism, so if you must criticise, then criticise the behaviour rather than the person. 'You're a bold boy' is a lot different to 'You did a bold thing' or 'That was a bold thing to do'. When people are hurt they are highly suggestible so be careful where you place the blame. If you give out to your daughter for doing a bold thing by telling her she is bold then she is most likely to make the jump and store the 'fact' that she is bold and that is certainly not what you want, is it?

- *Stick to the issue at hand.* Save your marriage or your partnership by dealing with one issue at a time. It is not useful to bring up your partner's entire past failings when you are arguing about why she took so long in the shower.

- *Validate the other person's position.* Sometimes people just need to be heard and to have their frustration acknowledged. You don't have to agree on everything to diffuse the tension. You can say stuff like 'I see where you are coming from.' 'I hear what you are saying.' 'I can imagine that I would be annoyed if I was in your shoes.' All of these statements acknowledge the importance that you place on the other person's opinion, once you do that you are more likely to get a reasonable solution to your differences by working on the things that you both have in common.

- *Don't be afraid to admit you are wrong.* Life gets easier when you do. Owen Fitzpatrick, my business partner, tells of an experience of his some time ago which demonstrates this concept perfectly. 'I am running to catch a plane, my luggage is overweight and I am late. The person at the ticket counter says I need to go to another desk to pay the extra charge on my baggage. When I go over to the desk, the lady there says I am too late. The plane is now boarding and I am going to miss my flight. She is obviously annoyed and tells me I should have given myself time for this. On and on she goes ... I listen. I agree. I say I am sorry. I do not defend or argue. She continues giving out to me as she is processing my payment and checking me in at the same time. I look at her seriously and say thank you very much. I get my plane, she keeps her rules – everybody is happy.' If Owen had stood his ground it could have been so different. He would have been left stranded in the airport, frustrated as hell and looking for another flight.

- *There is more than one truth.* You can agree to disagree. Nature has set us up in a way to believe that we are right most of the time. The problem is we often expect everyone to agree with our limited worldview. This is the stuff that wars are made of. Think of it this way, you believe you are right about something and because you do, you expect that your partner should agree too. If your partner did agree, your partner would be just like you. Now if that is how you would like the world to be, then really all you need is a mirror for a relationship because it will always agree with you – but that is a lonely place.

- *Be prepared at times to avoid the issue.* Sometimes agreement is simply not going to be reached. Some arguments do not have a solution that you can both be happy or equally unhappy with. Relationships that last over long periods of time recognise this and accept the difference. Every problem does not have to be addressed. For example, your partner had an affair but you have both talked and decided to give it another go. Once you have dealt with the reasons that gave rise to it and the motivations to end it then the only way forward is to draw a line in the sand and move on. This means that going through the sordid details is deliberately avoided because any reference to them will just re-ignite the bad feelings of jealousy and resentment and wreak havoc on what you have built up.

- *Forgive does not mean forget.* Be prepared to forgive. No one gets it right all of the time. You have been there too, it is only human, we all make mistakes and we all deserve more than one chance. However, whereas it is always important to forgive, it is not always wise to forget. If your boss takes advantage of your good nature and asks a little more than you can give, you can forgive her for being inconsiderate, but if you don't remind her of what it cost you, she is likely to do it again.

- *Be prepared to work through your issues.* Most people go out of their way to avoid conflict because they don't want to upset people or be upset themselves. This happens in business all of the time. It is why people settle for bad service, they simply won't complain. The fact of the matter is if you deal with your issues you will feel more positive and it will give you a sense of achievement. You will feel more relaxed and will sleep better at night. You will develop stronger relationships as a result and you will feel happier.

Coping with Conflicting Rule Sets within Families

There can be nothing like a good family get-together, family, friends, in-laws and outlaws all together under one roof drinking, eating, chatting, sharing stories and having a great time. At least that's how it starts out or how it is intended to be, but as we all know it doesn't always end up that way. Oftentimes we find ourselves in sensitive situations with difficult family members and as tensions run high and patience runs out festering resentment boils over and arguments unfold in front of our very eyes. This is because any social group that has existed over an extended period of time is bound to have its rules, its cliques and its scapegoats. Differences of opinion are bound to exist and where difference exists so too does tension.

Every group has a number of ways of releasing the build up of tension and that is typically by forming subgroups or cliques. Members of these subgroups often appoint themselves as moral supervisors or guardians of the wider group and react to non-conformity by a series of means. The choice of reaction will depend on the strength of individual members of the group. The basic idea is to get everybody to fit in. Initially this may be done subtly or overtly through welcoming outsiders and newcomers in with good-humoured persuasion and inclusion and the gradual assignment of roles and responsibilities.

All is well until there is a breach in conformity, then the demons show up and attempt to restore order and control. This can be done through high or low level aggression and is manifested through acts of bullying, complaining, criticising, spreading guilt, undermining and even ostracising the offenders until such time as they fit back in, are excluded or are kicked out. This process can be hell. So if you find yourself in this situation and don't want to end up as the scapegoat for group tension perhaps what you need are a few 'coping' strategies to help you survive.

- *Anticipate potential pitfalls.* Most of us have been there, you know what is most likely to happen and who is most likely to cause it to happen, so prepare in advance to avoid it or cope with it. It is no use relying on blind faith to take you through, you need to have a plan for each eventuality. Work out what could go wrong and work out how you will cope with it without making matters worse. If there is likely to be an encounter that could produce tension, say, for example, a family member holding a grudge or one that you don't particularly get on with, make sure that you visit them early in the day – there is less likely to be much alcohol consumed, which is the thing most likely to get you into difficulty. Once you have your plan in mind, visualise it going well as often as you can.

- *Set time limits* to your visits and stick to them no matter how well things appear to be going. You know what your tolerance levels are, you know how long it takes before your patience runs out (and that differs depending on the amount of alcohol consumed). So set it up in advance, have something or someone that you have genuinely got to visit or something you genuinely have to do after a set time, and politely excuse yourself, express your thanks and leave. Make it so that you leave on a good note not a strained one.

- *Focus on the present.* Avoid running over bad past experiences and focus solely and totally on the brief period that you will be in the particular situation. If someone brings up a past issue, whether alcohol-induced or not, use a 'Pattern Interrupt' or a sudden interruption to redirect attention and take control by bringing the focus back to the present again.

- *Focus on coping not resolving.* Do not assume that because you are in a happy mood that others are too and do not attempt to fix any longstanding family feuds, now is not the time. Keep your focus on 'coping', so you are always working to get through it rather than getting over it. Aim to have a pleasant gathering, to focus on the things that are going well and that are worth enjoying and to settle with coping with the things that are challenging.

If you have to meet someone and you know it is going to be a huge challenge, try and do so on neutral ground so that if tensions do erupt at least you can walk away.

Managing Difficult Adult Behaviour

It is useful to understand why people engage in difficult behaviours and the reason is simple: it works for them. As we move from childhood into our teenage years and later adulthood we tend to take on strict roles or make concrete decisions (rules) about how we will deal with people and life in general. We are not always consciously aware of these coping life strategies, but nonetheless they guide our behaviours, make up our personalities and determine our success or the lack thereof in life. These strategies or decisions are a natural part of the growing-up process and are reflected in the following manner:

- We like to be liked and because of this we engage in behaviours that are intended to achieve this objective so that the behaviour becomes habit. Later we even engage in it when we know it is not working. And then wonder why we feel so upset because it fails to work all of the time.

- We enjoy our polarity of response at the age of two and later again in the teenage years we begin to explore and experiment with the idea of not doing what our friends and family would like us to do or deliberately doing the opposite of what is expected of us. Again this behaviour can become habitual and we continue to limit ourselves by it even after we have forgotten the use behind it in the first place.

- We think we are our behaviours, however, the incorrect assumption that we are what we do can have disastrous consequences on our self-esteem and our general level of emotional health, never mind our efficiency in achieving our objectives. If it was true it would mean that when we did something stupid, which we all have done at some time or other, then we would be stupid. Conversely, if we did something intelligent then we would be intelligent, and as such we would be both intelligent and stupid at the one time. In short we are not our behaviours but we are responsible for our behaviours. As such we owe it to ourselves to engage in those behaviours that will best serve us in the achievement of our positive outcomes.

In order to best enjoy life we must become flexible. Being flexible means coming up with fresh responses to each challenge as it presents itself. Being flexible does not mean sacrificing your overall well-being or giving up your rules. Being flexible means being prepared to make alterations or changes in your words, your thinking, your reactions and your behaviours if only for this short period of time to ensure that life is a rewarding, enriching and enjoyable experience. For you, for your friends and for your family, being flexible makes sense.

In his book and audio series Dr Robert Bramson, an expert on conflict resolution, identified nine basic 'Difficult Behaviour Types' and provided some tools of interaction to help you cope with them. I have used his work as a basis to form my own categories of 'difficult people', described below.

1. *The Bully:* Avoid getting into a catfight but do stand up for yourself. Create eye contact. Call the bully by his first name. When he interrupts you, look him in the eye; tell him that he has interrupted you. Keep your tone non-accusatory. Use statements like 'I disagree with you but tell me more' or phrases such as 'in my opinion'. Once he has interrupted you a few times and you have stood up to him in an adult way, a change will occur, he will look at you as if he has seen you for the fist time and he will listen.

2. *The Sarcastic One:* Hit the nail on the head as soon as it starts. Sarcastic people rely on getting a group behind them to compensate for feeling powerless, so flush them out immediately. When she snipes, stay really quiet, smile and raise your eyebrow but keep looking at her when the group are looking at you. When she snipes again, keep the non-expressive look going and let the silence build. Give it a few seconds and then put a big smile on your face and say, 'Are you done yet?' When she has left

the cover of her group, meet her head on and challenge her behaviour. Keep the smile going but let her know you won't stand for it. Her objective is to make you the one that feels weak.

3. *The Emotional One:* When he first explodes, do nothing apart from maintaining eye contact. Let the rage subside and once you do you may notice his eyes falling to the floor as he becomes upset. He may at this stage begin to cry. Then say to him something along the lines of 'Look this is really important and I want to hear everything that you say. But not this way.' By taking him seriously you are in fact dealing with the threat that he is responding to, which is loss of control. Try to get some privacy. Next gather the facts, and then offer immediate help and work out a plan of action.

4. *The Indecisive One:* Find out the reason she is not making the decision. What specifically makes her hesitate? Help her to solve her dilemma. Make a personal statement of support. Watch for non-verbal signs, and be careful not to pressure her. Once you get her to make a decision, tell her that you believe that the decision she made was the best one for all concerned.

5. *The Complainer:* Never agree with him. Simply paraphrase back what he has said to you. Do not apologise to him for what you have failed to do. This will only give him the opportunity to criticise more (and another thing . . .). Get him into problem-solving mode. Ask him questions. Ask for his help. Get him to explain the problem and how he is going to fix it for you, as opposed to how he wants you to fix it for him. Put a time limit on him. Say something like 'Listen I am out of here in five minutes what would you like to have done by that time.'

6. *The Pessimist:* Save yourself and remain positive no matter what she puts in front of you. Never argue. Never nod in the affirmative while she is preaching her brand of doom and gloom. Say something like 'You are probably right' and don't expect help from her, get ready to motor on by yourself – but don't be surprised if it's offered.

7. *The Non-Responsive One:* Start the conversation yourself. Pause

and end each statement with a question: What do you think of that? What would you do in that situation? What's happening? What are you thinking? Enter into the silence yourself and wait and wait for a response. Next lean forward with an air of expectancy written on your face, put your hand on his forearm or shoulder, if that is acceptable, and say, 'You are not talking to me, what is happening?' Again enter the silence, while still demonstrating with your body language that you are expecting a response. If this fails to get a response, you need to tell him that you are reading his lack of response as a snub and a message for you to leave him alone. Tell him how that makes you feel and then leave him alone. Tell him that you will be happy to talk to him whenever he decides he is ready.

8. *The Know-It-All:* Listen and provide verbal feedback by paraphrasing what she has said. If you don't, she will think you did not understand her because you are stupid. If you disagree with her, you will have to use questions to get her attention otherwise she will not hear you because you are the dumb one. The two basic types of question to be used are:

   - The 'baby blue eyes' question – think of Marilyn Monroe, flicker your eyelids and say, 'I don't understand. Could you explain that to me one more time?' As she is doing that, get ready to launch in with question number two.

   - The extensional question – ask a question that draws out what she has already said, 'So what you are saying is . . . and that means . . .' (this is where you slip in your own thinking in the form of an extensional question that teases out her thinking in a safe way in an attempt to demonstrate the flaw in her thinking in the first place). Once she sees the flaw, she will have pointed it out to herself and so therefore it is less likely to cause you a problem.

9. *The Super-Agreeable One:* You have got to help him to be honest and give feedback, to say what he really thinks and do what he really wants. When you know that he has a problem with something, tease it out. For example, 'I know you're happy with

the job that I've done for you on the garden in general, but perhaps there is some minor area that could do with the slightest bit of improvement, after all nobody is perfect and we all need a little help at some time or other.' Once he squeezes out a strained, 'Well maybe the such and such could be a tiny bit better.' You know that is where he has his biggest problem and you must fix it immediately. Once you have done that thank him for his enormous help, it may actually encourage him to be more honest in the future. These people need plenty of encouragement so be lavish with your praise.

Techniques for Handling Difficult Behaviour in Children

1. *The Angry Child:* Avoid getting angry back. Talk and use reason with her. Elicit compassion from her. Offer alternatives to her behaviour. Highlight her good behaviour. Use a kind, attentive, firm tone of voice with her to let her know that you are the boss without having to say it.

2. *The Explosive Child:* Provide help and make him feel safe. Distract him, use humour, tickle him. Talk to him. Soothe and empathise with him. Help him prepare for the next time things don't work out the way he expects or wants. If you can, pre-empt a reoccurrence.

3. *The Disruptive/Noisy/Hyperactive Child:* Find out the reason for her behaviour. Reduce the amount of stimulation that she is exposed to. Give her a break to wind down. Provide an opportunity for her to work off energy. Help her regain control by paying attention, hugging and reassuring her.

Make up Your own Rules

All of these behaviours come from established and rigid rules sets. Rules, values and beliefs are all creatures of the same species. It is worth having a look at the beliefs that have been handed to you over time and to do as Timothy Leary suggested: 'question authority, question everything'. It's not about whose rule is the best one, whose value is the most important one or whose belief is the right one. The belief is only 'right' if it works for you.

There are certain things that we believe in, that we take for granted. Sometimes it's a good idea to find out where they came from. Now if it works for you, brilliant, knock yourself out. If, however, you begin to decide that someone else should believe it too, well then you are screwed. The purpose of this book is for you to develop your own belief system, to find out:

- What's the most important thing for you?
- What is it that makes you resonate?
- What is it that makes you happy?
- What is it that makes you enthusiastic?
- What is it that makes you motivated?
- What is it that inspires you?
- What is it that actually creates a better life for you?

At the end of the day you can look at any religious text and the basic idea is to do unto others as you would have done unto yourself. That's a pretty good rule.

Make up Your own Mind

My son Dylan is an exceptionally smart young chap and he performs really well academically too, so the teachers took a keen interest in him. When he was about eight years old they asked him if he would consider attending an educational programme for (academically) advanced children in Trinity College, Dublin during the summer. When Dylan arrived home from school, we had the following conversation:

'Dad, my teacher is saying maybe I could go to UCD or
    something like that.'
'Yeah.'

197

'It's supposed to be for special, gifted people.'

'Right.'

'And isn't that a little bit stupid?'

'Why Dylan?'

'Well, if I'm supposed to be gifted, if I'm supposed to be so smart and special, why do I need to work harder? Wouldn't it make sense to have the school for the people that are stuck?'

[What could I say? That made sense to me.]

'You know,' he says, 'is it smart to do more school when you are my age?'

'I don't think so.'

'Well, I won't be doing that either'.

When he was about nine years of age, Dylan said:

'Da, the Jesus and Mary thing?'

'Yeah, what?'

Raising his eyebrows, 'The Jesus and Mary thing?'

'What about it?'

In a sarcastic tone of voice, 'What's the story with that? That didn't happen sure it didn't?'

His mind was already made up and I thought to myself *God, he's starting too early.*

He's quite spiritual now but he doesn't have those beliefs and that's okay. If you have those beliefs that's great because it works for you and that's what matters. But he's got spiritual beliefs that work for him. If you believe there's a way to live life but it's not making you happy, why believe in it anymore? Because the idea of believing in something needs to be workable, it needs to produce good results. At the end of the day the only thing that you are here for on this planet is to get a full human experience and the baseline for that is to feel good. That's really what you are about.

Believe in What's Useful

One of the most useful beliefs is to believe that whatever happens happens for a reason and a purpose and it serves us. That may not be true, but who cares, it's a nice belief isn't it? If I have a bad day I ask myself 'What can I learn from this?' If something happens I say, 'Well, it's supposed to happen so I need to do something about that.' It's just the way I frame it. Remember you are a reality-building machine. Every single day you create ideas inside your head that literally dictate your reality and you can build whatever you want.

My younger son Cian comes into me and he says, 'Dad how come bad things happen in threes?' And I reply, 'That's not the rule Cian; the rule is this, when one bad thing happens, three good things happen after that, that's the rule.' Cian looks at me with a little scepticism and then goes off. Two days later he comes back to me and says, 'Dad you know that's true.' So I casually say, 'Yeah I know.' And he says, 'How come?' To which I answer, 'I don't know, I don't make the rules.' But in actual fact I did. You know, sometimes it's a good idea to lie to your children.

Words Can Build Reality

I was talking to a guy once in Waterford who began telling me that his hand was all busted; he had got annoyed and in a rant he banged his hand off a chair. I was with Michael Connolly in his yoga centre at the time and Michael interrupted and said, 'I've got the very thing for that' and he brought from his office this cream, which I found out later was pretty useless, and said, 'This is fantastic stuff Frank.' To which I responded, 'Aahh you got the cream Michael, that stuff is the business.' Michael agreed and he continued talking to me while he was really working on Frank. 'The way it works Brian is it seeps into the hand and it just softens it up and your hand begins to relax as the cream does its thing.' He continued on in this way, declaring the exceptional qualities of this wonderful miracle cream, and ten minutes later Frank's pain that had lasted for two days was gone and even he was saying how great the cream was.

It's how you add to a thing that very often creates reality, so is what you say about it. You might have experienced something like this in school when the teacher said, 'Right ladies and gentlemen, we are going to do maths today. Now maths is a very *difficult* subject, but we will *struggle* through and if you work *really hard* you might just *squeeze a pass* out of an honours paper.' So you said to yourself 'Oh man I'm not looking forward to this' and you set your mind on looking for what was really difficult and what was bad about it. The teacher had effectively hypnotised you into a negative belief about maths. Had he not said anything, you may have found it a lot more enjoyable. Very often the way you set up things dictates how people think and feel about them. The question for you is: What do you want to set up for yourself?

Techniques for Dealing with Conflict

- *Frustration Destroyer Patterns* (for changing your feelings around an immediate situation). Please refer to the Eliminating the Negative exercises (options 1 and 2) in Chapter 2. Both these exercises are occasionally referred to as 'The Frustration Destroyer Patterns'.
- *Genie Labordes' MYOUR Formula* (for resolving bigger issues of conflict). The MYOUR formula is an excellent tool for conflict resolution as it abides by the NLP principles of well-formedness and has at its heart a focus on a win–win scenario for the involved parties.

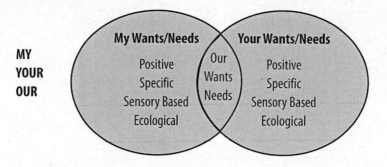

**MY
YOUR
OUR**

My Wants/Needs

Positive
Specific
Sensory Based
Ecological

**Our
Wants
Needs**

Your Wants/Needs

Positive
Specific
Sensory Based
Ecological

What's the Win–Win?
(How do we both get what we want?)

If the person you want to deal with is not there, put yourself in his or her shoes and work out what it is you feel they might want from the relationship or situation. This will prepare you better for when you have to negotiate with them at a later time.

CHAPTER 12

What Class of Thinker Are You?

Knowledge of the self is the mother of all knowledge. So it is incumbent on me to know my self, to know it completely, to know its minutiae, its characteristics, its subtleties, and its very atoms.

Kahlil Gibran

Are You a Big Picture or Finer Detail Type?

want you to give me permission to generalise for a little while, for demonstration purposes, as I outline a conversation that's typical for many couples.

Scenario One

Six o'clock and it's been a long day so far. Exhausted and frazzled you (Michael) arrive home into your warm, immaculately kept house to be greeted by your beautiful smiling wife (Christine). She 'dutifully' and 'rightfully' has prepared you a meal fit for a king, so after wolfing it down with a few words thrown at her you take the freshly brewed tea and plonk yourself on your luxurious leather recliner sofa. She knows your form so she remains quiet except for the occasional question, 'How was your day' and 'Was your food okay?' You know, the important stuff.

As you rest your weary bones to catch your daily dose of depression, the newsreader sings his usual ballad of doom and gloom from your new state-of-the-art, flat-screen television. The phone rings, you answer it and it's your good friend John.

Two hours later you return to the sitting room and sit yourself back down to resume watching *your* TV. No sooner have you picked up *your* remote control than your wife turns to you and asks, 'Well who was that?' With a little irritation over being interrupted, you answer:

'John.'

'So what were you talking about?'

'Ah just the usual.' (Thinking: W*hat's it got to do with her?*)

'You were on the phone for over two hours?'

'Yeah?' (*Is that a crime?*)

'So what were you talking about?'

Becoming increasingly more annoyed, 'Stuff.'

'How's Mary?'

'I *don't* know . . . Aaahhhh grand, yeah.'

'So how is little Katie?'

(*Holy Maloney!*) 'What? Yeah, she's great, yeah.'(*Anything for a peaceful life!*)

'And Katie is playing basketball now. How is she doing with that?'

'Why in God's name are you asking me so many questions?'

'I'm only making conversation. I don't know why I bother.' *(Fuming with frustration.)* 'Why don't you get back on to the phone and talk to your buddy he is obviously much more important than me. I am only your wife after all. You're supposed to love me. Some partner you turned out to be.'

'Now this is getting to be completely ridiculous. I don't love you anymore because I don't want to talk right now? I can never do right by you anyway can I? Yes, you're right, there's no point. No point at all.'

With that the two of you sulk for the rest of the evening, carrying out fully blown conversations in your own heads about how you have been wronged.

Scenario Two

The following day you arrive home from work and have since learned that the best way to communicate is to do so in the manner that the person you are communicating with prefers. So now that you know this you want to make up and create a great impression. This time, rather than not talking through dinner, you decide to make the effort and when you meet your beautiful wife you release a bright smile of enthusiasm and blurt out, 'How was your day?' You felt it was important that you got that in first because you want to win at this one. She smiles back at you and says, 'Oh what a day . . . Wait 'til I tell you.' She prepares for a nice long chat like she has with her girlfriends when talking about clothes and shoes and stuff that you know you can't handle. You immediately shrink inside knowing this is going to be a long one and the initially genuine smile becomes an effort to hold behind the anticipation of the excruciating pain about to be endured by you, poor thing. Bracing yourself, you say:

'I'm all ears. Tell me.' *(Liar.)*
'Do you remember this morning when the alarm went off? It was twenty-six minutes past seven . . . I could hear Cian getting up at that time too. He opened his bedroom door, made his way on to the landing and then opened the door to our bedroom. He was wearing his turtle PJs, you know the ones we got him for his birthday, the ones with the four Ninja mutant turtles on the front, the ones with the long black sleeves and the aquamarine body . . .'
'Yeah, oh yeah.' (Trying desperately not to glaze over.)
'You're not even listening to me are you?'
'I am so.'
'I know you're not because I know the way your eyes glaze over like that. You just don't care anymore. You never want to hear what I have to say. You are only interested in yourself. Never mind the day I had.'
In absolute frustration, 'I am interested. But would you just get to the point of the thing. What in God's name

happened to Cian this morning? Never mind what PJs he was wearing. I don't care about his silly PJs for Pete's sake. Just get to the point will you?'

'See I told you so, you don't love me. You just don't care, you'd prefer to go off now and phone your buddy John.'

'Oh here we go again. Could you not just tell me what the problem is?'

This is typical of what we do isn't it? We turn things from bad to worse by bellowing out stupid statements like 'Just get to the point will you?', 'Could you not just tell me what the problem is?', 'What *are* you talking about?' and in doing so we miss the point completely.

Another evening just bit the dust. All Christine wanted to do was to talk. Being a woman she 'knows' men are not capable of solving problems anyway. If she wanted to get a solution she would have talked to another woman, like one of her girlfriends, wouldn't she? Sometimes women just like to talk things through, not to solve a problem but merely as a means of expressing the emotions connected to the experience. In full male mode you arrived in and thought that you had to solve things. But she just wanted to talk to you, she was not looking for a solution, but you jumped ahead of things, straight in in all your efficient urgency and demanded that you be told the point of the story so that you could bring your magnificent problem-solving skills to bear on it.

Stereotyping is now over so if you haven't already figured it out by now I will explain what was happening. When any two human beings engage in communication they have certain preferences in the way that they like to receive, process and input information. These preferences extend to things like how you approach problems and challenges, how you store and react to time, how you are motivated, how you make decisions, how you think etc. These preferences tend to stabilise over time and become patterns. The technical name for these patterns is meta programs. Although these patterns are relatively constant, they can be changed, thus giving you a wider range of responses in any and all situations.

Meta programs operate in a similar way to your five senses. You use all of your senses but you are not consciously using all of them all of the time or all at the same time. Because of the predictability of these patterns we often label people, saying that this person is such and such a type of guy when in fact all he is doing is operating out of one of the many meta programs that he has available to him.

As demonstrated above, the operation of the preferences can lead to many an argument or misunderstanding. Awareness is the key with meta programs, once you recognise that these are just patterns or preferences it gives you the opportunity to change the ones that you are using in order to get a more successful result. In the example, the true cause of the conflict was the sorting processes that were being triggered naturally. Michael mostly focuses on the big picture. He doesn't sweat the small stuff. He likes to sum up and park away information, when he has, in his mind, it is done. It is in the filing cabinet and he doesn't care much for taking it back out and breaking it down into smaller parts whether it is to me, you, his wife or his friend John. Michael thinks in 'Big Chunks'.

This Big Chunk preference (often referred to as 'global') can be contrasted with a 'Little Chunk' preference (often referred to as 'detail') at the opposite end of the continuum and herein lies the problem. When Michael's wife Christine asked what he was talking to John about, he reluctantly offered single word responses using 'yeah', 'no', 'grand', 'stuff' and the like. Basically Michael was finished with the conversation and didn't believe that explaining all of what was discussed was worth the effort, thus the brief responses.

On the other hand, Christine believed it was necessary to fill in the finer details in order to understand or be understood. Christine thinks in terms of Little Chunks. She was sorting for detail each time she requested or supplied information. She did this because this was her preference. So when Michael said 'stuff', she immediately wanted to know what 'stuff' specifically he was referring to and in order to get more detail she asked specific questions that she thought would be relevant to the 'stuff'. She went on to ask about Mary and got a less than satisfactory reply that meant nothing to her, she needed more detail than 'grand'. So she moved on and asked about Katie, this time including a reference to Katie playing basketball to encourage a more detailed reply. Yet again she was met with an equally undesirable response at which point frustration got the better of her, she lashed out and asserted that she was only making conversation.

This simple statement reveals an example of how both Christine and Michael wrongly assumed that the manner in which they like to sort and input information is the right and only way to do it. Consequently they got frustrated when the information they were looking for was not presented as they expected it ought to have been. Michael lost his temper when Christine was telling him about what had happened earlier that morning with their son. As far as he was concerned Christine was supplying boring and unnecessary detail. He wanted the basics; she felt it important to supply the full story.

On occasions when I brought my youngest son Cian to the park play area he would often say, 'Dad, give me a challenge.' I'd say, 'Right. I want you to run all around the park and come back.' Cian would look at me and say something to the effect of, 'Okay, what do you want me to do? Run around *the entire* park? Where do you want me to run first, do you want me to run to the swings first and go over the log next? How do you want me to go over the log?' To which I would respond, 'For God's sake Cian will you just run around the park.'

Now little Cian didn't deserve a response like that, no more than I wanted to give one like it either. After all, what Cian was actually doing was sorting by detail and what I really needed to say was, 'Well the first thing you need to do is . . . and the next thing is . . .' and so on. Had Cian received that information I expect he would have checked and been really thorough about it so he knew what he'd be doing was exactly as I asked him. I cannot give him a Big Chunk instruction without him sorting it and breaking it down into detail.

What can happen is that I feel irritated sometimes and say, 'Come off it Cian stop making a mountain out of a molehill – just go and do it.' To which Cian will inevitably reply, 'You're getting angry with me now Dad.' When I deny it, he'll tell me he can see it in my face. I'll deny it again, 'I'm not son, I'm grand, just go and do your challenge.' To which Cian will respond, 'No you *are* getting angry with me Dad I know you are your face is getting all red, if you don't want to play with me I won't play.' At which point I feel like a complete bum and a useless father with no hope of redemption. I think to myself that I am emotionally and mentally damaging my child permanently. Isn't that what goes on? And there is nothing like a male mind to exaggerate the impact of one moment in time.

Now Cian and I sort in Big *and* Little Chunks at different times. It is when we are sorting differently at the same time that causes the tension. Therefore, it makes sense for one of us to adjust our behaviour and as I am the adult that really is my job.

You are going to meet lots of people who have no idea about what you are learning to do and what you are about to learn, so you cannot expect them to alter their responses in the light of your newfound insights. The onus is on you. We have a saying in the world of NLP:

IF WHAT YOU ARE DOING IS NOT WORKING THEN DO SOMETHING ELSE.

For you to make this work, it will be you that will be making most of the adjustments here, but as I have already pointed out, the person with the most flexibility is the one that has the most influence in any one system. So let's offer you some more of these meta programs.

Proactivity Versus Reactivity

Do you plan to react or do you react to the plan? Human beings are creatures of habit and when they find something that works they tend to do it lots. Because of this you will find that people who have happened on a meta program that works well will tend to use it in lots of situations. This is what makes certain elements of behaviour so predictable. This is very often how we label people.

Ever heard yourself accuse someone else of leaving things to the very last minute, or have you ever been accused of doing the very same thing yourself? Have you ever moaned at someone for being so boring, and scolded them for not being able to let their hair down once in a while? Maybe you told them to chill out, to relax and go with the flow, that not everything needs to be planned, not everything needs to be worked out. Some things are just best left be. 'Que sera, sera'. This song appears to have been written by someone who was in a very reactive mood.

If you are one who likes to plan things, if you like to know where you are going, when you will get there and how you are going to get there. If you think it is insane not to have a plan, if you subscribe to the philosophy 'Fail to plan then plan to fail' you are what we call proactive. You like to get things started; in fact most times you can't wait. You want to get the job over and done with. Oftentimes your enthusiasm can get the better of you and so you start before you get to check things thoroughly. This often gets you into trouble. You are the impatient one, the pencil-tapping, ants-in-your-pants, fidgety one. You just can't sit still, you want what you want and you want it now. You want to go for it, just to do it, to jump in, take charge, hurry up, you are a what are we waiting for let's get this show on the road type of person. Sound familiar or sound alien?

If this is an alien concept to you, it simply means you like to reflect a little. No point in barging ahead before you see what's going on. You like to think before you act.(Sometimes in truth you think too much until the pressure builds and then you have to act or it won't be done in time.) You like to wait and see. You like to let Lady Luck play her part. You like to roll the dice from time to time. You believe that your god has plans for you too and that everything that happens does so for a reason and a purpose. You just can't see the point in planning every last detail because it is just not spontaneous enough and as we said earlier it is so boring. This means that you have a reactive preference.

Can you see how two people of opposing preferences might at times drive each other insane? Here is a dialogue between me and my wife, Theresa, the love of my life. Theresa is very proactive, if she wasn't I would be a lost cause. On the other hand I am very reactive, most of the time. This conversation kicks off with Theresa asking me a familiar question:

'Did you put out the rubbish?'
'In a minute.'
'Why can't you do it now?'
'Why does everything have to be done right now?'
'If you don't put it out you will miss the pick-up time.'
'What are you on about? They won't be here for another hour.'
'Typical. Leave everything to the last minute why don't you?'
'Last minute – what are you like? There's loads of time. They won't be here until at least nine p.m.'

[Some time later.]

'Did you put out the rubbish yet?'
'Will you relax? I'm just waiting until this is over.'
'When is it over?'
'In about five minutes.'
'Well it's nearly five to nine now.'
'For God's sake, I can't get to watch anything I enjoy around here.'

[Moments later.]

'They're done. Are you happy now? The bin has been collected, nobody has died. There was no need to break out in a sweat. All that fuss over nothing and I missed the end of my programme. Thanks a million.'
'You wouldn't have missed your silly programme if you put the bin out when I asked you.'
'See, that's typical, even when I do what you ask I still get into trouble. Next time put it out yourself.'
'I will . . . at least it will be done.'

[Theresa picks up the remote control and switches channel.]
'I was watching that.'
'Well I am watching *Bones* now.'
'What?'
'It's a Wednesday. You know I always watch *Bones* on a
   Wednesday.'
'How am I supposed to know that you watch *Bones* every
   Wednesday?'
'If you weren't so busy chasing your tail you might be able to
   take your head out from up your arse and notice what's
   going on.'
'I'm going for a walk.'

Proactives plan, do and prepare for the future. Reactives react, deal
with things as they arise and live in the now. One is not better than
the other, both have their advantages and disadvantages.

Proactivity:
• Produces vision and leadership.
• Can cause one to step on other people's toes.
• Leaves you perched on the edge of your seat.

Reactivity:
• Produces spontaneity and the ability to solve problems.
• Can cause hesitation and stress.
• Forces you to stay stuck in it sometimes.

If both proactive and reactive preferences can accommodate one
another the result is perfection. In truth you are most likely
somewhere in between the two.

   Cian gets up in the morning and has his day planned out from
the day before: where he is going, what he's doing and stuff like that
because he is being proactive. So he is a planner in that way, he tends
to set up his morning, set up his day and just goes after it. He has all
of the detail in it. That's being very proactive; most people say that's

a great thing. NLP is designed to make you more proactive or to use more proactive programs more often. Because we like to compare and contrast things we are often guilty of saying reactivity must be wrong. Well it's not. You put a proactive person in a reactive situation and you've got mayhem.

Dylan is more reactive in certain areas than Cian. If you ask him what time he will be getting up at tomorrow and it is not a school day he is likely to tell you that he doesn't know. If you ask him is he going into town to meet his mates he will probably say yes. If you ask him what time he most likely will go into town he will say he doesn't know yet. He will get up when he feels like it and he will find out when he is going to town when one of his mates suggests a meeting time. Then he will shower in plenty of time (at the last minute) to get the bus and if he misses it he will just text the lads. There is no big deal, everything doesn't have to be planned out. Then he will be home later but it might be earlier depending on whether there is much happening in town. Dylan is a chip off the old block. But as he says, he is rarely in a bad mood and one of the reasons is that he doesn't sweat the small stuff. Plans and schedules are boring to him. He likes spontaneity, he is creative and why would you have it any other way?

When it comes to study though, he does plan it and is proactive, which helps him achieve As in his exams. This is what is known as flipping your meta programs and is captured in the phrase 'a change is as good as a rest'. This is an example of people running both programs in different contexts. My question to you is this: Would you have thought that Dylan would have done so well in school if you judged him on the basis of the story describing his weekend behaviour?

In life, it is pretty obvious that you need to plan for some things. Dylan needs to plan for his future. You and I need to plan how to pay our bills and so on. We all need to plan and that can include planning to be proactive about being reactive because that's what the reactive person does. The reactive person is driven to be proactive by circumstance. The proactive person tends to need to sit down and learn how to be reactive. Do you get the idea?

Those of you that would consider yourselves mostly reactive might have noticed that when you are planning things you never seem to have enough time. So when you are doing your plan, try planning it as though you are organising it for someone else, because otherwise you'll lower the standard. You think you are more proficient than anybody else, that you'll do your best and give it everything but the reality is time doesn't let you do that so if something takes an hour to do, give yourself an hour and twenty minutes to do it. Because something will likely come up.

When this happens to a reactive person they get pulled from Billy to Jack and they get unfocused, they want to get this done and that done and the other done and as result everything gets done under intense pressure. You are now starting to plan for your reactivity just as much as you are reacting to your plan. This is where you flip your meta programs and get more freedom because of your flexibility.

Sameness Versus Difference

I grew up in a recession so money was not as freely available as one might have liked. My Dad was a building contractor and quite a successful one at that. When he came home from work he always sat in the same armchair. He even had a thing called Daddy's mug (not referring to his face!), which would be set out on the table in his usual place on what was known as Daddy's side of the table. He even had his own butter (we were left to endure a particular brand of margarine, which tasted to me as if it was unfit for human consumption and in my opinion ought to have been blooming banned).

Are you a little like my Dad? Do you have your favourite chair that you like to sit on when you come home from being out? Are you one of those people who when taking the bus will always choose to sit pretty much in the same place if it is available? When you go out for a meal, do you like to go to the same restaurant or the same type of restaurant and do you mostly eat the same type of food? Would it irritate you if someone was sitting on *your* sunlounger in *your* spot by the pool when you are on your two-week holiday? Are you a bit territorial like that? If you are, chances are you like sorting by sameness. If someone shifts your stuff around in work, even if it is with the intention of helping you, does it do your head in? Do you have a place for everything and believe everything has its place? Do you not see the point of changing things around most of the time? Do you feel that if it's not broken don't fix it? Do you think that people would be better off leaving things alone? If you do, chances are now even stronger that you like to sort by sameness.

People that sort by sameness do not like change, they would prefer it if things would remain the same. They like routine and believe change should be by natural and gradual evolution rather than by a major revolutionary overhaul. One step at a time, baby steps, gradual changes; that is their preference as the opposite laces them with anxiety and overwhelms them with fear.

Although they only reluctantly accept major change they are likely to make a few major changes in their lifetime. This tolerance for change varies, some people will accept it once a year, and some people every five to seven years and others once every fifteen to twenty-five years. You will know these people by their employment history. If they choose a job for life, they are sorting by sameness. If they move around a lot, but the jobs they do are still pretty much the same in nature, they sort by sameness. If you ask them to compare one thing with another and they speak in terms of how this is similar to that, or this is the same as that, or the other is just more of the same, then you can be certain that their preference in each of those contexts is for sameness.

My Mum always taught us that it is nice to be different. In my case her lesson worked. My Mum was simply expressing her own preference for difference. That was and is her way. It worked for her and because it worked so well she expressed that fact to us repeatedly and for that I learned how to sort for difference. It continues to work for me in a myriad of different ways, however, now I have the benefit of knowing that it is a preference. There are other options available which are no better or worse, just different or in this case they are just the same.

If you love change, if you embrace it with open arms, if you adore the idea of turning things upside down and starting all over and getting a new perspective, chances are you are sorting by difference. If you get bored quickly and want to be doing new things all the time, if you like to try out new experiences often, if you go to the supermarket and try out the new brand of washing powder because it is something different, if you walk into a shop and notice a new bar on the shelf and feel compelled or attracted to taste it just because you never have, then you are sorting by difference. If you like to go to new places, new restaurants and new countries and try out new tastes, new experiences and new sensations, then you are most certainly sorting by difference.

If you are the type of person that gets bored doing the same task over and over again, it means you are in the wrong job and it is time to look for something different. You should look for a job that has lots of different things in it, so that your day is not predictable or subject to routine and so your day is not bound by rigidly enforced rules, regulations, formats and procedures. You most likely will embrace autonomy and unpredictability, but most of all variety. So your route to happiness is to work in accordance with your sorting preference. This will keep you motivated and out of harm's way.

In the context of a romantic relationship, people are usually attracted to their mate or partner because they are not like them. They exhibit qualities and attributes that they would like to have or just like to appreciate. Unfortunately then for most of the duration of the relationship they actively work on trying to make their partner become like them – to see things through their eyes, to do things as they do, to be as they are. Then they wonder why they get so bored, irritated or fed up with their partners. Relationships work, teams work, life works because of the diversity that is in it. One person can't be perfect but a couple can get pretty close to it. Meta programs make life interesting and when you learn yours and others' life can be more fun. If you decide that it's your way or the highway, then things can only get messy. I think my Mum was right, it is nice to be different, not essential just nice.

Towards Versus Away From

Are you motivated by pain or pleasure? Some people are motivated *towards the fun, enjoyment or pleasure* that their life experiences will give them and some people think first about what is likely to go wrong and are motivated to move *away from pain* to avoid the things that will cause them grief or hardship. These two approaches are very different and although we all want to have good things in our life, this is a question of what trigger is first activated in order to get you motivated. This is what is known as 'the carrot or the stick' approach in business.

If you are kicked into action by the thoughts of being late for work. If you do those reports because if you don't there will be hell to pay. If you do as you're told because you want to avoid getting an earful. Then chances are you are moving away from pain. If you hear yourself saying 'anything for a peaceful life' then you know you are operating an away from meta program. If you think of the worst case scenario first, if you concern yourself with what could go wrong, might go wrong and ought to be avoided, then you are most definitely moving away from pain. If you notice and focus on the problem long before you come up with the solution, then you are moving away from pain.

On the other hand, if you get out of bed because you have lots on, things to do and people to see and are in general looking forward to what the day will bring, then you are moving towards pleasure. If when you set out on a project you think of all the benefits that you will gain from it, then you are moving towards pleasure. If in general you make your mind up about things because of what you will get, gain, achieve and experience, then you are moving towards pleasure. If you anticipate the solution before you examine the problem, then you are moving towards pleasure.

You might well ask why it is useful to know this. Once you learn which trigger motivates first (because in truth we are all seeking more pleasure), then you can work this to your advantage. If you are struggling to get others to do something, once you learn their meta program, you can present it to them in a way that's more persuasive. For example, if you want to get your children to do their homework you can approach it in one of two ways:

- If a child is motivated towards pleasure: 'If you do your homework then you can watch the movie.'
- If a child is motivated away from pain: 'If you don't do your homework, I am not letting you watch the movie.'

Knowing the 'right' way will make all the difference.

Self Versus Other

Does the world revolve around you or are there others in it too?

Do you know of anyone who buys you presents that are more suited to their personal tastes and needs than to yours? For example, they may buy you an ornament for your home which you would never display but you know that if you visited their home you could expect that very type of ornament to be centre stage in their sitting room. The person doing this is most likely sorting by self – if it works for me, then it is bound to work for you.

This demonstrates an extreme lack of sensory acuity. 'I saw this in the store and I really liked it so I bought it. Here Happy Christmas.' Whoops. Not really on the mark. A person whose attention direction is on self will not notice your facial or gestural responses to receiving the gift, they will be convinced by what you say. If you say it is lovely, they will believe you because this is how they interpret the world. The world of body language is outside their awareness, so cynicism, sarcasm, tonal shifts, body slouches, grimaces are not part of their repertoire of understanding. They go by what you tell them and the rest quite literally goes over their heads. 'Well you said you liked it, so how was I supposed to know? I am not a mind reader you know? Why didn't you tell me you don't like garden gnomes? That way I wouldn't have been buying you one every year for the past twenty years. Anyway what's wrong with garden gnomes? I think they're beautiful. They brighten up my garden, I have loads, I've been collecting them for years.'

I remember sitting at a table for lunch in a hotel and watching my wife go to the counter to catch a waiter's attention. We had already been left waiting for around twenty minutes and I was delivering a seminar in the hotel and had a tight turnaround time to get ready for the afternoon session. As she approached the counter the waiter ignored her and kept working on folding napkins. When Theresa said, 'Excuse me,' he continued to ignore her. The second time she said it he looked up, expressionless and responded, 'I will be with you when I have finished this.' There was no one else in the restaurant, and this guy was doing what he had decided was important, his attention was obviously on self. This was a red rag to Theresa, who naturally sorts by other, and she insisted that he serve us immediately. He did because he had finished and he remained expressionless, no word of apology, no recognition of any wrongdoing, he robotically took our order and delivered it without as much as a by-your-leave. You can imagine how lunch went for both of us. This guy was never meant to be in the front end of the service industry.

Ever met a surgeon who appeared completely indifferent to your responses when she said that either you or someone belonging to you had a serious illness? If you were astounded by the surgeon's lack of tact in handling the situation, you are more than likely sorting by other. If any of the previous text resonated with you, you are most likely sorting by other. If you fail to understand how people cannot see when they are being manipulated, then you sort by other. If you tend to be animated when you talk and become absorbed and fully engaged using head nods and affirming sounds when in conversation (unless you have been trained specifically to do so), you are sorting by other. If you think it is imperative that you establish rapport with people, your attention direction is other. When little Cian said to me, 'I can see you are angry Dad . . .' he was reading my face, he was sorting by other.

Sorting Preferences Indicator Questionnaire

The following questionnaire will give you an indication of your psychological sorting preferences, use it and then get your partner's, friends' and work colleagues' opinions on it. Afterwards invite them to use it too and then enjoy exploring its relevance and accuracy. Have fun, you will learn lots.

Global – Detail
When looking for information do you find it irritating when people give you more detail than you asked for? (G)
When looking for information do you find the more detail the better? (D)
If you are asked about a movie that you went to recently are you likely to just give the person a general overview of the basic idea of what the movie was about with a handful of details thrown in? (G)
If you are asked about a movie that you went to recently do you think it only proper that you answer the question correctly and supply as much information about the genre, the actors, the events as they unfolded and your opinion and perhaps the opinion of the people that went with you? (D)
Do you think that sometimes you just have to get on with things and not be so preoccupied with knowing everything in advance? (G)
Before you make a decision do you think it is important that you gather as much detailed information as possible? (D)

Towards (Pleasure) – Away (from Pain)

What usually goes through your head first thing in the morning when you have to get up out of bed?

- Oh man I wonder what crap they will throw at me today. (AFP)
- As soon as I am up the first thing I am going to do is take a lovely shower and fix myself a nice breakfast that way the day will go well. (TP)
- I had better get up soon or I will be in trouble. (AFP)
- Oh great, today I have lots on and I get to go shopping later, love it. (TP)

When setting out on a project do you tend to watch out in particular for what could possibly go wrong? (AFP)

When making important decisions do you tend to get so excited by the benefits that you sometimes just fail to see the shortcomings? (TP)

Proactive – Reactive

When it comes to the weekend or to your holidays or even your working week in general:

- Do you like to have it planned out so as you know what is going to be happening from day to day? (P)
- Do you prefer to just wait and see what the day throws at you first? (R)

Do you have your own personal organiser, a diary or a planner that you like to use often? (P)

Do you get accused of leaving a lot of things to the last minute? (R)

Do you believe that if you fail to plan you plan to fail? (P)

Do you find that there is so much to do that it is easy to become distracted? (R)

Do you usually just get stuck in rather than waiting for someone else to make the call? (P)

Do you prefer to find out what is expected of you before you dive straight in? (R)

Sameness – Difference

When it comes to choosing or going out to a restaurant or going on holidays:

- Do you like to go to your favourite place as often as possible? (S)
- Do you like to choose somewhere new each time? (D)

When eating out do you usually tend to stick with a few dishes that you know you like and can trust? (S)
When eating out do you like to go for something on the menu that you haven't tasted before? (D)
On holidays do you go to the same place or the same type of place each time? (S)
Do you think holidays are a lot about seeking out new places, new locations, new adventures and fresh experiences? (D)

Self – Other

If a work colleague asks you a question do you think it is important to simply answer as briefly as possible so that you can get on with things? (S)
If a work colleague asks you a question do you like to answer the question in the way you know he will be most happy with? (O)
Do you feel that personal feedback from others is not that important because you know yourself when you have done a good job? (S)
Do you think the human touch is important and you like to hear from others that you are doing a good job? (O)
Do you consider yourself to be a people person? (O)
Do you occasionally get accused of being insensitive, cold or distant when all you are doing is working? (S)

CHAPTER 13

The Seven Pillars of Happiness

What doesn't kill you makes you stranger.
Heath Ledger as 'The Joker' in the Batman movie
The Dark Knight

Identifying Your Hierarchy of Values

So far you have been exploring and reading about the things that create and shape who you are as a person. The things that make you feel significant and validated. The things that make you feel good, the things that give you confidence, the things that inspire you and the things that motivate you. In earlier exercises when you recorded details about someone who inspired you, you were identifying what is important to you, what matters to you and that is in essence a reflection of your values.

Values are decisions about what is important in your life. Research has proven that if you pay attention to your values then you will be happier, it's as simple as that. The things that are important to you, the things that make you feel better, the things that make you feel empowered, the things that make you feel inspired, the things that make you feel motivated, all of these things that you have been exploring so far point in the direction of what is most important to you in your life, what you look for from life, what you value.

Any person that is happy most of the time, any person that is centred and comfortable in their own skin and anyone that you meet that has their house in order is almost certainly continuously paying attention to their values. Many may not even be consciously aware that they're doing this; it may be that they are simply perpetuating cultural patterns or assuming some traditional social or religious values. All of these things lead to fulfilment and fulfilment is all about making yourself (and the ones you love) happier, more often, more of the time. To ensure that you reach this worthwhile goal we need to dig a little deeper.

Basic Human Fulfilment Drives

Basic human fulfilment drives are the underlying motivations that give rise to things we call values. As human beings we have basic survival needs such as the need to have food, shelter and water and the need to reproduce. Once these needs are satisfied, there remain, in my opinion, seven further basic human needs. The need for *identity*; the need to feel *connected*; the need *to hold ourselves to a standard or code,* which is an expression of our need to feel right; the need *to feel and be free* at certain times; the need for *impact*; the need for *safety*; and the need to demonstrate *competence.* These needs can be explained in the following manner:

- *Identity:* Each of us feels the need to be happy with the person we are.
- *Connection:* Each of us feels the need to be loved and accepted by another person or group.
- *Code:* Each of us feels the need to have a standard that justifies our actions.
- *Freedom:* Each of us feels the need to exercise a certain degree of freedom.
- *Impact:* Each of us needs to feel that what we do counts.
- *Safety:* Each of us feels the need to have a safe place to withdraw from the world.
- *Competence:* Each of us needs to prove that we are really good at something.

The process of transforming these needs into satisfaction produces values. In other words these are the intentions behind your values, and these values are your personal beliefs about what is most important to you. Values govern your levels of motivation and guide your every decision. They are the rules, the principles and the standards that you live by. They reflect your beliefs about what is right and what is wrong, what is good and what is bad. Often these values are unconscious. All of us have values, but each of us assigns different levels of importance to them. Knowing the order of priority that you place on your values empowers you to take more focused action. True happiness and fulfilment can only be achieved if you live in accordance with your values. In life we have two basic directions: to move *towards pleasure* and to move *away from pain*. Knowing what you move away from is just as important as knowing what you move towards, as both actions involve the engagement of your values.

If you have ever experienced a prolonged feeling of dissatisfaction or unhappiness with your life or if you have ever had that feeling of being miserable for no apparent reason, you can be sure that one or more of your basic human fulfilment drives were not being met.

Identity

Time and time again I am approached by mothers who speak about feeling a little lost or useless, they tell me that their children are all grown up now and they are left with time on their hands and they don't know how to fill it. A little further into the conversation I get to hear the usual problem: 'I am so used to being a mum and looking after my children's needs that I have forgotten about my own and now that they are gone I just don't know what to do with myself.' What has happened here is that she has been carrying out the role of 'mum' for so long that she has assumed that role as her identity and then after twenty years or so, when the child leaves the nest, she feels stripped of her purpose. Our identity provides us with a much-needed sense of purpose to our lives, without which we are left in a state of confusion and with a feeling of emptiness or longing.

Our identity is created by the relationships we have and the behaviours we engage in. For example, in this case the lady refers to herself as a mum, she knows she is more than this, however, this is what has absorbed most of her attention and behaviour and as such this is who she describes herself as. In truth we are not our behaviours. In the literal sense she is doing the act of mothering, but she is much more than a mum, she may also be a wife, a friend, a daughter, an artist, a confidante, a party animal, a fun lover, a romantic and whatever else she relates to or identifies with. For twenty years her time has been dominated by one major role, i.e. that of mum, and those other roles took second place to the extent that she got to feel that all she is, is a mum. That situation can be and often is incredibly fulfilling for her and is of her own choosing, however, when she is mostly relieved of that role she needs to build new ones in its place in order to feel whole again.

She may do this by picking up with old friends or nurturing her relationship with her partner or returning to a neglected hobby or starting out in an entirely new area of interest. When this happens, she shines again. She assumes her new identity, feels useful and worthwhile and her levels of confidence and happiness reach new heights.

We often hear tell of men who retire from working life and whose physical and emotional health deteriorates rapidly to the point that shortly afterwards they die. This is no coincidence for a man stripped of his purpose and removed from his social setting can find adapting to the newly arrived lack of structure and isolation so overwhelming that his spirit dies and his body merely catches up a short while later. Work provided him with that sense of identity, that sense of purpose and the much-needed social setting where he felt he belonged. Once that was removed, his world literally fell apart.

Attitude has a powerful effect on our life force. We need only look at the statistics for the amount of heart attacks that occur on a Monday morning to know that how we feel about what we do can mean the difference between life and death. For this reason these things are so vital to keep track of and get in order. As human beings we need structure and a purpose to give us a sense of identity. When that is gone we are in perilous waters. Research continually demonstrates that profound personality changes occur with the unemployed when force or circumstance removes them from their jobs and leaves them without a sense of purpose. The gangs on the street that wreak havoc and pain do so on purpose and for a purpose. The connection to their group gives them a sense of self-worth and that drive is so compelling that they will inflict pain on others so that they can meet their basic human fulfilment drives.

We all need to belong to something or someone, we all need to know who we are and have that validated, we all need to show we are good at something and be recognised for it, we all need somewhere to feel safe and we all need to feel that what we are doing is valued and be shown respect for it. The longing, the yearning, the emptiness that human beings feel is simply the lack of any or all of these things. You are conditioned to meet your needs, you can do it unconsciously or consciously. I like the idea of doing it both ways so you get to be more accurate, you get to be more certain, you are the architect of your own destiny.

I would like you to do the following brainstorming exercise right now. Using the opening words 'I am . . .' write down without censorship whatever comes into your head. For example, if it was me I would write: I am a writer, I am a father, I am a husband, I am a friend, I am a trainer, I am a mind coach, I am a thinker, I am passionate, I am focused, I am driven, I am inspired, I am a son, I am a brother, I am a learner, I am a fighter, I am Irish, I am a survivor, I am what I am, I think I am all that I am, I am energised . . . This is just what came to mind in the moment. I am sure I am much more than this but for now I am bringing to mind the things that are nearest to the surface of my consciousness. Now I would like you to do the same.

Once you have that exercise done, I would like to you to repeat the exercise using the phrase 'I want . . .'. For example, I want to be fit, I want to be happier, I want to be healthy, I want to be rich, I want to be inspiring, I want to be really good at what I do, I want to be able to change people, I want to be having fun, I want to be a great dad, I want to be interesting, I want to be full of life, I want . . . Now it's your turn.

Present: Who are you?

_____
_____
_____
_____
_____
_____
_____

Desired: Who do you want to be?

_____
_____
_____
_____
_____
_____

Action: What has to happen for that to happen?

_____
_____
_____
_____
_____
_____
_____

Connection

Human beings are herd-like; they need to belong to a group, a sect, an organisation, a cause, a family, a religion, a something. Every one of us searches for a reference group, or a reference person. Everybody wants to belong to something or somewhere or someone, everybody wants to be connected in some way as it gives us that all-important sense of being okay, of being right, of being loved and above all of not being alone to face the world.

You can be sure that no matter how bizarre the behaviour of certain people, no matter how outside your own terms of reference their behaviour and actions are, you will find that somewhere along the line they belong to a group, an organisation or a set of ideas. Somewhere they will find that sense of connection and belonging, somewhere they feel that their behaviours or actions receive acknowledgment, justification and approval.

This process becomes more acutely evident when a switch occurs. Say, for example, when someone decides to trade one reference group for another, like in a relationship. It is not at all uncommon for a person choosing to leave or trade in one relationship for another to demonise the person being left. I have seen this many times during my client sessions. A client can present with feelings of guilt about being unfaithful in a relationship and go on to blame their soon to be ex-partner for failing to meet their needs. With a little space they begin to highlight all their partner's failings and shortcomings by way of justifying their reasons for leaving. Over time they build up their case. When they break the news or get found out, their partner reacts in a highly emotional way and gets justifiably angry. They act like a cornered animal and wreak havoc and revenge on the perpetrator – their world has been pulled apart in terms of their identity, connection, impact, security and competence.

Every action now becomes an endorsement for the case against them. Before long, resentment builds and the individual can't remember what they saw in that person in the first place. It's like they 'must have been in a dream' but they can see the light of day now and they leave in the 'fairest way that they can' because they 'really are a good person, it's just that it didn't work out for them'. They were in a dream, a trance of sorts, one that worked for a while and served their needs. They are deciding to trade one trance for another one with another person who they have decided will meet their pressing needs, which is why many second relationships fail to reach the heights of the first. Some do, but only the ones where real change takes place. Few people really change, they just trade trance partners and settle rather than undergo the upheaval of the first again.

I have witnessed both sides of so many relationship break-ups and their consequences that it makes me wonder how many would have survived with a deliberate change of focus. What would happen if every time you saw a failing in a person you took note of a quality too? It is so easy to demonise but it can be so worthwhile to see what is not shining so brightly in times of challenge. I often say that when you are in a bad mood treat your loved ones as you would a stranger, just be courteous and give them the time of day until you are better able to respond in a more loving and caring way.

Take a moment to think about your connections and relationships. Who do you like being with? Who do you want to connect with? Write your answers in the panel on page 230.

Code

No matter what behaviour we engage in, no matter what we do in life, each of us feels the need to have a standard that justifies our actions. Whether it is the criminal who murders someone, the husband who batters his wife or the businesswoman who rips off her client, each and every person will refer back to a personal standard, a rule, a principle, a cause, a reason for doing what they did. Often you will hear the phrase 'I did it *because*' in their justifications. The word 'because' may be absent but it is always inferred. The criminal murdered *because* 'it was either him or me' (the standard being to stay alive at all costs). The husband battered his wife *because* in his warped logic she was 'asking for it' (the rule being

Present: Who do you like being with?

_____

_____

_____

_____

_____

_____

_____

Desired: Who do you want to connect with?

_____

_____

_____

_____

_____

Action: What has to happen for that to happen?

_____

_____

_____

_____

_____

_____

no one speaks to me disrespectfully. I am the king in my own castle and I rule with an iron fist.) The businesswoman ripped off the client *because* 'it's a dog eat dog world' (the principle being 'you've got to get them before they get you').

The converse is also true. The priest adopts his god's rules and internalises them to justify his actions. This code becomes his modus operandi. The child internalises her parents' values and they become her rules as an adult. The politician adopts the party line and that becomes his justification for action. The important question here is whose rules do you want to live by anyway? I know whose rules works best for me. How about you?

Here are some of my rules. This is part of the code that runs in the background of my everyday interactions with life.

- I believe that what goes around comes around.
- I believe that everyone is my equal.
- I believe that honesty is the best policy.
- I believe that if it's worth doing it's worth doing well.
- I believe that you can't take life too seriously.
- I believe that most people are essentially good.
- I believe that whatever is for you won't pass you by.
- I believe that there is always a choice.

What do you believe? What is your code? What are your standards? What is your modus operandi? What are the rules that you hold to be self-evident? Jot down your answers on page 232.

Freedom

Although it would appear natural to want to be free, the truth is that with total freedom comes great uncertainty. As human beings we seek certainty. We like to be certain that our loved ones will always be there for us. We like the idea of knowing how the future is likely to pan out. We like to know that we have a home to go to. In short, we feel safe when we attach to things. Total freedom would necessitate the absence of these things and as such we choose to give up many of our freedoms. When we set up communities and decide

Present: What do you believe now?

_____

_____

_____

_____

_____

_____

_____

Desired: What new beliefs do you want to adopt?

_____

_____

_____

_____

_____

Action: What has to happen for that to happen?

_____

_____

_____

_____

_____

_____

Present: Who are you free to be now? What are you free to do now?

_____

_____

_____

_____

_____

_____

_____

Desired: What freedoms are you prepared to embrace?

_____

_____

_____

_____

_____

Action: What has to happen for that to happen?

_____

_____

_____

_____

_____

_____

to live together we subscribe to the idea of the common good and in doing so we give up the freedom to do what we want when we want and how we want. Despite the fact that most of us push in the direction of increasing our levels of personal freedom, few of us, if offered it, would accept the proposition in its totality. Instead we trade some freedoms for the comforting chains of compliance and subjugation.

Impact

Everybody wants to know that what they do counts. Every human being wants to know that their contribution and their efforts amount to something worthwhile. When you hear someone say 'there is no point in working here, nobody listens to a goddamn thing I say' – what they are actually saying is that they don't feel they are having an impact. Everyone needs that sense of control, that sense of knowing that they can control their own environment and that what they do matters, what they do counts. I am sure you have heard of people leaving their jobs because they believe they are not being listened to or taken seriously. This is all about their need to have an impact on their surroundings. People leave relationships for the same reasons. What we do gets mixed up with who we are and if we are not doing what we want it threatens our identity and that leads to dissatisfaction. Use the panel opposite to note down where you have the most impact now and where you would like to have the most impact.

Safety

You need a place to retreat from the world. Every human being needs it whether through prayer, meditation, reflection or simply having a bath. You might get it from going for a walk by yourself or closing your eyes and going to sleep. Everybody needs to know and feel that they can step away from the big, bad world at times to somewhere safe. One of the safest places is trance, that's why we use it a lot. What activities create safety for you? What new activities could enhance that experience? Write your answers in the panel on page 236.

Present: Where do you have the most impact currently?

_____

_____

_____

_____

_____

_____

Desired: Where would you like to have maximum impact?

_____

_____

_____

_____

_____

_____

Action: What has to happen for that to happen?

_____

_____

_____

_____

_____

_____

Present: What activities create safety for you?

_____

_____

_____

_____

_____

_____

_____

Desired: What new activities could enhance that experience?

_____

_____

_____

_____

_____

_____

Action: What has to happen for that to happen?

_____

_____

_____

_____

_____

_____

Competence

Buckminster Fuller talks about the fact that each of us needs to demonstrate that we are particularly good at something.

Very often when you speak to people who are carrying out what others would deem to be menial, unchallenging, repetitive jobs you find that many of them simply get their kicks elsewhere. All of us strive to meet our needs and it is not uncommon for us to accept positions, jobs and roles on the basis that the bills get paid, or for the social network that exists there. There are lots of well-founded reasons for accepting all sorts of jobs, however, if the job does not satisfy the need to demonstrate competence you will find that the need gets filled elsewhere.

For example, take a person who works on a production line in a factory and who considers the job to be boring. If you probe a little deeper into her life, you might find that she is consumed by a driving passion for music, dogs or some form of hobby that keeps her motivated and provides her with the outlet of being able to demonstrate her knowledge, ability and competence in a particular area. She may be an avid musician, marathon runner or fishing enthusiast, but ultimately you will find that she has something really good going on that she finds important and where she demonstrates competence.

Families work that way too, that's why family members often reject their parent and sibling group because they feel they are not being endorsed by it. They go somewhere else, to another group, to demonstrate that they are actually competent at something else. Sometimes they even create their own family and that gives them validation and recognition. Whatever your choice in this matter, it will seek to have your needs met. Many of the arguments that happen at family get-togethers are about this underlying fact and many a life has been shaped in response to it too. Take a moment to think about what you are really good at now and what you would like to get better at.

Present: What are you really good at now?

_____

_____

_____

_____

_____

_____

_____

Desired: What would you like to get better at?

_____

_____

_____

_____

_____

_____

Action: What has to happen for that to happen?

_____

_____

_____

_____

_____

_____

_____

CHAPTER 14

Making Every Moment Count

Happiness is that state of consciousness which proceeds from the achievement of one's values.

Ayn Rand

Operational Values Versus Aspirational Values

It is now time to pin your colours to the mast. I have an exercise that is going to give you a list of values. They are only words, labels that I have chosen to represent types of values. What I am looking for is what is important to you. This is about being clearer, sharper and more specific about what matters most. The more often you pay attention to the most important things, the more likely you are to get the better effect and subsequently be happier and live a fulfilling life.

Values come in different forms, some are called means values. Means values are the things that become important to get or achieve on your way to happiness. These derive from your basic human fulfilment drives, discussed in Chapter 13. Next are the end values. End values are your ultimate target. It's by focusing on these values that you can live a fuller, more successful and happier life. These values can be further broken down into two categories: those which you want and those which you reject.

All of the previous exercises in this book had the purpose of uncovering these values by bringing them into your everyday awareness. Each time you explored the exercises of happiness, reflection, inspiration, appreciation and motivation you were simply bringing to the surface that which resonates within, that which you value. Any time you thought or wrote about someone that is important to you or that inspired or influenced you, you were simply reflecting what is already in you. The world is just a mirror and everything you accept or reject is a reflection of what is already a part of you. To live in accordance with these values you need to increase your life experience of them. This means that if you say that honesty is important to you, that it is something you value, then you need to live it. Otherwise it is simply an aspirational value not a true operational value. Your happiness is dependent on your values becoming operational.

Some of you may think that you already know the things that are important to you. If I asked you whether family is important to you it is pretty likely you would answer yes. Almost everybody will say that. But guess what? It is not truly important if you are not working on it or towards it every single day. It's just an aspiration. It is like the constitution of a country, a statement, a declaration, but not necessarily an actualisation of intent. You could say, 'I love my wife and family.' In fact I could say that too, but am I being loving to my wife and family today or is that just the preserve of evenings and weekends because that's the only shot I get at it? If like me you travel in your job and are away for days on end, do you leave it until you're home to let your family know that you love them? You could be dead tomorrow! Values are only true if they are reflected in your actions.

I have broken down a list of values into two categories, the values that I want to experience and the values that I want to eliminate. This latter group are what I call negative values. They are values that prevent me from being at my best. For example, I believe that deception and bitterness are the birth of all evil. It doesn't matter whether you agree, it's just my version. I believe bitterness produces cancer. So if I sense for a second any bitterness in me I say, 'No way, I'm getting away from that. That's not who I am, that's not who I choose to be, I believe it will kill me.' So that's my rule in my head, that's how I set up my reality.

Making Every Moment Count

I remember Richard Bandler giving a seminar shortly after his wife Paula had passed into spirit and he said, 'I made every moment count and it still wasn't enough.' Richard is a man who squeezes life by the throat to get every last morsel. He lives life to the maximum, so he knows what he is talking about when he offers advice. Thankfully he is in a new relationship now and he's happy again. Richard carries good memories, he's had a beautiful life and a beautiful relationship and he holds that, although in his own mind he is saying I would like to have more. But he can qualify his experience and know at least he is doing his best in every moment. That's what will get him through it.

Even with a fantastic life something can happen so learn to say, 'F**k it, I'm going to make every moment count. I'm going to brighten up.' Remember you can waste years stressing about stuff. Treasure life and go after it, it is that important.

To move away from a value means to reject it in yourself and others. You are saying, for example, I don't accept lies in myself so if I sense I'm going to lie I back away from it or I tell the truth instead. If someone else is lying, well then I'll back off from them.

I also want you to select the things that you want to move towards. Family is one of my top moving towards values, that's what actually makes me feel alive. Family makes me happy, it makes me feel inspired. Now you can say family is not technically a value and you are right, but it's enough to capture a whole concept, it lets me know what is important.

I want you to choose the values that are most important to you. Values that you want more than just to aspire to, values that you want to bring about in your behaviour.

Exercise: Identifying Your Hierarchy of Values

Read through the list and find out what's important for you. Then select at least five positive values and five things that you want to move away from. Add in other values if your choices are not already on the list.

Moving Towards (MT) Values	My MT Values	My MA Values	Moving Away (MA) Values
Achievement			Aggression
Action			Anger
Admiration			Anxiety
Adventure			Bitterness
Ambition			Confusion
Awareness			Corruption
Beauty			Debt
Challenge			Deception
Character			Depression
Cheerfulness			Despair
Children			Distress
Comfort			Emptiness
Communication			Envy
Courage			Failure
Creativity			Fear
Dignity			Frustration
Education			Greed
Empowerment			Guilt
Enjoyment			Hate
Environment			Hostility
Equality			Humiliation
Excellence			Infidelity
Fairness			Insecurity
Family			Jealousy

Finances	Loneliness
Fitness	Manipulation
Flexibility	Negativity
Forgiveness	Nervousness
Freedom	Panic
Friendship	Rage
Fun	Recrimination
Generosity	Remorse
Gratitude	Resentment
Growth	Revenge
Happiness	Sadness
Health	Self-Criticism
Home	Self-Doubt
Honesty	Self-Pity
Honour	Shyness
Imagination	Stubbornness
Integrity	Uncertainty

Exercise: Personal Hierarchy of Values

Now it is time to prioritise your values. Working from your list above, select values in order of importance (i.e. number one being the most important, number two the second-most important and so on). Take your time selecting which is most important, perhaps writing your list out elsewhere a few times and examining it in detail before completing the chart overleaf. Bear in mind that this list will reflect your bottom line. The moving towards values are what you absolutely must have in order to feel fulfilled. So ensure that your needs of identity, connection, impact and security are each catered for. The moving away from values are those things that you will simply not tolerate from yourself or anyone else. You will notice that these work in direct contrast to your needs of identity, connection, impact and security.

243

What I want to attract	What I reject
1	1
2	2
3	3
4	4
5	5

Statements of Clarification

Now define what you mean. For example, let's imagine you chose 'friendship' as your top moving towards value. As friendship is something you'd like to move towards we've got to find out how you define friendship. However you define this is the correct definition because it is your definition. It's not up for judgment, it only needs to be defined for personal clarification, so your brain is clear about what you mean.

You are opening up your brain to say here's the deeper map of that: Mary, Anne, Tom, Jim, Jamie and John are important to me. You see their faces, and you can see that's what you mean by friendship. You've registered the image in your brain as important and the more you remind yourself by looking at the target(s) the more you are drawn towards it. This is all about awakening your senses so you can engage in those feelings and really draw from them, giving you both substance and detail. Having substance makes you feel good so you are already creating what you want.

When I choose 'family', I'll think of my wife and my sons. The hook for me is their smiling faces. You must choose one that fits your experience. Although I am a son, I don't think of my Mum. It doesn't mean my Mum is not important to me but it is not where I spend most of my time, so what I am doing here is an exercise as much in efficiency as in happiness. This is just my definition, yours might be different.

Exercise: Moving Towards Values

Look at each of your moving towards values in turn and write down two or three sentences that give each value substance.

Value 1

_____

_____

_____

_____

_____

_____

Value 2

_____

_____

_____

_____

_____

_____

Value 3

_____

_____

_____

_____

_____

_____

_____

Value 4

_____

_____

_____

_____

_____

_____

_____

Value 5

_____

_____

_____

_____

_____

_____

_____

Exercise: Moving Away From Values

Now look at each of the values you are rejecting and write down two or three sentences about them. Remember moving away from values are qualities in yourself or others that you don't like or accept. My top moving away from values are bitterness and deception. I don't like them in others and I definitely would be disappointed to see them in myself, so if I get as much as a sense of these in myself I immediately shut them down and change direction.

Value 1

_____

_____

_____

_____

_____

_____

Value 2

_____

_____

_____

_____

_____

_____

Value 3

_____

_____

_____

_____

_____

_____

Value 4

_____

_____

_____

_____

_____

Value 5

_____

_____

_____

_____

_____

_____

Once you complete this process you have enough to make your life better. Focus on what you've got and build on it, revisit it, go back to it and ask yourself how you can develop and improve on it. Now that you've tracked what matters and started to recognise that these are the things that you consider of prime importance, you are, by the process of attention, beginning to activate and draw it towards you. Remember you are feeding your unconscious, so flesh it out and make sure you see more of it so you can go there.

Know Your Role

As discussed in Chapter 13, we all play several roles in life. But for all the things that I say or think I am, the true measure of how the world will see me and how I will ultimately see myself will be through the roles that I perform not just some of the time, but most of the time.

We are not all faced with the same choices in life and not all of us get the same opportunities, however, one of the most important things you can do is to make sure that you do what you love more often. Find something that you are good at and do that. Think about how valuable your life is. If you are doing something that you are not really happy with, do something else until you find something that makes you feel happy. It can take a while to get there but do it.

Imagine working in a job for years and years and hating it. Yet many of us do it, we decide that we will do the job because we have to work and pay the bills and that we will do what we love as a hobby. That can work as long as you ensure you are doing what you love as often as you can. This is what makes you happy and if you are happy it doesn't matter whether you are sweeping up the roads, cleaning away someone else's rubbish or working behind a desk.

We only get one shot at life. I remind myself of this each day and try to imagine how I'd feel if I knew it was my last day on earth. Am I living a life worth living? Do I have purpose and live in accordance with what matters most to me? What would I do differently if the gun was to my head? I use this last question and a few others to provoke myself into action. I'd like to invite you to do as I do and ask yourself that question and the ones that follow overleaf.

Exercise: Provoke Yourself into Action

Present: What would you have done differently if a gun was put to your head?

_____

_____

_____

_____

_____

_____

_____

Desired: What could you do now in the light of this?

_____

_____

_____

_____

_____

_____

Action: What has to happen for that to happen?

_____

_____

_____

_____

_____

_____

For me to be happy I need to make sure that my values are met in my primary roles. I have loads of other relationships, I am a son, I am a therapist, I am a coach, but what I'm talking about now are the most important ones, the ones that I spend most of my time in. Because if I operate and express my values in those roles then I get a higher hit rate, I get a higher success rate on the personal happiness or personal fulfilment scales. I want you to identify your main roles. It doesn't mean you don't value your roles in other areas, it just means that they have a different priority and come to the surface less often than your dominant roles.

In the next exercise you will decide what's most important for you and include it as one of your key roles, the place where you spend most of your time. It may well be your job. Whether you like your job is not relevant for now because this exercise may lead to you making the decision to change it when and if you can so that you can increase your overall personal effectiveness. Once you have selected your roles, you go to the next level.

If I say that what's important to me is being a father, then I should think about how I want Dylan and Cian to introduce me or to talk about me when I'm not there. Do I want them to say, 'Dad's great craic, he's great fun, he spends time with me, he's a good friend to me and he's the world's best dad'? Yes. That would mean I am living in accordance with my values, that they are operational and not aspirational. Alternatively, if my children say, 'My Dad works too hard and he's never around, he is always grumpy and he falls asleep on the chair in front of the TV any time he is home', well that is self-explanatory. So if I say being with family is important, the real acid test is how my family experience my lofty claims. Are they just pie in the sky? Am I hitting the target most of the time? If I am, I don't have to worry about looking back when they get older and regretting I wasn't there for them more often.

Another one of my roles is as a mind coach/therapist and it doesn't matter whether *I* think I am good at this job, it's about what my clients say about me and what would they say about me in my absence, because that is more likely to reflect the reality. Do they value the work I do for them? Did they get the results or do they just think I am a nice guy? I would like to think that I am a nice guy, but what is of more value to me is that I am an effective one, meaning that I get the results irrespective of what the client thinks of my personality. I want every person that comes in contact with me to say, 'Brian is a really sound guy, he's very skilled, competent and efficient, if you go to him he will get the job done.'

Exercise: The Roles I Play

A role is a function that you serve in life. Roles represent your key relationships and responsibilities. You can bring a sense of order into your activities by separating the different areas of your life that require attention into roles. All of us play several different roles, and sometimes we play more than one role at a time. For example, I can be a father and a husband at the same time.

The manner in which we define our roles can help us to maintain balance, and increase our effectiveness in life. Please read through the chart opposite and identify only your *most important roles*, both professional and personal, and then rank them in order of priority. Select no more than five. I have provided a list but it is by no means exhaustive so feel free to add your own roles.

My key roles

_____

_____

_____

_____

_____

Sample Roles	My Roles	Sample Roles
Advisor		Homemaker
Aunt		Husband
Breadwinner		Instructor
Brother		Manager
Care Giver		Mother
Coach		Partner
Companion		Salesperson
Counsellor		Self
Daughter		Sister
Director		Student
Employee		Therapist
Facilitator		Trainer
Father		Uncle
Friend		Volunteer
Grandparent		Wife

Key People and Tribute Statements

From the roles that you have identified, you now need to identify your key people. A key person is someone who is directly affected by your performance in a particular role. If, for example, you are a manager, your key people in that role will be the people on your team. Your key people will usually come from your family, friends and work colleagues.

For each key person, you will need to produce a 'tribute statement'. A tribute statement is an account of something you would want a key person to say about you as you perform a particular role. Generally it will reflect the key person's own values, in other words what is more specifically important to them rather than what is important to you, although you can expect some considerable overlap in order for it to reflect your values on some level.

Here's an example for a father.

Role: Father	Key Person: Dylan and Cian

Tribute Statement: Dad is great fun to be with; he spends lots of time with me.
He treats me fairly, helps me, and makes me feel good, happy, confident and proud.
He praises and encourages me. He is the world's best dad.

Exercise: My Key People and Tribute Statements

Role:	Key Person:

Tribute Statement:

_____

_____

_____

_____

_____

_____

Role:	Key Person:

Tribute Statement:

_____

_____

_____

_____

_____

_____

Role: **Key Person:**

Tribute Statement:

_____
_____
_____
_____
_____
_____

Role: **Key Person:**

Tribute Statement:

_____
_____
_____
_____
_____
_____

Role: **Key Person:**

Tribute Statement:

_____
_____
_____
_____
_____
_____

Mind Technique: Succeeding in Your Roles

Now I want you to recall your roles and imagine that you're sitting at the head of a round table. As you look at the centre surface of the table you see in large, bold writing: **100%**. Now as you are doing that think of your roles: mother, daughter, teacher, friend etc. Select your five key roles. I want you to see another five versions of you arriving to sit with you at that same table. There you are as a mother, a daughter, a friend, a colleague etc. Each one of those five roles wants 100 per cent of your time. But you know you've only got 100 per cent, so you need to allocate how much each of the five can have. Some of the roles cross over and run at the same time but that doesn't matter. Designate in percentage terms how much time each role is worth giving.

You have only 100 per cent. Take your time and as soon as you've got the percentages sorted out write them down against your roles in the chart provided. You might choose to do this more than once. It doesn't have to be perfect yet. Once you've written them down, translate the percentages into hours of the day (24) and hours in the week (168). Check your calculations and determine if the figures are feasible, remembering to leave time for sleep! It's not so important yet to have it absolutely accurate, that can take a little time and some trial and error. For now, just sign up to the idea. Once you have the calculations, run with them for at least a few weeks. Decide now when you are going to re-evaluate because your life will always be a work in progress. You need to tweak things every now and then because stuff changes.

Give it enough time and then evaluate if the current time divisions are improving your happiness. If not, you need to adjust percentages somewhere. It's up to you what you choose to do. That way you already know how much you are deciding to improve so be sure to make it real and worthwhile – if it was too much you wouldn't commit to it so make it enough so that you know in your heart and soul that it is possible and this is the time to go do it really well.

It may take time to make up the difference but isn't that what it's always been about: moving from your present state of existence to your desired set of circumstances. You know what has to be so if there's a gap there you have to change it. Your time for yourself needs to be very specific as well. In a lot of other roles you are not actually paying attention to yourself as such, so you should give yourself time each week to focus on you.

Take the following steps to complete the role management chart overleaf:

1. Insert your five key roles in the spaces provided.
2. Assign a percentage of your time for each role.
3. Translate this figure into hours per day/week.
4. Try this out for a week and review and alter the figures if necessary.

There are two charts to assist you with this process. The first, your Personal Role Management Technique, will give you the big picture overview of your life. Following from that I suggest you complete the next chart, your Professional Role Management Technique, which will help you to manage both your time and your priorities at work.

Role Management Technique – Personal Sample

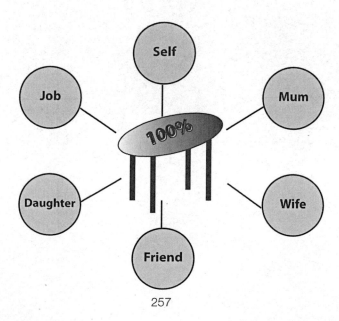

Role Management Technique – Personal

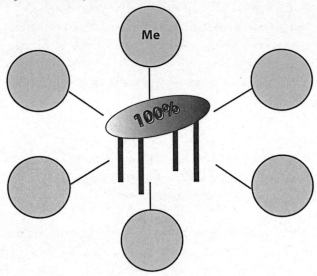

Role Management Technique – Professional Sample

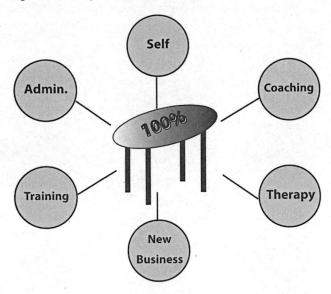

Role Management Technique – Professional

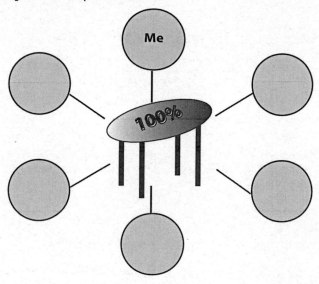

CHAPTER 15

The Secret Art of Living a Happy Life

To succeed in life you need three things: a wishbone, a backbone and a funny bone.

Reba McIntyre

Bio-Imprinting – Getting Done What Counts

Congratulations on taking the time and effort to look at your life more closely. You have almost completed your journey. You now have the skills, the ability, the direction and the focus to sustain the habit of happiness in your life.

This leaves you with one final exercise. I want you to pull all of this together. You can go back through your notes or even back through your thoughts to do it. This is about generating a template, a system, a little process that you can call upon whenever you want. This will be the future reference template that will act as a reminder for what you're all about. In times of challenge, if your thinking is not as clear as you want it to be, you can pick up this document and remind yourself of what is most important. This is what matters most; this is what you want to move towards. You can remind yourself that these are the standards you have set for yourself. You can say to yourself: this is who I choose to be. These are the people that are important to me. This is how I raise my mood. This is how I raise my game. This is the better me, the one that I am when I am at my very best. This is who I am and what I choose to project. This template is called your Bio-Imprint Statement.

I want you to read through what you've already done. Give

yourself the time to gather the information together. There are some guidelines and a template below for you, so that you can do it easily, clearly, effortlessly and naturally. Once you've written what's truly important to you in a more focused and concise way you'll be able to look back in time and say, 'If I want to find out how to feel good, if I want to remember how to continue to feel good, all I need to do is read the recipe.'

Create it so that you can read it in thirty seconds because in times of great challenge that's your time to pick it up and have a look at it. This is your map for happiness. Find a place to post it or display it. Put it somewhere where you can remind yourself often. If you choose, you can create a vision board and attach it to that.

A vision wall or board is simply a wall space that you set aside to fill with post-its, reminders and pictures of your goals, desires and dreams. For example, if you wanted to get back into shape, you might put a photo on it of yourself from a time when you were in excellent shape to look at and remind yourself each day of your goal. There are no strict rules to vision boards just create it in a way that works to inspire and motivate you. Remember the things that we are not reminded about are the things that we can do little about. Let this be your bible so to speak. Let these be the commandments that you live by. Let this be the document that defines you. Let this be filled with the source of your life's purpose.

Knowing what you want and what matters to you is crucial for success. Knowing how to get there is also critical. However, making the time to get there is the difference that will make the difference. When it comes to managing your time and organising your life, you won't get everything done so it is important then that you get done what counts.

In order to master your time rather than having it master you, you have to have a master plan. Your master plan is your Bio-Imprint Statement. Your Bio-Imprint Statement is in effect an overview of your life.

The question to keep in mind is: When all is said and done, when all my time is spent, what do I want to have achieved, what do I want to have done with my life? It is the answer to this question that needs to become the driver, the motivational force that shapes, creates and dictates how you respond to life and how you react to each presenting moment. Your Bio-Imprint Statement becomes your overall objective and will lead you to not only be more effective at time management but also to lead a happier life.

To help you on your way let me remind you of what needs to be included in your Bio-Imprint Statement:

Know What Matters Most

Before you craft your plan you have got to decide what and who matters most in your life. Who are the most important people? What are the most important things to get done? What do you want to have achieved by the end of your life?

Know Your Goals

Knowing what and who matters most will give substance to your goals. Once you decide what you want to do, when you want to do it and with whom you want to achieve it, then you are on your way.

Know Your Roles

This is a key and critical part of time management. It will determine your overall effectiveness. Whatever your plans are, whatever your goals are, they will amount to nothing unless you are in a position to execute them. Your time is spent carrying out certain roles. It is where you spend most of your time that will decide whether you achieve your goals. For you to have a workable plan you need to define this and then assign time to each role. Obviously this is not an exact science and there will be overlaps but the process of assigning times to it will keep your mind focused and your eye on the ball.

Know Your Relationships

Your roles can also be your key relationships, they might not always be the same but you need to define them one way or the other. For example, my key relationships as a father are with my two sons. For me to succeed I need to have specific plans for each of my sons. I need to ask myself questions like: What would I want Dylan and Cian to say about me if they were to talk about me to their friends? This means that I factor their values into my goals and that becomes a sure-fire model for success.

Know the Route

Your Bio-Imprint Statement needs to be properly aligned. You know you cannot do everything at once, you know that different things will crop up on a daily basis and you know even the best-made plans are bound to change. You need to keep one eye firmly on the present and another on the future so that each action and each reaction to every moment of every day is done with your higher purpose in mind, that way you are in a position to make effective decisions.

Write It Down

The most effective time managers write it down. Write it down. Write it down. Write it down. I cannot be more explicit than that. Once you write your goals down, you free up your mind for more stuff. You in effect instruct your mind to achieve and you are less likely to forget it or overlook it and end up with egg on your face as a result of it.

Do What You Can

You and I both know that life can put you to the test time and time again. No sooner have you climbed one mountain but the next one appears. No sooner have you put one challenge behind you but the next one comes rolling in. There are times that I think that somebody is just having a laugh, that the universe is deliberately conspiring against me. On my better days I choose to think that this is simply nature's way of ensuring that we remain on top of the evolutionary pecking order and that each challenge helps to make me stronger.

One thing for certain is that there are and will be challenges in your life and it is how you respond to each challenge that comes your way that will define and shape your character. In times of challenge I use a question that was taught to me and that has saved my life many times over. In my opinion it is one of the best questions to ask yourself when you are trying to get through. That question is:

WHAT'S THE MOST *USEFUL* THING TO DO NOW?

The beauty of this question is that it sends you in the right direction. It is worth noting that I said what is the most *useful* thing to do, not what do I want to do, not what is the best thing to do, not what should I do, but what is the most *useful* thing to do. This question is qualitatively different from the others in that it removes the emotional charge behind your actions and gives you some perspective so that you can step away from your feelings a little and not be bound by a knee-jerk or an emotionally fuelled response.

Often the most useful thing to do works out to be the best thing to do. The next time you are being challenged face it head on and ask yourself 'What is the most *useful* thing to do?' and as your actions are informed keep asking that same question until you are finding it is getting you through to the other side of that particular dilemma or challenge.

Opposite you will see a copy of my Bio-Imprint Statement, have a read through it and then prepare your own statement. Once you have your plan, you are ready to act. You are now ready to move from the big picture to the smaller detail. You are now in a better position to face daily challenges. Your Bio-Imprint Statement can be the barometer that you can check every moment against, now that you are aligned for success.

An A4 template of the Bio-Imprint Statement is available for free download at www.briancolbert.ie.

Sample Bio-Imprint Statement

Inspirational Quotation
The purpose of life is a life of purpose

Robert Byrne

My every waking hour will be dedicated towards paying attention to the things that matter most to me and the ones I love. I will spend some time each day with, or at the very least in contact with, each member of my family. I want them to experience the same feelings that they create in me. I intend to be a positive creative force in their lives, to be there when they need me, to help them to laugh and enjoy life. I want to teach them how to focus, and how to climb past fear and apprehension, to help them keep their youthful spirit of adventure and intrigue, to guide them towards health, happiness and prosperity. My goal in this life is to reach my full potential and to create the environment where they can fulfil theirs. I will do that by concentrating on my personal growth every day. This means that I will read often, daily if possible, so that I may continue to learn and keep my skills up to date. I will maintain inner harmony by connecting with the 'here and now'. When I am with Theresa, Dylan and Cian, I will frequently take stock of what I hear, feel, sense, touch and smell so that I may live in the present not in the past or off in the future. I will live every day as if it is my last.

In the morning I will set myself up for success by reviewing my goals and refocusing if required. I will end my day by giving gratitude for the things that I

What I Seek	What I Reject
Family	Mediocrity
Creative Expression	Manipulation
Self-Mastery	Inflexibility
Health/Fitness	Bitterness
Financial Security	Deception
Individuality	Negativity
Freedom	Revenge

Who I Am	Who I Affect
Father	Theresa
Husband	Dylan
Son	Cian
Friend	Owen
Mind Coach	Michael
Trainer	Richard
Therapist	John
Businessman	Dee
	Cora

Accomplishments
First Client
First Training
TV Appearances
Publishing First CD
Master Trainer
Ayahuasca
First Book

Inspirators
Dr Seuss
Richard Bandler
Maxwell Maltz
To boldly go…
Robin Williams
Mum
Dad

have. I trust that whatever I want out of life is already there, all I have to do is put in the effort. I know I can achieve whatever I want to, if I focus. The greatest gift in this life is time, it is also my most scarce resource, and I will never again have this moment. Happiness is just a habit. I am responsible for everything in my life. I refuse to accept or tolerate anything that goes against the principles of personal empowerment. Negativity, fear and self-doubt are the tools of failure; man is born to succeed not to fail. A mistake is just an opportunity to do it better next time. People hurt one another because they are hurting themselves. Forgiveness heals, resentment is a disease. Everyone is my equal, no more and no less. My friends help me to stay focused. I intend to earn a living by doing what I love, i.e. learning and growing. Creativity and flexibility get results. I want to be recognised as a hardworking, creative, sincere, compassionate, humorous, fun-loving family man that is dedicated to the development and empowerment of his fellow man. I want to leave this world with a definitive set of tools and techniques that are simple, ready to use, free from jargon and readily available to anyone that chooses to acquire them. My freedom of choice is my responsibility and not to be passed on to another. I am the architect of my own life.

Resources
Change Catalyst
Creative
Humorous
Deal with Conflict
Integrity
Perseverance
Skill Set

Appreciation
Friends
Laughter
Knowledge
Sunny Days
Sounds of the Sea

Motivators
Reading
Time Frames
New Challenges
New Ideas
TV Work
On Stage with JL
Training with RB

Mood Lifters
Learning
Comedy
Children Time
Time Out
Exercise
Eating Out
Music

My Bio-Imprint Statement

Inspirational Quotation

What I Seek		What I Reject

Who I Am		Who I Affect

Accomplishments

_____

Inspirators

_____

_____

_____

_____

_____

_____

Resources

_____

Appreciation

_____

_____

_____

_____

_____

_____

Motivators

_____

Mood Lifters

_____

_____

_____

_____

_____

Getting Done What Counts

So now we need to get down to the nitty-gritty of doing tasks, whether that is the mundane or the lofty, whether that is collecting the kids from school or writing a book. You need to focus on getting done what counts. This is the stuff that gives rise to your To Do List. Your To Do List needs to have structure to be effective. It needs to be organised in alignment with your Bio-Imprint Statement. The following approach can put structure to this process.

Your Five Task Options

Write down everything you have to do and with every task realise you have five task options:

1. *Do it.* Your questions: Does this fit in with my plan? Is it worthwhile? What will happen if I do it? What will not happen if I do it?
2. *Delegate it.* Your questions, assuming that it is worth doing: Do I need to do it? Can I get it done just as effectively if I give it to someone else? What will happen if I do this? Am I refusing to delegate because of an emotional insecurity (i.e. perfectionism)?
3. *Defer it.* Your questions, assuming that it is worth doing: Do I have to do it now? Can it wait? What will happen if I do it later? Can I get it done later and if so when specifically will I do it?
4. *Diminish it.* These questions are always worth asking: How can I get it done more efficiently? How can I save on time and not surrender quality and what has to happen for that to happen?
5. *Delete it.* Finally, if your master plan is well written, you will begin to refuse more. You will learn the art of saying no and do so gracefully because you know your mission is so important and worthwhile.

Your Four Fundamental Questions

On a simpler note and to ensure you stay focused, there are four simple, fundamental questions to ask each time you are faced with a request or a task to do:

1. *Who?* Who can do this? (Does it have to be me?)
2. *When?* When can it be done? (Does it have to be now?)
3. *How?* How can it be done? (Is it realistic to do this?)
4. *Why?* Why should I do it? (Does it fit in with my master plan?)

When you are armed with your plan, your goals and the right questions, you also need to allow for variables. Few plans go exactly as per the design. So you need to build in a margin for error. Research has shown that we tend to think we can do more than we can and we tend to suffer on account of others that don't do what they say they can.

The 20 Per Cent Rule
Overestimate for yourself
When planning a project and assigning a time add 20 per cent on to your own projection, this will allow for unforeseen circumstances and reduce the stress that goes with over-committing to do things.
Underestimate for others
When others give you a plan or a time commitment on something do likewise and add 20 per cent on to whatever they tell you (just don't let them know that you have done that).

Your Modus Operandi
- Begin with the end in mind.
- Approach each goal, each day with a view in mind of the end result.
- Plan, act and review. Few things go as planned, expect that. Be flexible and prepared to adjust as you go.
- Think twice before you commit. Hesitate and ask yourself if it fits in with your master plan?
- Think it through. What are your reasons for doing this? Is it to be liked or is it to do what counts?

- Learn how to say no if what you are about to do is not worthwhile or does not fit in with your master plan.

Time Parasites

We've all been there: you get up, go to work, are in flow, all psyched up and getting things done, then the phone rings or someone calls by and before you know it you've lost time and motivation. You have to get serious with time wasters and learn to plan in advance to get back control over your time. Here are some methods you can employ:

- *Distract:* When someone is using up your time by talking to you, appear distracted. Bring your attention to something unusual or not relevant to the conversation. The shirt they are wearing, the weather or whatever. This puts you back in the driving seat so you can close the conversation and get on with things.
- *Interrupt:* A less mannerly way of doing this is by interrupting the person, telling them that you would love to hear what they have to say and how about meeting up for lunch as you are busy right now.
- *Question:* People do not like to be asked questions in rapid succession; it interrupts their flow of thought, which is exactly what you need to do to reclaim control and end the conversation.

Feed Your Time Bank

Your overall objective is not only to manage your time but to attempt to create more of it. It makes sense. So feed your time bank with:

- *Me time:* Assign yourself time every day by yourself to enable you to plan your day. It will give you an overview and ensure you stay focused. This time needs to be non-negotiable.
- *Catch-up time:* Assign in your day or week a set amount of time for catch-up. This means that you will make consistent progress

and you will feel that you are getting places. If your calendar is full with tasks you are quite simply planning to fail, there has to be 'free space' for catch-up to account for everything that didn't go as you predicted.

- *Recovery time:* Life is hectic but it is critical that you take the time to recharge, time when you have absolutely nothing on, time to lounge around. This is not unproductive time, this is vital time that will recharge you to be able to approach everything from a clearer, fresher perspective and empower you to be at your best rather than flying at half-mast.

A Simple but Effective Daily To Do List

Preparing a daily To Do List will help you manage your time effectively. Write out a new list for each day and transfer what is not yet done to it.

To Do	Who	How long	When	First Step
Does this fit in with your Bio-Imprint Statement?	Can you delegate?	+/- 20%?	What else will be affected?	When?

Thirty-Second Navel-Gazing Review

It will be necessary over time to keep your psychic guardians in check. A good way of doing that is to consider the following points.

You are on the wrong track if:

- You believe you can do no wrong.
- You are convinced that others are always the wrongdoers.
- You feel you have to hype your own importance.
- You believe others never do their fair share.
- You believe there is no need for you to change.
- You believe other people should change.
- You always think circumstances are to blame for your own shortcomings.
- You believe others are always to be held personally responsible for their shortcomings.
- You are constantly tense, upset or unhappy for no obvious reason.
- You are rarely excited, enthusiastic or motivated by the things that are happening in your life.
- You suffer from chronic seriousness.

You are on the right track if:

- You have made happiness your priority.
- You have a purpose that inspires you.
- You have chosen the values and standards by which you live.
- You get your motivation from the goals you set for yourself.
- You write down and review these goals often.
- You accept that change is a constant part of your progress.
- You accept that your level of flexibility determines your success.
- You accept that there is no such thing as failure, only feedback.
- You treat life's challenges as an opportunity to improve.
- You realise that if what you are doing is not working you can always do something else.
- Your primary directive is to feel good more often.

- You make every moment count.
- You look for the positive in all situations.
- You view success in any endeavour as a matter of application.
- You use your imagination to shape your destiny.
- You realise that progress is determined by what you can do right now.
- You accept that we are all doing the best that we can in each given moment.
- You treat people how you would like to be treated yourself.
- You stop and take the time to notice and be grateful for what you have.
- You smile more and laugh often.
- You own this book.
- You think I'm great.
- You tell everyone you meet about me!

Remember the following four laws:

1. The Law of Reversed Effect (what you resist persists).
2. The Law of Attraction (you get more of what you focus on).
3. The Law of Requisite Variety (what works today might not necessarily work tomorrow so to guarantee success you must be continually prepared to come up with innovative ways of achieving the same goal).
4. The Law of Dominant Effect (a strong emotion will tend to replace a weaker one).

Conclusion

Thank you for taking the time to join me on this journey. You deserve the best that life can give and my sincere hope for you is that you take from it much that makes you happier. Just how far you take these learnings and skills is up to you.

It is my experience that not only is it essential to do what you love but it makes sense to do more of what works well for you too. If you are good at something, like singing, do more of that, do it loads, because when you sing it brightens you up, it brings spark into your life, you feel wonderful and you end up making other people feel wonderful because of it. So go do it, do it more often, find opportunities to do it. It shouldn't be a smaller part of your actions it should be a greater part. Do the things that are working well, find out what works well and do a lot of it. That's not really rocket science but guess how many people do it? Very few.

Take charge of your consciousness and work on it and with it daily. I have a consuming interest in altering my state of consciousness and I have done my share of experimenting, and I continue to do so. I have learned that the best effects are achieved when you alter your own consciousness internally as opposed to having it artificially altered using external stimulants. Thankfully I didn't feel the need to try out all avenues before I arrived at this point and for that I have two people to thank, one is Richard Bandler and the second is Timothy Leary, the man that President Nixon once described as 'the most dangerous man in America'. Timothy is given credit for his part as a spokesperson for LSD and the psychedelic movement of the 1960s. It was his statement 'turn on, tune in and drop out' that became the mantra of the hippy movement.

Leary stated that the best drugs are to be found inside your own brain (he even took it a step further saying that your brain is god). If you are doing drugs, fine if that's your thing, I've done enough to know some of them are good, some of them are not so good. The real trick though behind altering consciousness is to focus on generating good thoughts, that's what highs are all about, well the good ones that is. It's always good to find out where you can put your consciousness and I like to control my consciousness a lot. I like to know that when I'm putting my consciousness somewhere it's going to a good place so that I have control over it. It's a good idea to let go of control sometimes, but in general it's good to know where you are putting your consciousness because when you do you can make your life absolutely wonderful.

You've got enough power, enough capacity and enough stability inside your mind to generate and literally craft, create and sculpt a reality that is absolutely fantastic. It can be exceptional, you can do exceptional things, but you've got to go in and paint them first, you have to have that image, you have to have that focus, you have to have that idea. You have to think it through, not just wish it through, you have to run it through your neurology. You've got to see it, you've got to hear it, you've got to feel it, you've got to taste it, you've got to smell it, you've nearly got to wear it so that it's inside your mind.

Every time you input something into that bio-computer of yours you are altering frequencies, changing to higher level vibrations by sending out specific signals that begin drawing your goals to you like a magnet attracts bits of iron. But you absolutely need to input cleanly first. There is no point in having muddy images, that's not good enough. If you say that you want to be happy, then you have got to go back to the target and look at the target, and ask yourself 'What does happiness look like? What does it feel like? What do I see? What do I hear? What do I feel? What will be happening in my world when I am happy? Who am I going to be with? Where am I going to belong? How am I going to feel about myself? Who am I when I am a happier person?' As you put that into your imagination you are vibrating at the precise frequency to activate what others have called The Law of Attraction.

It is just like you did when you were a child. Remember as a child you were happy because you had all these ideas and you lived in the magical worlds that you created daily. Whether it was playing with dolls or toy cars or dressing in uniforms or costumes, whatever it was you used your imagination to achieve it, to activate it. Children tend to be full of energy, excitement and imagination. The imagination is what is creating everything for you and it is creating the very reality you find yourself in. When a child is down on all fours playing with toys, he or she is in that world.

That world is the training ground for this world. The only question is: What do you want? The only limit is put there by your imagination, which itself is limitless. So the real question is: What would you do if you could only succeed? All you need to do is to climb back into your own fantastic imagination world. A world that too many of us leave behind in our childhood because we are told it is time to put away childish things. If you are not used to exercising your imagination and have children of your own join them in some of their games. Self-hypnosis is also a good gateway into this world.

Every time that you soften, every time that you tune in, you can simply sit down and say, 'Okay how do I want to feel? What would it be like if I had a magic wand? How would I make my world?' And do that and do it often. Do it frequently. This will begin to draw things towards you.

You have the resources to clear the debris from your thinking, to 'shut the f**k up' and become freer again. You can program yourself to feel younger, to be younger if you choose. Play around with those things. Recognise that life is important. Do some planning; plan to be relaxed, to be able to deal with changes, to have a great day. Plan so that it's easy. Plan to be effective, efficient, industrious and successful. Whatever sounds or looks good to you just throw it into the mix. You may not get all of what you want in exactly the way that you planned it, but that is how the universe works. You are unlikely to get any of it if you fail to plan it in.

You can also use your imagination to do other things. At the end of your day finish off by imagining everything being perfect. If something went wrong during your day why not go inside your mind just before you go to sleep and imagine fixing it. It doesn't have to be fixed in the real world, but your brain gets the idea that it's finished and that makes it feel good.

Play with your imagination as you did when you were a child. It is powerful, creative and effective, it can do so much for you. My life is dramatically different now from what it was like when I set out on this journey. It is absolutely, completely and totally different, because I have changed it. The things that you think are stopping you don't necessarily need to, they can be changed.

While my life is not all hunky-dory, it is most of the time. It's not that challenge doesn't happen, or that problems or stresses don't occur – they do, but I tend to get through them a lot quicker than I used to and you will too. When things go wrong I look at it in more useful ways and reach the 'f**k it' threshold faster. That's what it's all about. To really give yourself that permission, say to yourself 'I *can* do this and I *will* do it.' You've already overcome challenges, there is stuff you have already got through and you've got this far. If you were to look back at all the crap you came through you'll see that you must be pretty good, you must be pretty strong. There is nobody who hasn't had some crap in their life. You got this far without these new skills. Now that you have these skills, how far do you want to go? That's the question.

When you really get your system and neurology lined up so that it's backing you all of the time, you are on your own side. You've had enough criticism of yourself, you've had enough giving out to yourself. It's time to shut the f**k up, shut the f**k up. Where do I want to go? How do I want to feel? What do I want to have happen? These are useful questions; they are the questions that lead to the habit, the happiness habit. Get that habit and you will have happier days. Every day can be a happier day on some level. You wake up and you can say to yourself or the world, 'F**k it. Despite what they throw at me, I'll still feel good anyway.'

When you release the valve of your imagination and give it permission to run full flight, when you allow yourself to daydream, to stand like an infant mesmerised by a starlit sky, when you become curious about how wonderful the universe can be, then you release its creative power. Stop for a moment and consider that you are not just in this universe, you are the universe experiencing itself. Inside of you there is the same creative force that has shaped everything you see and all that you experience. Everything is preceded by mind. Whether you choose to just get your feet wet or plunge right in, is entirely up to you. There are so many levels to consciousness and we know only of a few. Plant consciousness differs from animal consciousness and animal consciousness from human consciousness. Within human consciousness there are also huge variables. There are worlds within your world and worlds you have yet to experience.

The universe is a friendly place. The three million cells that work in harmony to allow you to be who you are can't be wrong. I believe that Charles Darwin got it wrong: co-operation not competition is the fundamental survival tool of the species. Take a look around you, everything is interdependent. Our very biosphere relies on the interconnection of so many things.

If you want to be successful, be part of this co-operative force. Give and you will get in abundance. Dare to trust and you will be rewarded. Life is waiting for you to add your imprint. Be sure to make it both wonderful and memorable. You are designed to be happy. You can be if you follow the guidelines. Life never stands still and the only thing that you can predict is that change will happen. Get used to it, befriend it and be prepared to flow with it.

Take control of your life and remove those self-imposed limitations. Accept that most solutions are inside your own mind. Realise that every thought draws you like a magnet towards your success. See yourself through kinder eyes. Become your own best friend. Give yourself permission to encourage yourself, to inspire yourself, to motivate yourself, to be kind to yourself. Realise that you can create much more that way. Embrace life as a rare and unprecedented opportunity to develop, to grow, to evolve, to expand your consciousness in new and more useful directions.

Focus on how much pleasure you can stand, how much more fun you can have, how much adventure you can venture into. Travel often through the corridors of your imagination and open wide your unconscious because it's your time to have a better time for the rest of time. Success is drawn to you in so many different ways, so sometimes be prepared to be unprepared because that works too. Remember that the best thing about the past is that it's over and your future is beckoning you with open arms. Your happiness and your success are waiting for you. Everything in your body, every cell, every nerve, every fibre of your being can become attracted towards health and well-being and become attracted towards having a wonderful time, as long as you make it your goal. Being happier is about learning how to run good feelings in every moment that you can and doing what matters most.

I wish you well as you develop your own habit of happiness and wonder about the imprint you will leave on your way. May this simply be the beginning of many beginnings. Journey well, my friend. Happy days are ahead of you. I wish you every success on your glorious journey of personal evolution and I would just love to hear how well you're doing. My wish for you is that you do great things and if you can't do great things just simply be, as you are already great.

The Eight Levels: Complete Chart

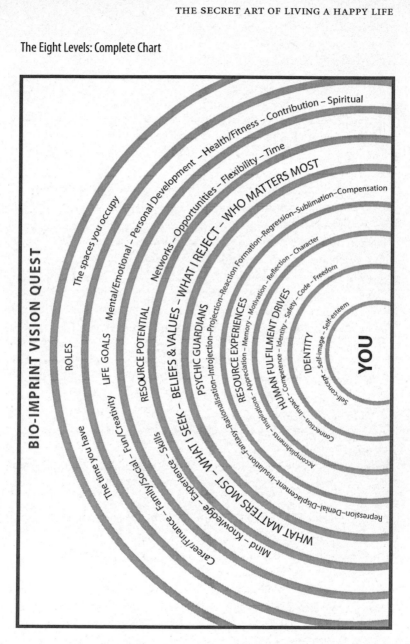

Bibliography

Bandler, Richard, *The Adventures of Anybody*, Meta Publications, 1993.

Bandler, Richard, *Get the Life You Want: The Secrets to Quick and Lasting Life Change with Neuro-Linguistic Programming*, HCI, 2008.

Bandler, Richard, *Richard Bandler's Guide to Trance-formation: How to Harness the Power of Hypnosis to Ignite Effortless and Lasting Change*, HCI, 2008.

Bandler, Richard and Owen Fitzpatrick, *Conversations: Freedom is Everything and Love is All the Rest*, Mysterious Publications, 2005.

Bandler, Richard and John Grinder, *The Structure of Magic I: A Book about Language and Therapy*, Science & Behavior Books, 1975.

Bandler, Richard and John Grinder, *The Structure of Magic II: A Book about Communication and Change*, Science & Behavior Books, 1975.

Bandler, Richard and John La Valle, *Persuasion Engineering*, Meta Publications, 1996.

Bandler, Richard and Will McDonald, *An Insiders' Guide to Submodalities*, Meta Publications, 1989.

Bramson, Robert M., *Coping with Difficult People*, Simon & Schuster, 1986.

Byrne, Rhonda, *The Secret*, Beyond Words Publishing, 2006.

Charvet, Shelle Rose, *Words that Change Minds*, Kendall/Hunt Publishing, 1997.

Covey, Stephen R., *The Seven Habits of Highly Effective People*, Simon & Schuster, 1989.

Crowley, Aleister, *Collected Works of Aleister Crowley 1905–1907*, Gordon Press, 1974.

Crowley, Aleister, *The Book of Lies*, Samuel Weiser, 1981.

Crowley, Aleister, *The Book of the Law*, Red Wheel/Weiser, 2004.

DeLozier, Judith and Robert Dilts, *Encyclopedia of Systemic Neuro-Linguistic Programming and NLP New Coding*, NLP University Press, 2000.

Dilts, Robert, *Applications of Neuro-Linguistic Programming*, Meta Publications, 1983.

Dilts, Robert, *Roots of Neuro-Linguistic Programming*, Meta Publications, 1983.

Dilts, Robert, *Changing Belief Systems with NLP*, Meta Publications, 1990.

Dilts, Robert, *Cognitive Patterns of Jesus of Nazareth*, *Dynamic Learning Publications*, Ben Lomond, 1992.

Dilts, Robert, *Effective Presentation Skills*, Meta Publications, 1994.

Dilts, Robert, *Strategies of Genius Volumes I, II & III*, Meta Publications, 1994–1995.

Dilts, Robert, *Visionary Leadership Skills: Creating a World to which People Want to Belong*, Meta Publications, 1996.

Dilts, Robert, *Modeling with NLP*, Meta Publications, 1998.

Dilts, Robert, *Sleight of Mouth: The Magic of Conversational Belief Change*, Meta Publications, 1999.

Dilts, Robert, *From Coach to Awakener*, Meta Publications, 2003.

Dilts, Robert and Gino Bonissone, *Skills for the Future*, Meta Publications, 1993.

Dilts, Robert with Todd Epstein, *Dynamic Learning*, Meta Publications, 1995.

Dilts, Robert B., Todd Epstein and Robert W. Dilts, *Tools for Dreamers: Strategies of Creativity and the Structure of Innovation*, Meta Publications, 1991.

Dispenza, Joe, *The Science of Changing Your Mind*, HCI, 2007.

Dr Seuss, *Did I Ever Tell You How Lucky You Are*, Harper Collins, 2004.

Farrelly, Frank and Jeffery Brandsma, *Provocative Therapy*, Meta Publications, 1974.

Fitzpatrick, Owen, *Not Enough Hours*, Poolbeg, 2009.

Fordyce, Michael W., 'Development of a Program to Increase Personal Happiness', *Journal of Counseling Psychology*, 24(6), 511–521, 1977.

Fordyce, Michael W., 'A Program to Increase Happiness: Further Studies', *Journal of Counseling Psychology*, 30(4), 483–498, 1983.

Fordyce, Michael W., 'The Psychap Inventory; A Multi-Scale Test to Measure Happiness and Its Concomitants', *Social Indicators Research*, 18(1), 1–33, 1986.

Fordyce, Michael W., 'A Review of Research on the Happiness Measures; A Sixty Second Index of Happiness and Mental Health', *Social Indicators Research*, 20, 355–381, 1988.

Fordyce, Michael W., 'Educating for Happiness', *Quebec Review of Psychology*, 1997.

Frankl, Victor E., *Man's Search for Meaning*, Washington Square Press, 1984.

Fuller, Richard Buckminster, *Only Integrity Is Going to Count*, Critical Path Publishing, 2003.

Gordon, David, *Graham Davies Expanding Your World*, Desert Rain, 2005.

Gosling, Sam, *Snoop*, Profile Books, 2008.

Goswami, Amit, *The Self-Aware Universe*, Tarcher Penguin, 1995.

Grinder, John and Richard Bandler, *Patterns of the Hypnotic Techniques of Milton H. Erickson, M.D., Volume I*, Cupertino, 1976.

Grinder, John and Richard Bandler, *Frogs into Princes: Neuro Linguistic Programming*, Real People Press, 1979.

Grinder, John and Richard Bandler, *Reframing: Neurolinguistic Programming and the Transformation of Meaning*, Real People Press, 1983.

Grinder, John and Richard Bandler, *Using Your Brain for a Change*, Real People Press, 1985.

Grinder, John and Richard Bandler, *Magic in Action*, Meta Publications, 1992.

Grinder, John and Richard Bandler, *Time for a Change*, Meta Publications, 1993.

Grinder, John, Richard Bandler and Andreas Connirae (eds), *Trance-Formations: Neuro-Linguistic Programming and the Structure of Hypnosis*, Real People Press, 1981.

Grinder, John, Richard Bandler and Judith Delozier, *Patterns of the Hypnotic Techniques of Milton H. Erickson, M.D., Volume II*, Meta Publications, 1977.

Grinder, John, Richard Bandler, Judith DeLozier and Robert Dilts, *Neuro-Linguistic Programming: The Study of the Structure of Subjective Experience, Volume I*, Meta Publications, 1980.

Hallbom, Tim, Suzi Smith and Robert Dilts, *Beliefs: Pathways to Health & Well-Being*, Metamorphous Press, 1990.

Hamacheck, Don E., *Encounters with the Self*, West Publishing Company, 1991.

Harner, Michael, *The Way of the Shaman*, Harper, 1990.

La Valle, John and Richard Bandler, *Persuasion Engineering*, Meta Publications, 1996.

Laborde, Z. Genie, *Influencing with Integrity*, The Anglo American Book Co., 1984.

Laborde, Z. Genie, *Fine Tune Your Brain*, Syntony Publishing, 1988.

Leary, Timothy, *The Politics of Ecstasy*, Ronin Publishing, 1998.

Leary, Timothy, *Change Your Brain*, Ronin Publishing, 2000.

Leary, Timothy, *Info Psychology*, New Falcon, 2004.

Leary, Timothy, *Your Brain is God*, Ronin Publishing, 2008.

Lichter, S., K. Haye and R. Kammann, 'Increasing Happiness through Cognitive Retraining', *New Zealand Psychologist*, 9, 57–64, 1980.

Maltz, Maxwell, *Insights for the Quest for Happiness*, Psycho-Cybernetics Foundation, 1997.

McDonald, Robert and Robert Dilts, *Tools of the Spirit*, Meta Publications, 1997.

McKenna, Paul, *I Can Make You Thin*, Bantam Press, 2005.

McKenna, Paul, *Instant Confidence*, Bantam Press, 2006.

McKenna, Paul, *I Can Make You Rich*, Bantam Press, 2007.

McKenna, Paul, *Quit Smoking Today Without Gaining Weight*, Bantam Press, 2007.

McKenna, Paul with Hugh Willbourn, *Change Your Life in Seven Days*, Bantam Press, 2005.

Nwosu, Eugene, *Cut Your Own Firewood*, Collins Press, 1998.

Pert, Candace B., *Molecules of Emotion*, Pocket Books, 1997.

Pert, Candace B., *Everything You Need to Know to Feel Good*, Hay House, 2006.

Robbins, Anthony, *Unlimited Power: The New Science of Personal Achievement*, New York: Simon & Schuster, 1986.

Robbins, Anthony, *Awaken the Giant Within*, New York: Simon & Schuster, 1992.

Thaler, Richard and Cass Sunstein, *Nudge*, Penguin Books, 2009.

Tyson, Donald, *Enochian Magic*, Llewellyn Publications, 2005.

Vitale, Joe, *Buying Trances*, John Wiley & Sons, 2007.

Vitale, Joe, *Hypnotic Writing*, John Wiley & Sons, 2007.

Vitale, Joe, *The Attractor Factor*, John Wiley & Sons, 2008.

Wenger, Win, *Brain Boosters*, Nightingale Conant, 2003.

Wenger, Win and Richard Poe, *The Einstein Factor*, Prima Publishing, 2000.

Wilber, Ken, *Quantum Questions*, Shamabala, 2001.

Wilson, Robert Anton, *Prometheus Rising*, New Falcon Press, 1983.

Wilson, Robert Anton, *Quantum Psychology*, New Falcon Press, 1990.

Wiseman, Richard, *59 Seconds*, Macmillan, 2009.

Irish Institute of NLP

Brian Colbert and Owen Fitzpatrick co-founded the Irish Institute of NLP (Neuro-Linguistic Programming) in 2001. Brian is well known for his work as the mind coach on RTÉ's daytime magazine television programme *The Afternoon Show* and is one of the top NLP Master Trainers in the world. Owen is known for his popular RTÉ television series *Not Enough Hours* and is also a Master Trainer of NLP. There are only two NLP Master Trainers in Ireland.

Owen and Brian are highly recommended by Dr Richard Bandler (co-founder of NLP) and the Society of NLP, the largest and oldest NLP training body in the world. They are known for their remarkable ability to work together seamlessly and with great humour. Their unique training style reveals their great friendship and complementarity.

Since they founded the Institute they have presented NLP seminars in Ireland, Britain, Europe and America. They provide regular NLP Evenings, Life-Enhancement Weekends, Art of Charisma Workshops, Trance Tripping, NLP Practitioners, NLP Business Practitioners, NLP Master Practitioners and NLP Coaching Certification Programmes.

Brian and Owen also offer corporate consulting and present in-house training to the corporate sector in the areas of communication, sales, motivation, stress management, creativity and business applications of NLP.

To learn NLP in Ireland or to make your life and business better, visit the Institute's website today.

Irish Institute of NLP
84 Sundrive Road
Kimmage
Dublin 12
Ireland

Tel: +353 (0)1 490 2923
Website: www.nlp.ie
E-mail: theresa@nlp.ie

EXCLUSIVE OFFER TO READERS OF
THE HAPPINESS HABIT

As a thank you for investing in buying and reading this book, you can download a free A4 accompanying e-book that will allow you to record your answers to the exercises in a more spacious format. Simply go to www.briancolbert.ie and download your free e-book today!